PRIME TIME
TENNIS

PRIME TIME TENNIS

VIC SEIXAS

WITH

JOEL H. COHEN

CHARLES SCRIBNER'S SONS   NEW YORK

Copyright © 1983 Vic Seixas and Joel H. Cohen

Library of Congress Cataloging in Publication Data

Seixas, Vic.
   Prime time tennis.

   Includes index.
   1. Tennis.   2. Middle age.   I. Cohen, Joel H.
II. Title.
GV995.S395   1983   796.342'2   82–42660
ISBN 0–684–17904–0

1 3 5 7 9 11 13 15 17 19   F/C   20 18 16 14 12 10 8 6 4 2

Printed in the United States of America.

To Toni and Tori,
the women in my life

ACKNOWLEDGMENTS

With grateful appreciation to the following:

Eve Kraft of the USTA who, more than any other one person, is responsible for my starting and completing this book. She constantly urged me on when I periodically slowed down, and was always ready to give whatever assistance was necessary. Many thanks, Eve.

The Tennis Grand Masters—Al Bunis, Sven Davidson, Frank Sedgman, Alex Olmedo, Mal Anderson, Torben Ulrich, and Bobby Riggs—for their willingness to contribute their years of valuable knowledge of the game in often used quotes. These are my tennis contemporaries and, more importantly, my close friends of many, many years.

Joel Cohen, who came to my rescue when I was virtually stalled. Working with Joel was a distinct pleasure, and getting to know him and his love of tennis was an extra delight I hadn't counted on.

Vic Seixas

CONTENTS

PRIME TIME
TENNIS

TIMELESS TOY

■|■

> Age, I make light of it,
> Fear not the sight of it,
> Time's but our playmate, whose toys are divine.
> —Thomas Wentworth Higginson,
> *Sixty and Six: A Fountain of Youth*

Maybe I'm biased, but I'm convinced that one of the most divine toys available to us mortals, at just about any age, is the game of tennis.

To paraphrase a popular song of the 1970s, I've seen that world from both sides now—first as a hotshot amateur and then as a cooled-down professional . . . as a full-timer and as a part-timer . . . as a youngster who whipped players twice my age, and as a middle-ager outclassed by kids half my age.

For more than half a century, tennis has been both vocation and avocation for me, and whatever my role in it, I've found the game consistently challenging, exhilarating, healthful, and sociable. Judging from what I read and see around me, growing multitudes of men and women feel the same way. Presumably you're among them, and very probably you're in the age group that I like to refer to as prime time players—people over forty who play the game for relaxation, exercise, camaraderie, competition, or a combination of these motivating factors.

1

You may have been playing the game since you could barely see over the net, taken it up for the first time in your middle years, or just returned to it after a long hiatus. You may be an advanced player or a hacker or at some level in between. Whatever your level of skill or time in the game, you're going to find that age is forcing you to make changes. That's true, of course, not only in tennis but in virtually every aspect of life—and it's not all bad. Just different.

In this book, I want to share with fellow prime time players the fun and frustration, the conditioning and psychology, and the necessary physical and emotional adjustments that characterize tennis in the middle years and beyond.

Drawing on my own experiences and those of contemporaries who are former world-class players, I'll try to give a panoramic overview of the joys of tennis for the older tennis player—including suggested ways for you to get maximum pleasure from the game—as a spectator as well as a player, how to discipline yourself to avoid injury, how to behave on the court, and how to rate yourself as a player.

The effect of different surfaces on aging knees and different rackets on aging elbows will be covered, and I'll offer some playing tips of particular interest to the older player, along with five basic principles that can help players of any age improve their game. Since you're likely to be playing a lot more doubles than singles, I'll go into doubles in some detail, covering such matters as how to pick a partner and who plays which side, as well as how to maintain the delicate balance of mixed doubles.

Some of the characters who have lent color to the game both on and off the court will appear on these pages, and nostalgia buffs should enjoy some reminiscences of great Wimbledon, U.S. Open, and Davis Cup matches. There will also be a discussion of the tennis boom, whose effects we're still enjoying, the Grand Masters (great old-time players who are still in lively competition); and how to outplay youth with wisdom and experience.

I'll also venture some opinions about champion "brats," so-called "shamateur" tennis, tennis officiating, and my top ten men players of the past fifty years.

SENIORITIS

Technically, a *competitive* male tennis player is counted as a senior from the age of forty-five on up,* although the United States Tennis Association (USTA) includes players thirty-five and older in senior competitive tournaments. As someone approaching sixty, I feel I'm going to be a senior any year now.

The saying, "Different strokes for different folks," is more than a tennis pun. We've all known people who look and act young for their age, and others who act old for their age. Everything else being equal, it's really a state of mind. Some people at forty are a lot older than some who are sixty. Furthermore, you can't really predict your lift span. At forty-five, you might be two-thirds of the way through your life, or only half.

Heredity plays a part, of course, but so does your attitude. Thinking young and keeping physically fit are a good prescription for a long and happy life. Playing tennis is an excellent reflection of this. Those who have played tennis a good part of their lives are in better shape physically and mentally than those who haven't taken up the game or other activities.

So be glad to be part of the growing population of mid-life tennis enthusiasts.

Playing opportunities are constantly expanding. More clinics, more programs, and more senior men's and women's tournaments are being scheduled throughout the country.

With the children grown, your time should be more your own. There should be fewer demands, and consequently free hours available for leisure, physical fitness, and self-improvement, all of which spell TENNIS.

At the prime of your life, you should be having the time of your life.

I'm confident you're already finding the game rewarding, and I hope some of the suggestions and observations in this book will contribute to your heightened enjoyment.

---

* In many areas, Australia and Europe among them, the term *veteran* is still used for the senior player. In the United States, however, probably because *veteran* conjured up the vision of a disabled returnee from combat, the term was changed to *senior*.

In tennis—as in life—there's no reason why you can't improve with age, like fine wine. Approach it with enthusiasm, use common sense, sharpen your skills, stay in condition, make the necessary concessions to age without capitulating, and you'll surprise yourself with your progress.

In the words of Robert Browning's poem "Rabbi Ben Ezra," "Grow old along with me,/ The best is yet to be . . ."

Welcome to prime time tennis.

WHAT WAS, WAS

It seems to be the destiny of people growing older to want to dwell in the past, those times when the mind was sharper, the body stronger, and, in retrospect at least, life rosier.

Aging tennis players are no different. The urge to relive triumphs, celebrate the vigor of youth, and recall the "good old days" dies hard. Not that you can—or should—live in the past. What was, was and can't be recaptured except in reminiscence, too much of which can be depressing.

But, as noted, an important aspect of prime time tennis for many players is how we adjust, physically and psychologically, to changes in our playing levels over the years. In order to understand and come to grips with the necessary adjustments in your own tennis playing, it might be helpful to know what players in my peer group have gone through. And that means starting in the past.

So bear with me, if you will, as I recount some tennis experiences of years gone by to give you some idea of "the way we were," contrasted with the way we are now.

WIMBLEDON

On a crisp autumn day in the hills of West Virginia, the finals of the Almaden (vintage 1980) Grand Masters Tennis circuit were being played in the beautiful indoor facility of the Greenbrier Hotel. I was drawn against Sven Davidson in the first match of this round robin competition. We were being introduced by Alvin W. Bunis, president and founder of the Tennis Grand Masters, in his usual flowery manner. While some of our major accomplishments were being recounted, I could not help but recall my first meeting with Sven.

The dream of every tennis player the world over is to win Wimbledon. For many, just playing in this, the greatest of all tournaments, is the realization of a lifetime ambition. I made a rather late debut there in 1950 at the age of twenty-six. This was caused partly by World War II, which delayed all of us in that age group a few years, and partly by the fact that there were so many good American players around after the war that I could not raise enough money for the trip. In 1950, however, I was fortunate enough to be selected by the United States Lawn Tennis Association (USLTA) as part of a team of four (with Art Larsen, Doris Hart, and Shirley Fry) to tour South Africa during February and March. We returned by way of Europe and England, ending the trip at Wimbledon. So part of my dream was to become a reality at last.

I remember attending the draw, which takes place on the grounds of the All-England Lawn Tennis Club, and hearing my name called out against Sven Davidson of Sweden. I had heard of him, for he was already on his way to becoming one of the top players in Europe and was heralded as the best player ever to come out of Sweden. Sven was only twenty-one at the time, but he was already one of the mainstays of his country's Davis Cup team. I thought to myself that this had to be one of the better first-round matches in the tournament. Apparently, this opinion was shared by the committee, for our match was scheduled second on the Centre Court on opening day. There's a tradition at Wimbledon that the defending men's champion, if present, always plays the opening match on the Centre Court. If he is not in the tournament, this honor falls to the runner-up. After that, the committee tries to present on Centre Court the matches that they believe will be the most appealing and interesting to the crowd. Obviously, ours was high on the list. Since it was also Sven's first Wimbledon, it was to be a memorable occasion for both of us.

For those playing matches on the Centre Court, a practice court is made available for a short warm-up prior to their match. Since Wimbledon is very strict regarding the three-minute warm-up time allotted players once they enter the stadium, most players make use of the practice court whenever possible. I can remember looking at Sven as we walked into the stadium together, wondering if he was as nervous as I was. We have since discussed this many times and concluded that no other two people in the world could have been as nervous as we were at that moment!

It seemed we had only started to rally when the umpire called for play. We really hadn't had one decent exchange, and no ball had crossed the net more than twice. This pattern was to continue for the first eight games of the match. It was four-all in roughly ten minutes with barely a return of serve by either of us. Your nerves don't affect you when you serve as much as they do when you're receiving serve. You can get set, throw the ball up and hit it. But once it's coming at you, and you're nervous, you stiffen up, your arm gets tight, and you don't really take a good swipe at the ball. Also, because we played on the first day, the court was lightning-fast, and we both had pretty good serves, so there was tremendous difficulty trying to return the serves. We were so nervous that we couldn't get a rally going.

I recall thinking how crazy I must have been all my tennis-playing life to have longed to be as miserable as I was at that instant. All I could think of was how much I wanted to be somewhere else, *anywhere* else. Sven has since told me that he felt exactly the same, which at the time would have been small consolation.

Perhaps because I was a bit older and had more experience, I got over the nerves sooner than Sven did and managed to win the match. Looking back, I recall very little of the tennis, only the overpowering atmosphere of the Centre Court. I was to play probably close to a hundred matches on that famed court during the next ten years and would come to know it and love it. Once a player is over the initial shock, it's the greatest stage in the world for bringing out the best in him or her.

With the full cooperation of the notorious English weather, the tournament schedule proceeded nicely through the first week, and I was to play John Bromwich on Saturday in round sixteen. Our match was set for the Centre Court, probably because Queen Mother Mary was coming to the matches that day and Brom was one of her great favorites. He had always been loved by the English fans, who were bitterly disappointed when he narrowly lost in the finals in 1948 to the American Bob Falkenburg after having match point. Although only thirty-one, Brom seemed older. He'd been around a long time. At eighteen he was on the 1937 Australian Davis Cup team and had served five years in the Australian Army during the war. In fact, it was in 1939, during the last Davis Cup Challenge Round before World War II, that I first met him.

The Aussies and the Americans were playing in Philadelphia, my home town, and I was head ball boy for the matches. As a sixteen-year-old, it was a memorable occasion for me, a chance to see and mingle with the greats of the game, and an unforgettable experience.

The U.S. team jumped out to a 2–0 lead on the first day, as Bobby Riggs defeated Bromwich and Frank Parker beat Adrian Quist. It looked good for the Americans, even after Jack Kramer and Joe Hunt lost the doubles to Quist and Bromwich on the second day, because Riggs and Parker were fresh for the remaining singles while Quist and Bromwich had had no rest. In one of the great matches in Davis Cup play, Quist defeated Riggs in five sets to even the score at 2–2, setting the stage for Bromwich and Parker. Frankie Parker was known throughout the tennis world as one of the steadiest if not *the* steadiest player in the game. The only possible equal to Parker in this category was his opponent that day, John Bromwich. Brom had a strange way of striking the ball, serving right-handed, with a left-handed forehand and a two-hander on the right side. He was known to go for days without making an unforced error! This match shaped up as a war of attrition, a battle of nerves and concentration between two adversaries, each of whom believed he was the best at his way of playing and neither of whom would concede or change for a moment. It had all the earmarks of a match that would go down to the wire, a long five-setter that would be a fitting climax to an exciting Challenge Round. The fact that the match was on grass made no difference to these two players; neither would go near the net unless he was forced to, and both were determined not to miss. I remember that during the warm-up they hit the first ball back and forth so many times that it became green from the grass. Finally, Brom deliberately hit the ball to the fence so that another could be thrown into play.

They played almost three hours with endless exchanges; every point was close and hard fought, with almost all of them going to the Aussie, and Brom won 6–0, 6–3, 6–1! The proof of their evenness ultimately became evident when they next met eight years later in 1947 at Forest Hills in the semifinals of the U.S. Championships. Parker won 8–6 in the fifth set.

Fortunately for me, the Bromwich on this Saturday afternoon at Wimbledon in 1950 was not the Bromwich of 1939, and I was able to beat him, much to the chagrin of Queen Mary and most of the rest of the Centre Court spectators. While Brom and I remain good friends to this day, I often wonder if he appreciated the fact that I reminded him before we went out to play that day that I had ball-boyed for him eleven years earlier. (Since then, I have been on the other side of that same kind of relationship more times than I care to remember.)

There is no play at Wimbledon on the middle Sunday, so everyone looks for a way to get away from the tennis briefly. Trips to the country are usually in order, or just plain looking around if you don't care to leave town. If you are still alive in the tournament, it's a day to recharge the system and prepare for the all-important second week, which is quite a grind. Contrary to present-day trends, in the 1950s most of us played three events: singles, doubles, and mixed doubles. If you were good enough to be involved in all three the second week, you were in for a lot of tough tennis. Also, since there were no tiebreakers, stamina played an even bigger role. I was scheduled to meet Eric Sturgess from South Africa in the quarterfinals on Monday, but the first rainy day of the fortnight postponed our match until Tuesday. On the South African tour earlier in the year, I had met and lost to Eric five or six straight times; I had never beaten him.

All his countrymen thought this was his year to win Wimbledon; no doubt they felt some relief when they saw that I was to be his quarterfinal opponent. Eric, nicknamed the Greyhound, was a good all-court player. He was more at home on clay than grass but much more adaptable to grass than most clay-court players.

In what was by far my toughest match, I narrowly eked out a win over Eric, 9–7, 6–8, 3–6, 6–2, 7–5. I consider this one of the better victories in my career, but it took its toll on my reserves and left me drained physically and mentally for the semis the next day. Had I had a day to recover, I might have beaten Budge Patty in the next round. That's something we'll never know. Patty went on to win the tournament, defeating Frank Sedgman in the finals. Taking nothing away from Patty, one of the finest match players the game has known, he had the luck of the draw; Sedgman had had long singles matches and an unbelievable four-hour doubles match the day before the final.

I left London that year feeling that I would win Wimbledon one day; I was determined that I would never again lose a tennis match because of lack of stamina. I had always prided myself on being in top shape, but I learned in 1950 that to win Wimbledon, you had to be in peak condition both physically and mentally.

I didn't go to Europe or England in 1951, but in 1952 I set my sights on Wimbledon. Instead of playing all the European clay-court tournaments, I stayed at home. I practiced constantly on grass, even had tennis balls sent from London so that I could prepare with the very balls that would be used. Since England was still suffering some food shortages from the war, I took thirty steaks packed in dry ice with me to London. A restaurateur friend kept the steaks in his freezer. I asked him not to make any fuss when I came in for dinner but rather to serve me a steak quietly so as not to create any kind of unpleasantness in the restaurant. I didn't want my English friends to think there was an American eating their meat when they couldn't get any. Needless to say, the very first night, the steak came out on a platter amid fanfare and ceremony, and I felt like a real heel.

My playing preparations also went for naught, as I lost in the quarterfinals to Herbie Flam. Of all the Wimbledons I played, this one was about the worst. Looking back, I think I overtrained and was much too tight during the tournament. The night after losing, I went back to my restaurant and asked how many steaks were left. I was told that there were nineteen, which I promptly distributed to the folks in the restaurant. I lost my match, but I did make a number of friends in London that night.

In 1953 I changed my tactics completely. Playing all through Italy, France, Spain, and England, I arrived at Wimbledon the week before the tournament. I had done well, reaching the finals of the French Championships and winning tournaments in Barcelona and in Bristol, England. I took Wimbledon in stride and played very well, getting through the first week without too much difficulty. In the quarterfinals I had a real cliff-hanger with Lew Hoad that I won 9–7 in the fifth set. At 6–6 in that set, I was down love–40 but managed to pull out my service game. Lew double-faulted on match point, and I don't think I was ever so glad to see a double-fault as I was at that moment.

In the semis, I had yet another scare from Mervyn Rose, the tough

Aussie lefty. We always had long, close matches, and this was no exception. I was down two sets to one, and trailing 3–4 and 15–40 on my serve in the fourth set, and it looked bleak. But this time, unlike in 1950, my reserve was there and I fought back to win 6–3 in the fifth set.

The final was a bit anticlimactic as I defeated Kurt Nielsen of Denmark in straight sets. Kurt had surprised everyone getting through to the final, though unseeded, a feat he accomplished again two years later. To reach the final, he very obligingly eliminated Ken Rosewall and Jaroslav Drobny, either of whom might well have been tougher for me.

As much as this was a great Wimbledon for me—the realization of a dream, and the biggest thrill of my career thus far—it probably is remembered by all those present as the year of the Drobny–Patty match. Starting their third-round match on the Centre Court about 5 P.M., they battled continuously until 9:20 P.M. when, with the light fading, Drob finally won. The scores in this incredibly well-played and hard-fought match were 8–6, 16–18, 3–6, 8–6, 12–10! Budge Patty had six match points in the fourth and fifth sets, Drobny fighting back each time. To give you some idea of the length of this struggle, I watched most of the first set before changing for my singles match. I played three sets against Philippe Washer of Belgium, changed back into regular clothes, watched a few more games, and then returned to the locker room to change again for doubles. We played four sets of doubles and I returned to Centre Court in my tennis clothes in time to see the end of the match. To the very end, both players served and volleyed at a very high level; the caliber of tennis after four hours was astounding. In all my years in the game, I rate this match as the finest I have ever witnessed. To commemorate the occasion, both men were presented with inscribed gold cigarette cases by the All-England Lawn Tennis Club.

Amazing as it seems, Drobny, in spite of a severely strained leg muscle, survived two more rounds before being beaten by Nielsen in the semifinals. It was an all-out effort by a great competitor who would realize his dream the following year.

It is never a problem for me to remember the year I won Wimbledon, for it was coronation year in England. I always tell everyone it was a big year for the queen and me! In fact, when Wimbledon celebrated its centenary of the championships in 1977, there was a coincidental celebration taking place, the twenty-fifth anniversary of Queen Elizabeth's reign. Knowing that the coronation took place in May of 1953, I was sure that all of England was making a horrendous mistake celebrating her twenty-fifth jubilee in 1977! My panic abated when I finally learned that the years were counted from the time she actually assumed the throne in 1952, not from the time the coronation took place a few months later.

Indicative of the high esteem in which Wimbledon is held by the world's leading tennis players, in 1977 a total of forty out of the fifty-two living past singles champions (men and women) returned to the scene of their triumphs for the one-hundredth anniversary of the championships. While a few were still competing, most made their way back at their own expense, drawn by the incomparable magnetism of this great event.

I returned to Wimbledon every year from 1953 through 1957 and, with one exception, reached the quarters or semis every year. Only once, however, was I really in contention to win the tournament again. In 1956 I had Ken Rosewall 5–3, 30–15 in the final set in the semifinals but was unable to put him away. He was beaten in the finals that year by Lew Hoad, against whom I'd been doing well while having my chronic troubles with Kenny. In any event, after 1957 I returned sporadically, playing in the men's singles several more times and winning the veteran's doubles twice. Ironically, I played and won one singles match on the Centre Court in 1967, ten years after retiring from full-time play. It was quite a thrill to play and win on that great court at age forty-three and feel the tension one more time.

To my mind, the finals of the women's singles at Wimbledon in 1953, won by Maureen Connolly, 8–6, 7–5, over Doris Hart, was one of the finest displays of women's tennis I have ever seen. They had long baseline exchanges with well-placed, hard-hit shots, often ending points with outright winners. Maureen, or Little Mo, as she was always called, was virtually invincible during her brief but brilliant career, and to many, including me, was the greatest of all women tennis players. On that day, Doris played her almost dead even, and I feel she would have beaten any other opponent but Little Mo.

The list of women's champions at Wimbledon contains just about all the greats over the years. Attempting to rank them is nearly impossible. But, for pure watching pleasure, Alice Marble, Maria

Bueno, Karen Susman, and Evonne Goolagong Cawley stand out in my memory. Here athleticism combined perfectly with classic grace to produce greatness.

At this writing, I still hope to return to Wimbledon in the future, if only to compete in the veteran's doubles. The thrill of being there, especially on opening day, is something that must be experienced to be believed. Many changes have taken place in tennis recently, almost all for the better, but it is still a good feeling to know that much remains the same at Wimbledon. Tradition thrives there, and one gets the feeling that nothing can change it very much. At the same time, Wimbledon led the way into open tennis, being the first major tournament to open its draw to all tennis players. Not at all stagnant, Wimbledon is willing to adapt, but not at the expense of what has made and kept it the greatest of all tennis championships.

My flashback is over, Mr. Bunis having completed his introduction of Sven Davidson and me. As we prepare to hit the first ball in the warm-up of this Grand Masters singles match, I dare say we will keep it in play a bit longer than we did thirty years earlier.

THE QUEST

It's now the second day of the round robin at the Greenbrier, and my opponent is Frank Sedgman.

Of the many times we've met over the years, our first encounter will always stand out most vividly in my memory. It was the finals of the U.S. Championship at Forest Hills in 1951. It wasn't the first in the tournament for Frank or for me (in fact, it was already my tenth), but it was the first time in the finals for both of us, and the first of several crucial meetings between us.

Frank cruised into the finals rather easily, extended to five sets only by Tony Trabert in the quarterfinals. On the other hand, I had my usual quota of long matches, for which I was becoming known. As we started the finals, however, I felt fine physically and thought I was playing quite well. Let the record show that I got a total of six games and the match lasted less than one hour!

Frank was absolutely devastating, and although I tried everything I could to stem the tide, nothing helped. I can honestly say I have never been beaten so badly while feeling that I was playing quite well. I always felt I had an edge in speed over most of my opponents, but on this day Frank proved to me that he was the fastest player ever on the tennis court. Whenever we've discussed that match, Frank has always said it was perhaps the finest tennis he ever played.

In the locker room after the match, Allison Danzig, the dean of American tennis writers, approached me with a look of pure astonishment on his face. Never one to get overly excited at a tennis match, he seemed ready to explode. He had kept the statistics on our contest, as he often did in the press box, as an aid for his newspaper stories. He told me that over the years he had been doing this, he had arrived at the conclusion that, in an average match of four sets, the winner would make about eight errors to five winning placements. In our match, Frank had made twenty-eight errors and fifty-three placements, almost double the amount of placements to errors! He labeled it *unbelievable*. I could assure him that I, too, had never encountered anything quite like it before.

Largely due to the emergence of Frank Sedgman, Australia wrested the Davis Cup from the United States in 1950, after it had resided in this country since the resumption of the competition in 1946 after the war. Thus, for the first time in quite awhile, the United States became a challenging nation. Since the Challenge Round would take place in Australia between Christmas and New Year's, our team had to be selected shortly after Forest Hills in order to journey down under in October. It was customary for players to arrive there a couple of months earlier in order to play in two major grass court tournaments as well as the Interzone Final prior to the Challenge Round.

Frank Shields was named captain of the U.S. team (a rather surprising selection since he hadn't been closely connected with the game for several years), and I was named to the team along with Dick Savitt, then the current Wimbledon champion, and Tony Trabert. We were all Easterners, so we assembled in New York and flew to Palm Springs, California, for a few days' layover and practice before taking off for Australia. It wasn't until we arrived on the West Coast that we learned that Ted Schroeder had been added to the team and that Jack Kramer would be along as coach and adviser. Schroeder had been a stalwart on the U.S. teams since the war, although he had pretty much limited his play during the previous season and hadn't played at Forest Hills since 1949. His addition to the team came as a surprise, but more important to me, it was an indication that my chances to play were greatly reduced. Everyone felt that Ted had a virtual guarantee before leaving that he would play singles and doubles. Trabert was the left-court doubles player for sure, and it looked as if Savitt, being the Wimbledon champion, would be the other singles player. That left you-know-who along for the ride. I was convinced that I was the fourth man on a three-man team.

In a way, the intrigue was good for me and started me on the best part of my career. Feeling that I was the extra man, I realized that if I were going to play at all, I had to prove it over there. I had to put it all together at that time, because if there was any way for them not to use me, they probably wouldn't have.

So while at the time I felt a little indignant, as things turned out, it probably was just what I needed. In the first of the two tournaments, the New South Wales Championships in Sydney, I beat Trabert, Ken McGregor, and Sedgman to win the tournament. Furthermore, this win took place at White City in Sydney, the site of the Challenge Round a few weeks hence. It was quite an accomplishment and placed me squarely in the picture as a singles player on our team. Meanwhile, Schroeder and Trabert played doubles together and carried Sedgman and McGregor to five sets in the finals. I was to be paired with Tony at the next tournament in an attempt to discover the best possible combination for our side. So Trabert was going to play doubles for sure, which was as it should have been. After their excellent showing in Sydney, Shields, our team captain, decided to keep Trabert and Schroeder together in Melbourne, where the Victorian Championships were to be played at Kooyong the next week. He felt that another tournament together might prove valuable to them. But in a countermove, Harry Hopman, who was captain of the Australian team, split up Sedgman and McGregor so as not to give our pair any additional practice against them. This was a smart move on the part of the canny Aussie, for Trabert and Schroeder won the tournament and became our Challenge Round doubles team, just as he wanted.

I continued my excellent play in Melbourne, beating Schroeder and losing to Sedgman in the finals in a good match. By now, I couldn't be kept out of the singles in the Challenge Round, and the problem for Shields and Kramer now became who the other singles player would be. Savitt felt sure that he would play and Schroeder knew that *he* would play, so you can see the problem developing.

Meanwhile, the Australian team was having troubles, too. Sedgman was a fixture in singles and he and Ken McGregor were the doubles team, but their second singles presented a dilemma. McGregor had played extremely well the year before, upsetting Schroeder in the key match. He was an excellent big-match player and Hopman's favorite. But Sir Norman Brookes, head of the Australian selection committee, favored Mervyn Rose, the other top Aussie, who had beaten McGregor in most of their meetings. Also, Rose had an excellent record against Savitt (who the Aussies figured would be our other singles player), whereas Savitt had beaten McGregor in the finals at Wimbledon rather decisively. Also, Rose was left-handed, as was Sir Norman Brookes.

It's easy to see why this 1951 Challenge Round would be the most intriguing of the seven I was to take part in. We still had to play the Interzone Final against Sweden, whose team included Lennart Bergelin and Sven Davidson, not exactly pushovers, to say the least. However, we were confident of victory, especially since the matches were to be played on grass, a decided advantage to us since we were used to playing on it, and the Swedes were not.

At this point, I approached Frank Shields and asked not to be considered for the Interzone Final against Sweden. I was concerned about trying to peak for the Challenge Round, and I had reached the finals in both the New South Wales and Victorian tournaments and was in need of some rest. Also, bear in mind that all matches there were best-of-five sets, and there was considerable tension because of the upcoming Davis Cup series. I was willing to take my chances on being selected for the Challenge Round, which I was confident we'd reach.

Schroeder and Trabert played against Sweden and they won 5–0, setting the stage for White City and the Challenge Round. The moment of truth arrived: the teams had to be named, and all the masterminding and second-guessing had to come to an end. Australia went with Rose and Sedgman in singles, and the Americans went with Schroeder and Seixas. The doubles were Sedgman and McGregor against Schroeder and Trabert. Savitt was out. Dick has always felt that Kramer influenced Shields to use Schroeder because Jack and

Ted were such good friends. While I think that's true, I still believe that Ted was assured of a spot before he left the States. I defeated Rose in the first match, and Sedgman prevailed over Schroeder. After the Australians beat us in doubles in straight sets, Schroeder salvaged a win against Rose on the third day, making it 2–2 and forcing a showdown that I hoped would be a replay of what had transpired several weeks earlier on the same court.

In the locker room, a few moments before going onto the court, Frank and I joked nervously about how maybe we didn't feel like playing unless we each got ten thousand dollars before going on the court. We were receiving fifteen dollars a day living expenses, while some twenty thousand fans in the stands had already swelled the tills of the USLTA and the Lawn Tennis Association of Australia (LTAA) by thousands of dollars. Funny, the things you think of at crucial moments.

In a great day for Australia, Sedgman played what I believe to be his second best match ever and virtually repeated his Forest Hills win over me, 6–4, 6–2, 6–2. As before, I didn't play badly, but once again I had run into a Sedgman who was invincible. Naturally, the Americans were all greatly disappointed; I personally would have considered it a perfect ending to a fairy tale trip if I could have beaten Frank that day. It was not to be, however, and as I look back upon it, I honestly believe the results would have been the same no matter who played for us or for them. We would have beaten their number two player, Rose or McGregor, and they would have won the doubles. For us to win, someone had to beat Sedgman, and the two with the best chances were Schroeder and I. To this day, though, I can still picture Hopman smiling as he "played" Schroeder onto our doubles team.

It was difficult for Americans, and indeed, the rest of the world, to realize or even imagine the fanaticism toward tennis that existed in Australia in the early to mid-1950s. It was the number one sport in that country, elevated to that position largely as a result of the success of the Davis Cup team against the mighty United States beginning in 1950. Though Australia is as large in area as the United States, its population at the time was only about eight million to our one hundred fifty million. The difference was that about six million Australians played or closely followed tennis. I can remember flying into Sydney at night in 1951 and seeing a great many tennis courts with lights. I later found out there were over eight hundred lighted courts in Sydney alone, quite possibly more than in all the rest of the world at the time.

Tennis and cricket were the biggest sports, with Australian Rules football also quite popular, and of course, the Aussies love the horses and the water. Most of the major cities are near the sea. The Aussies are an outdoor, sports-loving people, and when their players brought the prestigious Davis Cup to their shores, they were quick to recognize and promote them to superstar status. This, of course, attracted more and more of their top young athletes into tennis and in the end was responsible for Australia's domination of the sport in the 1950s. Americans used to ask me how a country with such a small population could produce so many top tennis players. Aussies who played and dominated tennis in the 1950s included Frank Sedgman, Ken McGregor, John Bromwich, Mervyn Rose, Lewis Hoad, Ken Rosewall, Rex Hartwig, Mal Anderson, Ashley Cooper, Neale Fraser, Rod Laver, and Roy Emerson. Among those dozen players, there are six Wimbledon singles champions, seven U.S. singles champions, nine Wimbledon doubles champions, and ten U.S. doubles champions, in addition to many other major titles garnered along the way. They were products of the boom that had hit Australia in 1950, eighteen years before it hit the United States.

An example of Australia's tennis fanaticism occurred shortly after their victory in the 1951 Challenge Round. Sedgman was being courted for the pro ranks by Jack Kramer, and the money sounded good to Frank, who was planning to marry. He was seriously considering the move. The Australian officials were so fearful of losing their Davis Cup hero to the pros, that they initiated a nationwide collection and presented Frank's fiancée with approximately twenty-five thousand dollars, ostensibly as a wedding gift. To show his gratitude, Frank remained an "amateur" for one more year.

Sedgman's decision helped make 1952 a frustrating year for U.S. Davis Cup fortunes. The USLTA, seeing the handwriting on the wall, decided to send what I labeled the *economy team* to Australia. I was appointed playing captain, which cut down expenses. Tony Trabert was in the navy but was granted leave to play, and Ham Richardson and Straight Clark were the other members of the team. We defeated Italy in the Interzone Final, but Sedgman and McGregor were too much for us in the Challenge Round in Adelaide. My win over

McGregor was the only point we managed. Tony just hadn't been able to get enough tough match play during the previous few months, although I doubt seriously if the results would have been much different anyway.

The last match was played on the day of New Year's Eve, so we all decided to drown our sorrows by doing some serious celebrating. Both teams had been invited to a party at a very nice home in Adelaide, so after a bit of preparty warming-up, the team loaded into our car, and I proceeded to follow Frank Sedgman, who claimed to know the way. Shortly after starting out, we were stopped by the local police for exceeding the speed limit. I was getting nowhere with the policeman until I mentioned that we were the U.S. Davis Cup team and we were following Frank Sedgman. The last part was the magic ingredient and, after we all signed autographs, we were joyously sent on our way. We arrived at the party and were welcomed whole-heartedly by many friendly Aussies. After spending an hour or so thoroughly enjoying ourselves, we discovered we were at the wrong party! After many apologies, everyone was gradually gathered to-gether and we went down the street to the house where we belonged. This was an even bigger affair, black-tie, with music and plenty to eat and drink. It was a bit stuffy, though, so after a few minutes we all slipped out and returned to the first place. I don't recall too much else about the night, but from the way I felt the next day, it must have been a successful party.

So many people clamored for tickets to the Davis Cup Challenge Round in Australia that lots even had to be drawn for some of the seats. As in 1951 in Sydney, the stands were full in Adelaide, with perhaps eighteen thousand spectators. To enable some of the tennis-hungry fans who couldn't get seats to the Challenge Round to see the players in action, the International Lawn Tennis Club of Australia staged one-set exhibitions on the day following the Chal-lenge Round, with all the members of both teams taking part. The feature match on this occasion was a doubles contest with Sedgman and McGregor playing Mervyn Rose and me.

The reason for this match needs a little explaining. Earlier in the year, Rose and I paired up at the last minute to play in the U.S. National Doubles Championships at Longwood Cricket Club in Brookline, Massachusetts. Suddenly, we were without partners, and Merv was able to get permission from Harry Hopman to play with me. After all, Hoppy reckoned, no team was going to upset Sedgman and McGregor, who needed only this title to wrap up the grand slam of doubles for the year. You guessed it. Rose and I beat Talbert and Mulloy in the semifinals and took Sedgman and McGregor in five sets in the finals. It was a bitter defeat for the great Aussie pair, but an especially sweet victory for Rose, who had been the third man in the Australian camp for so long and who was never one of Hopman's favorites. In fact, when we wanted to defend our title the following year, Hopman refused to allow Rose to play with me.

In any event, our exhibition at the International Club was to give Frank and Ken one last chance to show that this lone loss of theirs in 1952 had been a fluke. As mentioned, we had all celebrated far too much the night before, with the possible exception of Ken McGregor, who lived in Adelaide and spent a more quiet evening. It was over 100 degrees on the court and, after a few games and some consumption of water, we were a bit woozy again. The game gradually got funnier and funnier, and play deteriorated. Frank, who was so quick, was going just as fast as ever, but often in the wrong direction. Finally, it went too far, and some of the fifteen thousand or so fans who paid ten bob (about one dollar) to get in on a first-come basis, started to complain. One irate spectator shouted at Frank, "What do you think we paid our ten bob for!," to which Frank replied, "I don't know, *we're* not getting any of it." With that, the governor general of the state left his box and the jeering got worse. This was Frank's last day as an amateur, so I guess he really didn't care too much, but knowing him, I'd say it was more likely the effects of the night before overtaking him. Calm was finally restored, and we resumed playing more seriously, but I shall never forget seeing Frank across the net, with a grin on his face, serve a ball up into the stands. I hardly need to mention the capper to the story: Merv and I defeated them again, keeping our brief career as a team without a loss.

Coming up to Forest Hills, I had probably the best overall record of the top players, and 1953 was developing as a great year for me. But then came a moment when everything went from good to bad. In the finals of the Newport Invitational about three weeks before the Nationals, I was playing Tony Trabert and leading two sets to love, with a service break in the third set. I was well on my way to victory when I slipped while volleying and twisted my right knee.

Looking back on my career, it's probably the only fairly serious injury I ever incurred. It is also the only time I ever considered stopping in a match and I probably should have. Unable to move well, I decided to finish, losing to Tony in five sets. Foolish as I might have been to continue, I'm glad now that I did, for I can still say to this day that I have never defaulted a tennis match.

Strangely, when reading the writeups on the tournament the next day, I noted that Al Laney, one of the top tennis writers of the time, never mentioned my injury in his coverage. I later learned that he had not been present at the match but had written two articles, one to be used if I won and one if Tony did. They printed the right article, but I could never understand that bit of journalistic skulduggery. Al never said a word to me about it.

My knee seemed to recover fairly quickly, although I was not able to do my share in the National doubles the next week. At Forest Hills, however, the knee seemed okay, and I managed to get through to the finals once again. My opponent was Trabert and I suffered a defeat almost as humiliating as the one to Sedgman in 1951. During the tournament Tony suddenly seemed to get it all together and was flawless and overpowering. It came at a bad time from my point of view, but it augured well for our chances in the upcoming Davis Cup season against Australia, especially since, in the semifinals, Tony had beaten Rosewall and I had beaten Hoad, both in straight sets. Also, by now Tony and I were well on our way to becoming a really good doubles team, as our eventual record would prove.

With Sedgman and McGregor gone, Australia turned to the whiz kids, Hoad and Rosewall. Hopman still had Rose in reserve, along with Rex Hartwig, probably the finest doubles player of all the Aussies. Bill Talbert was appointed captain of our team and Ham Richardson was our third player.

My troubles started shortly after our arrival. While practicing in Melbourne, my knee suddenly gave way and felt much the same as it had in Newport. I could hardly walk and the joint began to swell. We contacted several of the leading orthopedic doctors in Melbourne, all of whom suggested rest and therapy. Time, however, was the one thing we didn't have too much of, since the Interzone Final against Belgium in Brisbane was only about two weeks away. I was virtually unable to practice and soon began to wonder whether I would be able to get in shape in time.

Arriving in Brisbane, I found a note in my box at the hotel from a Milton Conn, who described himself as an American osteopath living in Brisbane. I immediately contacted Dr. Conn and was somewhat heartened when he said he thought he could help me. I should mention that I have always been a believer in osteopathy, and I'm grateful for the help I've had over the years from these doctors around the world. With two short sessions per day, in which simple exercises (but the right ones) were utilized, my knee responded almost immediately. Within ten days it felt completely normal and has never bothered me again. But I had lost a month of preparation, and it was apparent in my play.

FOR USLTA AND COUNTRY

Belgium had two of the best players in Europe at that time—Jacques Brichant and Philippe Washer—and we knew it would not be easy for us to beat them for the chance to enter the Challenge Round against Australia a couple of weeks later.

Incidentally, in those days, the Challenge Round was a big event in Australia that drew tremendous crowds and resulted in a large gate. The countries (not the players, of course) shared the proceeds of up to 100,000 dollars on a 50–50 basis. It so happened that the USLTA was in poor financial straits back then, and had already spent the money from the Challenge Round. Most of the time in that era it was a foregone conclusion that we'd get to the Challenge Round. We seldom beat Australia, but at least we generally got to challenge the Aussies.

In the 1957 Interzone Final, for example, against these same Belgians, Herbie Flam won the opening match against Brichant, after which I beat Washer. But we lost the doubles and Washer beat Flam, so at the end of four, Belgium had two victories and so did we. It came down to a match between Brichant and me.

I suspect USLTA officials felt the pressure as much as I did, because if I lost that match, it meant that the United States would not go to the Challenge Round, and the USLTA would be out the expected gate money. I personally had nothing to lose but pride, but I was aware of the financial subplot. Fortunately, Brichant had had to play a tough five-set singles match the first day, and then four sets of doubles the next day, so he was pretty tired. The first set of our match was close, but then he folded. I won the match, the United States got to the Challenge Round, and the USLTA was saved. If I hadn't won, we wouldn't have made it to the Challenge Round and the USLTA wouldn't have received that fifty thousand dollars and would have been bankrupt. For years, the association had been operating on deficit financing, spending money in anticipation of funds coming in from Challenge Rounds. They were so confident we'd get there that they didn't feel they were taking any risk at all.

Amateur, "Shamateur"

It's ironic that the players who were, in effect, earning thousands of dollars (which was then a large sum) for their associations were not being remunerated themselves. Thousands of stories have been written about how players survived in the days of amateur tennis. There may have been some sporadic subsidization, but there were no wholesale under-the-table payments that I ever heard about. If there were, I can't imagine the sums being anywhere near the levels some have claimed. If there was money to be had, I was probably in a position to be a recipient, so either I was very naive or correct in my feeling that the idea of anyone having played amateur tennis for money is hokum. Nobody in his right mind would have played for that purpose. It wasn't "shamateur" tennis, as far as I was concerned.

We amateurs were entitled to receive expense money for ourselves and, if we were married, for our wives. The amount increased somewhat as the cost of living increased.

If a tournament was being held in Europe, the couple would be entitled to first-class airfare, plus per diem expense money. Some players may have converted first-class tickets to economy and kept the difference, received tickets to the same place from two sources and cashed one in, or padded their expense accounts. But it couldn't have amounted to more than a pittance. The amount of expense money varied, depending on the player's stature, with the top-ranked players receiving the maximum. At the time, I was playing my best tennis and was among the top half-dozen or better U.S. players, so I got all the expense money I was entitled to. But I was happy if I could come out even at the end of the year. I never made any money playing as an amateur; I never played with that intention, and they'll never convince me that *anybody* played amateur tennis to make money. Anyone wanting to make money from the game had to turn professional.

On the other hand, although we merely "existed" on our tennis playing, we were treated very well everywhere. We received the VIP treatment and found that it was possible to live like a king, though we didn't have a nickel.

The sad part was that players were put in the position of having to scrounge around to do things that were considered "shamateur," like selling rackets they'd been given.

Although I got my rackets free for years, I was never in the right place at the right time to sign as an endorser of one. I was never subsidized. Jack Kramer, for one, had that kind of deal. When Jack played, his one intention was to turn professional, and the racket manufacturer knew he was going to. The same thing was true of Tony Trabert, and I know that the manufacturers helped each along when he was an amateur, realizing that he'd be on their staff when he turned pro. But I never indicated to anyone any intention of turning pro, and so was never helped.

Not counting senior tournaments, I played in the men's singles at Forest Hills a record twenty-nine times, of which I reached the finals three times and won the event once. During each of those twenty-nine tournaments, I lived in New York about ten days, for a total of nearly three hundred days in the big city. In all that time, I got *one* free dinner. The night after I won the tournament, someone treated me at the club.

Even on that occasion, my host wasn't someone connected with the tournament, but just a friend who came over to say he'd enjoyed the match and wanted to buy me dinner. Ironically, I had already ordered—a hamburger—so that was my free dinner.

For the national championships, we didn't get a nickel in expense money, even though it meant living in New York in addition to traveling to the city from our hometowns. These were the U.S. National Championships at Forest Hills, something a ranking player could not afford to miss from the standpoint of prestige. The tennis establishment knew that you couldn't very well skip the tournament, so they didn't have to give you anything. If you didn't want to play, too bad.

It wasn't considered wrong for someone to buy you a dinner or for a person or business to sponsor a tournament. But there were no sponsors around that I knew of. Of the five times I went to Culver, Indiana, to play in the junior and boys finals, we used the family car three or four times, and, in fact, gave a lift to some others who were going. But there was no such thing as help from any of the local associations. There just wasn't any money. Most of the tournaments would put you up and give you meals for as long as you stayed in the tournament. But once you were eliminated, you were on your own.

TROUBLE DOWN UNDER

Getting back to 1953, we managed to defeat Belgium 4–1, but I was anything but pleased with my condition, and the Challenge Round in Melbourne was only a few days away.

Tony Trabert was playing well and we were considered the favorites by the press, especially since we were the seasoned players and Hoad and Rosewall were the untried youngsters. Another large crowd was on hand at Kooyong to cheer their countrymen on. I lost the opening match to Hoad, but Tony defeated Rosewall, who seemed to suffer a bit from the overwhelming pressure of being in his first Challenge Round. In fact, Hopman pulled Kenny out of the doubles and inserted Rex Hartwig one hour before match time, a perfectly legal maneuver but one not designed to calm the nerves of the player involved. We won in three straight sets, to take a 2–1 lead.

On the final day, Lew Hoad and Tony Trabert played what many feel was one of the best Davis Cup matches ever. After Lew won the first two sets, it started to drizzle slightly and both players donned spikes. As the balls grew heavier with the moisture from the court, Tony gradually began to get back into the match. He evened the sets at 2–2 and serves held in the fifth until it was 5–5. During the next game, Lew slipped on the wet grass and, although unhurt, did get a bit dirty. Harry Hopman threw him a towel to dry off, a gesture that was blown out of proportion.

The press called Hopman a genius for relieving the tension just at the right moment, and people still talk about the brilliant move by the foxy Australian captain. In reality, all he did was toss a towel to Hoad so that he could dry off. But when Trabert, serving with new balls, was broken at love, giving Hoad the match, Hopman was credited with having performed a near miracle. Maybe it had some mysterious effect on Lew, but I choose to think the new balls, being lighter and faster, responded to his touch and, instead of being an advantage to the server as they usually are, in this case helped the receiver. In any event, the Challenge Round was suddenly 2–2, and I had to play Rosewall in the deciding match.

The rain had not let up, and the court was quite slippery, so they postponed our match until the next day. Needless to say, neither Kenny nor I slept very well that night, which, added to all the other troubles I had been having, made it a rough trip. I lost to Ken in four sets and felt just about as dejected as a tennis player could feel. All I could think of was how a year that had been so great a few months earlier could have wound up being so horrible.

Before leaving Australia, Billy, Tony, and I got together and made a solemn vow that we would be back, one year later, and that we would win the Davis Cup.

VICTOR VICTORIOUS

In many ways, 1954 was just the opposite of 1953. I played just so-so on the continent and at Wimbledon, and had, at best, a rather spotty record coming into Forest Hills. However, after twelve previous tries, including two as runner-up, it all came together for me just a few days after my thirty-first birthday. Rex Hartwig was a surprise finalist, having beaten Trabert and Rosewall, and, in my side of the draw, Ham Richardson upset Lew Hoad in the quarters and played a good match against me in the semis. In beating Rex in four sets, I became and still am the oldest first-time winner of the U.S. Singles Championships. I have always considered this a dubious honor, but, if nothing else, it showed stick-to-itive-ness. This is also one of those records that is not likely to be broken since players seem to be getting better at younger ages nowadays.

After Forest Hills, my winning ways continued and I was victorious for the second time (without the loss of a set) at the prestigious Pacific Southwest Championships in Los Angeles. In passing, I might mention what an enjoyable tournament this always was, under the able direction and supervision of Perry Jones. There were always many movie stars in the stands all week long, a fact that prompted someone to suggest that it was the only tournament in the world in which the players watched the spectators.

After the Pacific Southwest, the Davis Cup team assembled for a trip to Mexico City and a zone final with the Mexicans. Although we were successful, 4–1, against them, I became famous for losing the first-ever Davis Cup match to Mexico. I lost to Gus Palafox, a fine player. To this day, there is a plaque hanging in the stadium at Centro Deportivo Chapultepec, honoring his victory. Things have changed around quite a bit over recent years, and I doubt that such a result now would seem so noteworthy. The fact is that it was so much a foregone conclusion in the 1950s that the United States and Australia would meet in the Challenge Round that an individual match won by any other country caused raised eyebrows (or plaques).

Of the seven years I played on our team, we were in the Challenge Round every year. I played in a total of sixteen zone matches, finishing with a 20–2 record in singles and a 12–1 in doubles. The fact that I was only 6–14 overall in Challenge Rounds those years points out the domination by the Australians.

Shortly after returning from Mexico, we took off for Australia. Billy Talbert was again the captain, and young Mike Green joined Ham Richardson as the other member of our team. Tony Trabert and I, however, had no thoughts of sharing playing time with them against the Swedes in the Interzone Final or the Aussies in the Challenge Round, unless or until the ties were decided. *This was our quest!* During the tournaments, unlike the year before, the Aussies were getting the buildup from the press. Hoad and Rosewall were a year older, more experienced, and considered capable of beating the U.S. team of Trabert (not having as good a year as in 1953) and Seixas (getting along in years). When, in fact, Rosewall beat me in the finals of the Victorian Championships, it marked his eighth straight win over me. I recall in the aftermatch speech, however, warning him that no one had ever beaten me *nine* times in a row! While this was intended to sound humorous, I was deadly serious. Without meaning to pass over it lightly, we did defeat Sweden, 5–0, in Brisbane in the Interzone Final, with our old friends, Bergelin and Davidson, still at a slight disadvantage on the lightning-fast grass courts.

The Challenge Round draw in Sydney paired Hoad and Trabert in the first match, with Rosewall and Seixas to follow. This was regarded as favorable for Australia, especially since Rosewall and

I were to meet on the first day. In a friendly moment in the locker room after the draw, I asked Adrian Quist, the Aussie great, what odds he would give me that we wouldn't win the first three matches. He offered 10 to 1 and I wagered a bob with him. I reckoned Tony would win, as his form had greatly improved since our arrival, and we would also win the doubles, so I thought 10 to 1 on my match with Ken was good odds. Tony played well and very intelligently against Lew to win in four sets, and I garnered some sweet revenge in four sets over Ken. I can still say no one ever beat me nine times running. In the doubles the next day, we beat the whiz kids 10–8 in the fourth set, to win the Davis Cup for the United States. It was a great moment, one of those once-in-a-lifetime thrills and the culmination of many months of physical and mental preparation. Although it was the only victory I experienced in seven tries against the Aussies, somehow it seemed to make up for the losses.

Almost twenty-six thousand people attended that Challenge Round, the largest crowd ever to witness a tennis match (with the exception of the Bobby Riggs–Billie Jean King match in Houston).

Looking back, I suppose that what made the success so sweet was the sacrifice and then the reward for the hard work. I was filled with pride and joy when the big mug was presented to us formally by Prime Minister Robert Menzies, who, incidentally, was a loyal fan, attending all the Davis Cup matches over the years. He also became a good friend of mine and wrote several fine letters on my behalf when I decided to go into business in 1958. He was widely regarded as, next to Winston Churchill, the greatest English-language orator in the world.

And so, the year 1954 ended just the opposite from the way 1953 had, and whenever Tony and I have a chance to reminisce a little, we inevitably recall the night we got together after losing in 1953. And whenever I see Adrian Quist, I remind him that he still owes me ten shillings, which I will never let him pay me.

The Cup went back to Australia in 1955, and I made two more attempts to help return it. Trabert turned pro after winning both Wimbledon and Forest Hills in 1955, so the U.S. Davis Cup doubles was never quite as strong again. About as close as we came to winning was in 1957, when all four singles matches went five sets. We lost 3–2, however, as the Aussies proved too tough in the doubles. This was my final Davis Cup, and I had the happy experience of winning my last match. It was 13–11 in the fifth set against Mal Anderson who is, coincidentally, one of the rookies on our Grand Masters tour. At age thirty-four, after fifty-five Davis Cup matches, I was finally convinced that I couldn't weather another wave of Australians. Sedgman and McGregor, Hoad and Rosewall, Cooper and Anderson, along with Rose and Hartwig, had been enough. In the wings were Fraser and Emerson and an up-and-coming youngster named Rod Laver. I was known as a fighter, but this was ridiculous. They were using clubs and I had a toothpick.

But here I am back at the Greenbrier, still battling Australians, as Sedgman prepares to serve first. I kind of suspect I'll have the same trouble with him now that I did some twenty-nine years ago. He's slowed down to near normal human speed now, but he's still just a little faster than I am.

THE GRAND MASTERS

On a weekend afternoon on a sunbaked court at a suburban tennis club, a former stock broker, a part-time musician, a lawyer, and a hotel owner, each in his late forties or fifties, are locked in a hotly contested doubles match. They play the game good-naturedly but intensely, as if money, reputations, and memories are on the line.

And indeed they are. For while in many respects the scene described could be taking place in any of hundreds of tennis clubs (including yours) among any four middle-aged, occasional players, this one involves a quartet of former tennis greats who still play professionally against their old-time rivals in something called the Grand Masters. I'm happy to have been a part of it.

The Grand Masters tour came to life in 1973, "fathered" by a Cincinnati businessman, Alvin W. (Al) Bunis, who had been a nationally ranked junior tennis player and had competed against some of the better players, including Frank Sedgman. He turned his attention to a business career but kept his hand in the game, doing volunteer work for the United States Lawn Tennis Association (which has since taken the *Lawn* from its name) and playing tennis locally and, occasionally, on a national level.

When he reached forty-five, he started playing "senior tennis," which at that point was basically an amateur game. In the first round of the first tournament he played in, at Forest Hills, Al had the misfortune of drawing as his opponent the number one ranked senior, Gardnar Mulloy, but had the good fortune (and skill) to beat him.

"I told myself, 'This is fun, this is exciting,' " Bunis said, "and I started to play in all the senior tournaments and had a lot of fun with it. Yet I knew, because I was chairman of the U.S. Tennis Association Senior Committee, that the really great players of the time weren't playing. Many of them were professionals, and couldn't play. So I just fantasized about it and thought it would be a great thing if I could prevail upon a few of them to play a little tennis on a formalized basis. Since most were professionals, I knew there was no way I could prevail upon them to play, unless there was prize money."

"There were no professional sports for middle-aged people at all in those days," Bunis continued. "I talked to a few people about my idea and most thought it was highly impractical. I was laughed off the courts at the West Side Tennis Club by someone who was heavily involved in the professional world of tennis at that time."

But Bunis stuck to his guns. He came to Philadelphia to tell me his idea. He said he would put up the prize money himself—something unheard-of, but he did it. "The only commitment you have to make, Vic, is to play." I agreed.

He then flew to California to see Tom Brown, who once was the runner-up at Wimbledon, once runner-up in the U.S. championships, and had won the Wimbledon doubles with Jack Kramer. Al and Tom watched Bobby Riggs defeat Margaret Court, and Bunis presented his idea. Brown agreed to play.

Bunis had been studying the field closely and had established three criteria for being a Grand Master: a player had to be at least forty-five years old (that's easy; you get there without trying); he had to have won a major national or world championship, and he still had to be able to play tennis at a level that was interesting enough to the public to make people come out and watch. Otherwise, Bunis said, "You have nothing."

The last criterion narrowed the field tremendously. There were plenty of good senior tennis players around, but few of them, Bunis included (as he is the first to admit), could draw flies with honey. Players would tell him, "Oh, I could beat this guy," and Bunis would respond, "But I can't find anybody to buy a ticket to see you play. And don't talk to me about it. I beat Gardnar Mulloy the first time we played, and I can assure you nobody would buy a ticket to see *me* play."

Bunis's next stop was London. In the locker room at Wimbledon he met Frank Sedgman, who readily qualified on all counts, and told him of his idea. Says Bunis, "He listened to me because he remembered me and knew I was a reasonably successful businessman and that I'd been around tennis. I'm sure he thought it wasn't a practical idea. To prove how serious I was, I said we were going to have our first pilot tournament the week after Wimbledon. I said, 'Go home to Australia via the United States and I will buy you a ticket.' I guess he thought I was possibly joking. We took a taxi down to the Pan Am office and I bought him a ticket, which I stuck in his hand and said, 'Here's a ticket to Milwaukee, see you next week.' So he knew I was serious."

In July of 1973 in Milwaukee the Grand Masters played its first tournament, and, in Bunis's words, "really had a surprising response.

"The matches were played in a tennis community, at a club where people had seen the players play earlier in their career. The media grabbed it up. The *Wall Street Journal* ran a front-page article about senior professional sports and this obscure guy in Cincinnati and his idea. That was terribly meaningful, and then almost on the heels of it, *Sports Illustrated* called and did a six-page article on us in color. Those two things sort of made it explode."

The Grand Masters could claim early in its life that its players represented more national and world titles than any other age group ever assembled. Among the players (no more than eight in a given tournament) were Bobby Riggs, Billy Talbert, Gardnar Mulloy, Sven Davidson, Torben Ulrich, Pancho Segura, Frank Parker, Gustavo Palafox, Jaroslav Drobny, Hugh Stewart, Torsten Johannsen, Pancho Gonzales, and Sam Match, in addition to Tom Brown, Frank Sedgman, and me. More tennis champions joined over the years.

Bunis is convinced that when the Grand Masters started, his were the best forty-five-year-old (and over) players around. "These men are now older, and there are some forty-five-year-olds who can beat some of our fifty-eight-year-olds," he said in 1982, "but each one of these guys is about the best player in the world *for his age*. There is no sixty-four-year-old player in the world who can come close to Bobby Riggs, no forty-five-year-old better than Gene Scott; no forty-six-year-old better than Alex Olmedo; no forty-eight-year-old better than Mal Anderson. I make the world's rankings, so I'm quite familiar. . . . Ramanathan Krishnan and Scott, both the same age, would probably be quite close. There's nobody at fifty-nine who can beat Vic Seixas. So, in a sense, they are the best; it's just that they're not all forty-five."

NOSTALGIA TRIP

In 1973, when the Grand Masters began, tennis was still booming, and media coverage was getting bigger. Added to the onset of open tennis, which contributed to popularization by the media, was a big wave of nostalgia. The Grand Masters was a logical device for capitalizing on the boom in the game and this wave of nostalgia.

You could not have imagined anything like the Grand Masters happening eight or nine years earlier, when no one cared whether I played tennis in my backyard or anywhere else.

One of the drawbacks that we faced at the beginning—and still face—is that about 85 percent of the current tennis fans were not fans when we were playing, so they didn't know who we were. With a few exceptions (Pancho Gonzales, notably) our names were unknown, and that took some educating and promoting to overcome. As the "household" names, the Lavers and Rosewalls and other popular stars and "legends" of the tennis-boom era come into the Grand Masters—provided that the purses offered are enough to attract them—the Grand Masters will become more popular and easier to promote. Now the challenge is to get people to come to the matches. Once they come, they're pleasantly surprised at the quality and intensity of the play, and they love the matches.

Strange as it may seem, I think there's some truth to the claim made in a 1973 press release that the country's new middle-aged player "can relate far better to these Grand Masters than to the sleek young greyhounds like Smith, Ashe and Laver . . . he can readily relate his own tennis problems to those he views on the court. After all, these middle aged players have all the problems of middle age."

One of the elements that has made our tour successful is the fact that we are as competitive as ever. Sedgman tries and drives himself just as hard now as he ever did. Most fight to the bitter end and fall down. That's the way we used to play, and still do. That press release also was on the mark when it said, "Senior tennis is a thinking man's game. The players have to compensate for the lack of power with science and strategy." But it's far from a powder-puff competition.

The tennis has been amazingly good, to the surprise of many of the spectators, who half expect something like an old-timer's baseball game. I'd say our level is somewhere between those of today's men's and women's games. It's neither too fast nor too slow, which makes it attractive to the public. In the Grand Masters we've discovered that we've all aged, and so no one has an edge on anyone else. We play longer points, which has made our brand of tennis more interesting to watch from the average spectator's point of view. Also, it's no longer the big serve-and-volley game, although it depends to a degree on the type of surface we're playing on. If the surface dictates that that's the way to win, we'll attempt it, but not on a slower court because obviously we can't cover as well. Besides, we know we're less likely to win playing that way on that type of surface.

AUDIENCES

The size of the Grand Masters audience varies, depending on where the event is held and how well it's promoted. It seems to work much better in a smaller town or a club-type atmosphere than in a big arena in a big city. As I mentioned, the big problem is that four out of five tennis fans were not fans when we were playing, so our names are remembered at best only vaguely (except in Australia, which has a tradition of tennis involvement). But once they come to the match, they're not disappointed. If the tournament is staged for the benefit of a charity, attendance is usually larger. We've had more than six thousand spectators and as few as a few hundred. The prize money is guaranteed, no matter how many show up. The local promoters pay a fee to the Grand Masters and provide eight or nine hotel rooms. Whatever proceeds come in belong to them. Some new condominium developments have scheduled us as an inexpensive way of getting publicity for themselves.

PLAYING EVERYWHERE

Grand Masters tournaments have been played all over the world—Manila, Sydney, Hong Kong, Jakarta, Indonesia, Bahrain, Saudi

Arabia, Brazil, Johannesburg (where the largest crowd ever—between six thousand and seven thousand spectators—saw the finals between Pancho Gonzales and Frank Sedgman). Our largest U.S. audience was about five thousand at Pauley Pavilion on the campus of UCLA.

SCHEDULE

A Grand Masters tournament is a three-day event, beginning on Friday, with the scheduling such that only one court is needed for all the singles and doubles competition. (On rare occasions, weather problems have caused us to start a second match on another court.) The one-court format helps make the Grand Masters a neat package to sell.

The court we play on can be indoors or out and be any surface (we've played on them all). "In that respect," Bunis claims, "we consider ourselves the ultimate professionals. We will adjust to any court, and quickly. I've never heard a Grand Master say, 'I don't like grass' or 'I don't like clay.' That would be unprofessional. He might say, 'My style is a little better suited to one surface or another,' but then he'll add, 'I'm experienced enough that I'll just change my style.' "

There are usually four singles matches on Friday and two singles and two doubles on Saturday. The finals are played on Sunday, with a third-place play-off or something else if the host wants it.

Part of our package is to have our eight Grand Masters play a pro-am doubles on the preceding Thursday. The amateurs might be eight or more of the best local players, or eight top businessmen or media people who might buy the privilege of playing for a few hundred dollars. Sometimes it's presented as quite a big event, and the local participants get a lot of fun out of it. Most of the time, too, we put on a clinic on Saturday morning for children and/or adults —any group the host selects.

Unlike other tournaments, there is no pick-from-a-hat kind of draw for the Grand Masters. Essentially, the way the pairings are made is that the winner of the previous tournament is seeded number one and the player who was runner-up, number two. The two losing semifinalists from the previous competition are seeded three and four. The balance of the field is so constructed that players who competed against each other in the prior tournament meet someone else this time.

"We make no concessions to age whatsoever," says Bunis. "We play the same rules as the young people—the best of three sets with a 12-point tiebreaker."

MAKING A LIVING

It's not exactly a matter of butcher, baker, candlestick maker, but a variety of professions and occupations are represented in the Grand Masters. Tom Brown, one of the first to play, is a lawyer. Sedgman, who turned pro and played a couple of tours, owns a hotel in Australia and has a company there that sponsors the Australian Open. Hartwig was a farmer. He lived on a farm outside of Melbourne and hadn't touched a racket for seventeen years. Neale Fraser as recently as 1982 was captain of the Australian Davis Cup team. Mal Anderson had varied business interests and worked as a teaching pro in Australia. Torben Ulrich, our "guru" who brings along his own health food on tours, never stopped playing tennis but over the years has also been a correspondent for a Danish newspaper and a jazz musician, among other pastimes.

People ask, "Can you eat from the Grand Masters?" If you're Sedgman, you can. He probably made close to sixty thousand dollars one recent year. Bunis refers to it as "the world's best moonlighting," which may be just a slight exaggeration. He views the Grand Masters as a pleasant, profitable weekend activity that enables a player to have a job during the week.

But I don't think anybody is playing in it just to eat. There are too many risks to try and make a living out of between sixteen and twenty tournaments a year. Almaden Vineyards has been sponsoring us for about a decade (as of 1983). The prize money they put up, coupled with other prize money in senior men's tennis events, totals about 300,000 dollars.

In a given Grand Masters tournament, the prize money is divided on a percentage basis. The singles winner gets 23 percent; the runner-up, 15 percent. In some events we have a third-place play-off, in which case the number three finisher gets 10 percent; and the fourth-place finisher, 8 percent. If there's no third-place play-off, they each get 9 percent. The four losing quarterfinalists (only eight players compete in a tournament) each get 6 percent. So this accounts for 80 percent of the prize money.

The remaining 20 percent goes for doubles. The average tournament now has prize money of about fifteen thousand dollars, so if you lose in the first round of both the singles and the doubles, you come away with about a thousand dollars, plus a little bit from the pro-am play we engage in preceding the tournament. Our room is paid for, but not meals or travel expenses. Depending on the distance traveled, I can break even or make a little bit of money if I lose in the first round.

I haven't won any of the singles tournaments but have managed to finish second several times. For the first few years, I won a lot of the doubles tournaments, the first year taking almost all of them as Sedgman's partner. I then teamed with Hartwig; we won seven tournaments in a row. The second year of the Grand Masters, Sedgman and Hartwig were partners, but then Sedgman hurt his Achilles tendon and was out for most of the year. So Rex and I became partners. When Frank got back into action, he and Rex teamed up again, and I started playing with Sven Davidson. We didn't win any of the tournaments, but have made it to the finals quite often.

The tennis Grand Masters is a profit-making corporation, not bound by the regulations of any tennis associations. But naturally we follow tennis rules as far as game play is concerned.

A HUSTLER'S PURSE

On the subject of purses, Al Bunis recalls how delighted he was to receive the unheard-of sum of one thousand dollars to put together a pilot tournament in Cincinnati in November 1972 as a way of determining whether the whole Grand Masters concept was feasible. (I think today more than that goes to the lowest-ranked player in a pro tournament who loses in the first round.)

Al was going to assemble eight good players over forty-five and have them compete in a three-day tournament. He reached Gardnar Mulloy and Billy Talbert and offered to pay their air fare, and they received his offer enthusiastically, Bunis said. He made the same offer by telephone to Bobby Riggs.

"There was silence for a moment," Bunis remembers. "Then he said, 'Oh, Al, I couldn't come for a cent less than five hundred dollars.' "

"Bobby," I said, "I couldn't possibly do it. I have only a thousand dollars for the whole operation."

"It's out of the question, Al, I need five hundred."

Bunis said he'd see Riggs before the summer was over and asked him to say hello to mutual friends back east. Two weeks later, Bunis's secretary told him there was a Mr. Riggs on the line.

"Hi, Al, what did you decide?"

"What do you mean, 'What did I decide?' "

"You know, the five hundred."

"Bobby, it's out of the question," Bunis responded. "There are eight guys to divide that thousand. It comes to less than one hundred fifty each. I can't do it, Bobby."

Again, there was silence. Then Riggs asked, "How about three hundred?"

"Bobby, it's ridiculous," Bunis said, relating how the others were coming in, just for the air fare.

"Can't do it. But I'll see you before the summer's over. Say hello to anyone who remembers me."

Some weeks later, Bunis and his wife were at the bar of the Carlisle Hotel in New York, when he was called to the phone. Al heard the unmistakably squeaky Riggs voice say, "Al, it's Bobby."

"Hi, Bobby, how are you?"

"What did you decide?"

"Decide?"

"About the three hundred dollars?"

"It's out of the question, but I'll tell you what I'll do. The air fare between Cincinnati and New York is a hundred dollars. It costs eighteen dollars a night to stay at the Holiday Inn across from the courts, so if you want to do it, I'll give you a hundred and fifty-four dollars. But, Bobby, the tournament's next Friday. You've got to tell me now—in this conversation—whether you're coming or not."

There was silence for a good forty-five seconds. Then finally Riggs spoke. "Dammit, why do *I* always have to be the good guy!"

(The "good guy" is still hustling. He had me play backgammon with him for fourteen straight hours because I started off beating him and he wouldn't let me quit until he drew even.)

THE YOUNGER GRAND MASTERS

A lot of the Australians who were top players in the 1950s are now hitting the forty-five mark, which makes them eligible for the Grand Masters. We look forward to their joining us.

In a couple of cases, a "youngster" of forty-five has come into the Grand Masters confident of walking away with every match. The forty-five-year-old calculates quite correctly that, compared with the players in their fifties, he is relatively fit. One newcomer, for example, was in peak physical shape but hadn't been playing tournament tennis. So instead of breezing through the matches, he found himself a loser (albeit to the likes of Gonzales, Ulrich, and Davidson, three of the better players). Rosewall joining the Grand Masters presents a different story, however, because he's been playing and winning in the thirty-five-year-old group, the Legends.

Mal Anderson, who was playing almost as well as, if not equal to, Rosewall, joined the group and was expected to sweep all the competition. He won two or three tournaments in a row, but then lost two finals to Frank Sedgman, much his senior.

Although the age span between the oldest and youngest player in the Grand Masters is sometimes as much as fifteen years, we're essentially all contemporaries who have known and liked each other for decades. I've known Sven Davidson for more than thirty years (since we played each other at Wimbledon in 1950), and I've known Sedgman even longer. We all get along famously and have as much fun off the court as we do on. We all figure it's just gravy and we're happy to be playing.

GRAND MAESTRO

It's no wonder that sometimes the players have sought out the Grand Masters rather than the other way around. One day, Al received a letter from Guiseppe Merlo, an Italian player he had known in Italy years earlier. As he remembers it, the letter read: "Dear Mr. Bunis, I know you have circuit for older players. My name is Guiseppe Merlo. I am four times national champion. I am Italian Davis Cup player. I have beaten Rod Laver, I have beaten . . . I would like to play on your circuit. I am yours sincerely, . . ."

Bunis wrote back, "Dear Mr. Merlo, I remember you well. You've had a distinguished tennis career. Unfortunately, we use only eight men in a tournament and we already have a commitment for eight, and so I would not be able to make any commitment to you at this time, but if an opening occurs, you can rest assured that . . ."

About four weeks later, Al received a two-page cable. "Dear Mr. Bunis, I am Giuseppe Merlo, I am four times national champion of Italy, I understand you have circuit for senior players, I have beaten Rod Laver, . . ."

It went on just as the letter had.

Bunis cabled back, "Dear Mr. Merlo, I remember you well. You've had a distinguished tennis career, . . ."

At the tournament, who should show up but Guiseppe Merlo, ready to play! Bunis capitulated. "We used him for six years, he was a cute guy, and we never regretted it."

He's never regretted introducing the Grand Masters concept either.

"It was treated as a joke at the beginning," Bunis declares, "yet the public and media responded, and we struck a blow for an aging country and maybe an aging world. Over half this country is going to be over fifty years of age some time in the 1990s. Maybe you find that depressing, but it's sure as hell a fact."

Bunis, who has sold the Grand Masters to International Management Group and remains as a consultant, refers to us as a "geriatric band of warriors . . . an elitist bunch of guys. . . . Just go down the roll of great champions—Don Budge, Pancho Segura, Pancho Gonzales—and they've been in our midst."

Not only greatness, but great geographical diversity, is represented by the Grand Masters. For example, the eight participants in competition at the Longwood Cricket Club in Brookline, Massachusetts, in the summer of 1982, spanned five continents: Europe was represented by the Scandinavians Davidson and Ulrich; Australia, by Anderson; South America, by Olmedo, originally from Peru; Asia by the Indian star Ramanathan Krishnan; and North America, by the U.S. players Riggs, Scott, and me. We've had players, too, from Africa. Only Antarctica is missing, but we're working on that. One of the things that makes us attractive, I think, is that we have a good variety of players from all over the world.

NOTICING
YOU'VE AGED
■|■

It's like growing old, you don't realize it, it's such a creepy thing, it happens so slowly. Does anybody make an adjustment for that?

I think the same thing happens in tennis. It's such a slow process, you're not even aware of it. Then all of a sudden you realize you can't get to the ball, you can't cover the court, and you wonder what happened.

—Bobby Riggs, 1982

The aging of a tennis player takes place very gradually. But you don't have to consult a calendar or count the candles on your birthday cake to know that changes are occurring. The clues—that we've lost a step or a breath—are there all along. But we prefer not to notice.

For the world-class player, the physical changes happen more gradually, especially if you've been relatively free of injury. The psychological change may occur suddenly.

It happened to me first on my serve. My game was built heavily around my serve, and suddenly I noticed that it was coming back a lot harder, a lot more often, and with a lot more on it than I thought it should. It was the first clue I had that my game wasn't as good as it used to be. I was in my mid-forties when I made the discovery. Someone else might have noticed the change at a much younger age, but I'd been playing pretty well in my forties; my reflexes were still pretty good.

While the first realization that I wasn't the player I once was came to me on my serve, with someone else it might be on the volley or some other shot. I noticed a difference, too, in hitting a volley, especially on the forehand side. This had always been one of my strong points, but now I was sure that my reflexes had become a little slower and so I was instinctively bringing the racket back a little farther to give myself a little more time to hit the volley. And, of course, meeting the volley back a little, instead of out front, is not the recommended way. Thus, I missed more. Although I knew what was happening, for some reason I couldn't correct it. I couldn't speed up the reflex power. So my volley was another early victim of the aging process.

About the same time, I noticed that even though I was swinging harder than ever at the ball and hitting it in the middle of the racket, the ball wasn't coming off the racket as fast. The only answer I could come up with was that, like most older players, I wasn't *hitting* it as hard, though I might be *swinging* as hard. This was even true of an overhead, where you can really crank up and let go.

It may be that while the speed of the racket is the same, there's less rigidity at the moment of impact than there used to be. Possibly I wasn't getting a solid hit because the strength in my muscles or tendons was less at the moment of impact. Whatever the cause—whether it was because my racket wasn't moving as quickly, because I was experiencing some muscular deterioration, or because I was bringing my racket down at an angle a few degrees different or farther back—the ball wasn't coming off as fast.

What could I do about it? Live with it, and adjust. Other players have come to the same conclusion, and so should you. Alex Olmedo, at forty-six one of the youngest players of the Grand Masters, says, "When I was younger, one of my big assets was serve-and-volley. Now I rely more on my ground strokes to make a few points. I used to have a more dependable net game and more mobility on the court. The mobility factor is getting away from me now." (Wait a few years, Alex.) As Alex points out, as you get older, you learn to rely on different parts of your game, and eventually you stop volleying and coming to the net.

As far as mental adjustments are concerned, according to Alex, the aging topflight player has to play a more patient game. "In the old days, all you'd think of was serve, volley, put the ball away. Now you have to tell yourself, 'I've got to get three or four ground strokes and wait for the weak shot to come in on.' And you have to know exactly what position you're going to take on the court. You don't rely so much on speed." He learned to play that way on a clay court, he says, which wasn't his forte. Pancho Segura, whose two-handed forehand was one of the best shots in the game, used to tell him that on a clay court he had to be prepared to play three or four hours, as opposed to a fast court where a match was completed in half the time.

Alex can still blow an opponent off the court on occasion, but in another ten years he's going to find he has to win the points a different way. We all have to rely on not making many mistakes. We don't get easy points, so we have to work more for them.

Even though we realize all these things, it doesn't do us much good because everyone else in our peer group realizes them too, and any possible edge is canceled out. As Bobby Riggs says, "We're all on the same plane. Everybody's five steps slower. Everybody's doing what they used to do. The age factor is the same."

Riggs, who was an outstanding tennis player, one of the best in the world, declares, "I have a hard time remembering back to the time when I was really quick and fast and covered the court. I realize at one time I must have been able to do it, like all the young guys, but I can't remember *really* what I could do then."

What, if any, adjustments has Bobby made?

"I can't honestly say that I try to play any differently now than I ever played," he says. "I still make a nice lob, I still try to make a passing shot. The most notable fact is I can't cover the court. I don't have the strength on the backhand. I don't seem to have the comfort or the strength to be able to come back and really get it."

His forehand, he notes, has kept up much better than his backhand, but "My serve has gone way back. I get so used to just lobbing the ball over. Hey, I used to be able to serve real good. I always tried to place the ball. I always did everything smart and right and perfect. That was my style, that was my game. I always had great talent. I did everything.

"The only thing that I don't have is I cannot cover the court and my backhand has deteriorated, and my serve has gone away, and I don't have the quickness. And I don't have the reach. I come to the net—nobody could pass me—but now the ball is passing me. I look at the ball and, wow, these guys are making great passing shots."

Some players are bothered more than others about what aging has done to their tennis game, but Alex Olmedo, for one, declares, "It doesn't upset me at all. I admit that I'm getting older and there's nothing I can do about it. I realize I'm getting older and a bit slower, but I still have fun and enjoy the game. I'm glad I'm playing tennis and still enjoying the competition. I'm thankful I'm able to perform the way we do. . . . At least we go out there and get some exercise."

Alex, a teaching pro at the Beverly Hills Hotel, whose pupils include some of Hollywood's best-known stars, emphasizes the game's "lifetime sport" aspect.

"Tennis is such a great game, you can start when you're a youth and keep playing it into your seventies or eighties. You can continue to compete at your own level. Of course, you don't try to compete against the young kids. I realize that I'm not as quick as Borg and that I don't have the ability to hit the ball as hard. But when he gets a little older, I'll be able to give him a little better game."

Sven Davidson, the remarkable Swedish quinquagenarian (that means he's in his fifties), points out, "We're not competing with Borg and McEnroe and Connors, but among ourselves."

Another player Sven is not competing with, he says, is "the Sven Davidson of the 1950s." Accordingly, he's not bothered by the fact that he no longer can do quite what he did on the tennis court three decades ago. A vigorous survivor of a multiple-bypass heart operation in 1980, he hasn't made any deliberate adjustments in his playing style, Sven says, but he hasn't had to, because they've come about "automatically."

"One's legs are not as fast, one's eyes are not as fast, one's reflexes are not as fast. Okay, so one doesn't charge the net like a bull (although on fast courts, one tries to get to the net as soon as possible). You play within your physiological limits."

The players in the Grand Masters—and in other senior competitions—have all made adjustments of the type Sven mentioned, or they wouldn't be playing. Yet there are a few great players from the past who still have the ability to play but won't because apparently they've been unable to make this mental adjustment. They're not satisfied to compete at a level below what they used to play. Players like Dick Savitt and Tony Trabert have decided, in effect, "If I can't play at the level I used to when I was at my best, then I won't play."

Others of us, however, have made that adjustment. It's not that we enjoy being beaten or not playing as we once did. But we've rationalized that we'd rather play and enjoy the competition and pure fun of playing and the feeling of fitness, even it if means having to accept a little different, lower standard. Perfectionists sometimes miss out on fun.

A world-class player is more likely to become frustrated if he stops playing early in his career, or when he's right at the top of it. Chuck McKinley, for one, was a topflight player, but he really stopped when he was about twenty-four. He could very easily have played another four or five years without any physical problems.

I pushed a little bit, stretching my full-time career until I was thirty-four, but I think that was the reason I felt less frustration when I played later on. I had played a lot more than most players and had done everything I wanted to do.

At first, switching to part-time play didn't cause me any particular frustration. I still thought I could do what I formerly had, and in fact I played pretty well for a while in the nationals and some other tournaments before the gradual drop-off began.

It's such a gradual decline that, if you keep playing, you really don't notice it. If you could suddenly go back ten years, you'd see it, but as it is you're not aware of it.

The ability to see clearly the difference in how I played before didn't really hit home until I was about fifty. Gardnar Mulloy hasn't noticed it yet and he's about seventy. It depends on the individual.

Mal Anderson, the Australian star who recently joined the Grand Masters, is only forty-eight. He hasn't noticed any significant changes in his game as he's entered prime time. In fact, he speculates, contrary to the changes most world-class players have experienced as they've become seniors, he probably plays "more of an aggressive game" than he did previously. Why? "Maybe I don't want to get involved in long rallies and, secondly, I believe I move well enough to pressure the [other] guys."

While for a younger player running is no object, Mal says that an older player doesn't *want* to get involved in a long match in hot, humid weather that will tire him and leave him open to a pulled muscle. "So basically I attack a bit more."

Anderson says he hasn't noticed any real psychological changes in himself as a player, although he thinks, "My temperament is a lot better than when I was younger. Not that I ever got mad or anything of the kind, but I sort of handle the day-in and day-out situation much better."

"They seem to pace themselves a little bit," comments Al Bunis, the "headmaster" of the Grand Masters, "but in terms of the way in which they hit a tennis ball, I'd say there's little or no change at all."

BOOM!

It was in 1968 when the tennis boom began, the result, I think, of a combination of two major phenomena. First was the onset of open tennis. Open tennis (which means that pros and amateurs can compete together in the same major tournaments for out-in-the-open prize money) stimulated media interest, and the publicity began to feed on itself. We began to see widespread sponsorship, larger purses, and the infusion of a lot of money into the game. At the same time, our country was on a fitness kick, inspired somewhat by John Kennedy's leadership. When so much was being said and written about getting and staying in shape, people discovered that tennis was a fine way to become fit while having a good time. They found it was more entertaining and challenging than jogging, which was already enjoying popularity at that time, and unlike golf, didn't require a whole day to play.

Whole families took up the game. People in their thirties and forties started hitting the tennis ball. Housewives who had never been interested in sports either as spectators or participants and men who were spending most of their lives behind a desk and in front of a television set got into tennis. They were joined by people who'd played it years earlier and given it up, and by others who'd been athletic but had participated in sports other than tennis.

TV OR NOT TV

I'm convinced that television had nothing to do with the tennis boom. In the 1950s, TV coverage of tennis was only a token thing—maybe three hours of the finals from Forest Hills, and nothing else.

It wasn't for lack of trying on the part of the tennis establishment that TV wasn't interested. Tennis people told the TV broadcasters that, compared with golf, baseball, and other sports, tennis was the perfect game to be televised; put the camera at a certain angle and you don't have to move it. But the TV people weren't interested. Tennis was not a popular enough game, in their opinion.

But as soon as the boom came and tennis did start to enjoy widespread popularity, TV jumped on the bandwagon. At that stage, television helped nurture the boom, but had the boom not already developed, TV people wouldn't have become involved. If nothing else, TV's attention meant that tennis had arrived.

UNNECESSARY TRIP?

So tennis has finally become a major sport in the United States, a far cry from what it was when I was playing at world-class level. It's gratifying to see it reach that point. When we were playing, few people knew anything about the game. You'd find tennis on the back page of the sports section, probably in small type.

To give you an idea of what the recognition factor was way back then, I'd like to tell you about a conversation I had in the early 1950s with a customer of my father's.

After playing in the 1951 Challenge Round in Australia, I came back to Philadelphia and began working in my father's plumbing supply business. I'd been away three months. One day I was working at the counter when a tobacco-chewing journeyman plumber came in to buy some fittings.

"Where you been?" he asked me. "Haven't seen you around."

"I was away for awhile."

"Where?"

"Australia."

"Australia!" shrieked the plumber, who seldom even left the neighborhood. "What were you doing in Australia?"

"Uh, I was playing tennis."

"Playing tennis? Why'd you wanna go all the way over there to play? You could've played on the courts here, at Thirty-third and Columbia."

I think that today, most Americans are more sophisticated about the sport.

Once thought of as an elitist, "sissy" pastime, tennis is recognized as a sport for the people, "he-men" included. Years ago, there was a stigma attached to the game—the impression was that you had to belong to a country club and that you had to be wealthy to play. That wasn't true. In big cities there have always been public courts available, and tennis rackets have always been available through patron associations. If kids wanted to play tennis, all they had to have was a pair of sneakers. Tennis never really was an expensive sport. In the past fifty years, almost all the great players have *not* come from wealthy backgrounds.

SPORT FOR A LIFETIME

Tennis is definitely a sport for a lifetime—whether you've been playing it regularly since you could barely see over the net, you're learning the sport for the first time in your middle years, or you've just resumed playing after a hiatus of some years.

A substantial segment of the tennis-playing population of the United States is in the forties and fifties age groups, many of them players who came into the game in the 1960s when they were in their thirties. And, while years ago you'd see a lot of players hopelessly trying to hit the tennis ball, today there are many more good players at the intermediate level.

The fact that you can play and enjoy tennis all your life (within reason) helps you keep fit and feel younger and better. The fellows who play in the Grand Masters tournaments are living proof of that.

Tennis has been a very important part of my life for as long as I can remember. There's something terrifically gratifying about hitting that ball with a reasonable amount of power and directing it with some accuracy. I'm sure that others derive similar pleasure from other endeavors, whether it's the musician playing a piano concerto or the surgeon performing a delicate operation. It's tennis that continues to be thrilling for me.

One of the attractions of tennis is that you don't need vast numbers of players or a lot of expensive equipment to play and enjoy the sport. It's easier to get a game up because you don't have to assemble a group, and it's relatively simple to find someone to play with and somewhere to play.

YOU CAN BEGIN AT ANY AGE

I think if you're physically healthy—and you go about it gradually and wisely—you can start playing tennis at almost any age. No one should take the attitude, "Well, I'm forty now and too old to start playing." Obviously if you start to play at age forty, you can't expect to be a champion. But you *can* play most enjoyably, and that's the important thing.

One thing you have going for you is that you're going to learn more quickly than someone younger who is just starting out. You may not be able to respond physically as rapidly as a youngster learning the game, but intellectually you should be quicker.

I can't overstress the importance of making sure that you have a checkup before you take up the game seriously for the first time or resume after a long layoff because this is a very vigorous sport that is frequently played in high humidity under the hot sun. Once you do get the medical go-ahead, don't foolishly overextend yourself to the point that you risk suffering a heart attack. Actually, even though it does not involve any physical contact between players, tennis is a lot tougher than most sports from the standpoint of having to be fit to play well. It's not a sport you should play if you're out of shape or out of breath. So exercise discretion. It's as important to get in shape to play tennis as it is to play tennis to get in shape.

LATECOMERS

It seems to me that those who take up tennis later in life are one of two types of individuals. They might be men and women who were pretty athletic when they were younger but gave up the sport they were involved in. Now they find they're physically out of shape and feel the need to get exercise, so they try tennis, a sport they hadn't thought about playing before. Or they may be people who were never athletic at all, but after reading and hearing how much better off they would be if they were physically fit (less danger of heart attack, etc.), they pick tennis, one of the few sports that isn't too strenuous or impractical to take up later in life.

TOUGHER TO RETURN

It's probably more difficult for older people who left tennis for some years to "relearn" the game. Breaking habits is a very difficult thing to do. But that doesn't mean the potential pleasure from the game is any less.

Many great athletes from other sports—Bob Cousy, Ted Williams, Otto Graham, Bob Mathias—have taken up tennis and they all say the same thing: they're crazy about the game and wish they had taken it up earlier. But you don't have to be a great athlete or tennis player to enjoy the game tremendously. In fact, I think the people who aren't great players enjoy the game a lot more.

PICKUP GAMES

Tennis is an excellent socializer: you can strike up great friendships on your local courts or at vacation resorts. I've even heard of a non–tennis player using tennis to meet a prospective husband. A good-looking divorcée, she bought herself an attractive tennis outfit and racket and parked herself on a bench near the public courts, a pleasant and safe place to meet appealing men. When anyone asked her to play, she'd say, "Thanks, but I just finished three sets of singles." One fellow invited her to play, and when she gave her standard reply, he said, "Maybe next week." They chatted awhile. The following weekend, the same dialogue ensued about her having just played. They got to talking more, began dating, eventually became engaged, and married. It was only after her marriage that she confessed she didn't play tennis. He didn't care.

LIKE PRIME TIME ROMANCE

Some people compare prime time tennis with prime time romance: you're probably going to be less energetic and more deliberate than in former years, and adjustments have to be made. But the fundamentals still apply ("as time goes by"), and you'll probably derive a feeling of fulfillment equal to or greater than you did previously.

Those of us in the Grand Masters are pretty much all in the same boat as far as the aging aspect of our tennis is concerned. We've all come up with pretty much the same solutions, so it hasn't changed the outcome of our matches very much. We've all decided that we can't hit the ball as hard as we used to, and therefore we're not going to blast anyone off the court the way we did when we were younger. We realize that the only way we're going to win is to keep down the number of errors. This means not taking as many chances as we used to, and, as a result, we end up having longer rallies. For the fans, this is beneficial because they can see points being planned a little more and they can relate more to the strategy that's involved.

MAKING THE ADJUSTMENT

Because today's social players weren't at the level we were years ago, the adjustments they have to make to accommodate increasing years are not going to have to be that drastic. But they are going to have to make some adjustments. For instance, players in the prime time category are likely to be playing doubles more and serving-and-volleying less in singles or doubles than they did formerly.

As a young player, your inclination probably was just to bash the ball back without concern whether it went to your opponent's backhand or forehand. If you hit it hard enough, you figured, you were going to win the point. Now, however, you can't win the point that way any more, so you've got to find what and where your opponent's weaknesses are and start playing to them more. Maybe certain types of serves give him trouble, or ground strokes that spin into him. You have to be more resourceful about your shot selection than you used to be. If you're smart you'll realize that you've lost a step or two, and you're not going to get to the ball as well or as quickly as you once did. So you'll play a little steadier, try not to make errors, and let your opponent be the one to miss the ball. "Get it over one more time than your opponent" is a good motto to keep in mind.

Every aging player has to compete with physical changes. But if you were a once-good or once-great player, I think the psychological aspects of aging are more important than the physical. Chances are, throughout your life, you've had some athletic injuries and been aware of the possibility that they could occur. You've learned to guard against them and keep them to a minimum. So, as a competitive player you learned to understand injuries and how to cope with them better than you can cope with some harsh realities: the fact that you can't make the shot you used to make, that you can't run as fast as you used to, or that your reflexes are not as good as they once were.

On the other hand, if you're someone who started playing the game relatively late, your ability has probably stayed on a pretty even keel, and it will be more important to learn to cope with physical problems as you get older. You'll want to know how to warm up properly, how long you can play, and how to avoid injury. For example, the average person starting out to play might not know that if he runs too fast he's liable to pull a hamstring, but he would not have to learn to cope with not being able to make a shot he once could or having an unexpected shot come back to him.

The better player you were, the harder it becomes to cope psychologically with changes of aging. The less ability you had as a player, the less difficult the psychological adjustment but the more difficult the physical one. An example of this would be a player once capable of being on the Junior Davis Cup team who, for a number of reasons, stopped playing at an early age. He went into the business world and just recently started playing again, at age forty-five or forty-six. He can still remember the shots he used to make easily as a youngster, and he tries to play that way now, but can't. This can be very frustrating for him—and it can also be very dangerous physically, because he imagines himself as he was at sixteen or seventeen when he never thought about the possibility of hurting himself.

MIDLIFE CRISIS: YOUNG RIVALS

∎|∎

I was ten years old when I entered my first tournament, which happened to be a men's* tournament at a local club in Philadelphia. I was barely able to see over the net; I remember measuring the net with my racket and discovering that I was just about the same height.

My first-round opponent was Sam Pruitt, a player more than twice my age (somewhere in his twenties). I beat him. We came into the locker room after the match, and he threw his rackets up against the locker and swore off tennis for life. He figured if he couldn't beat a ten-year-old he should quit. Twenty years later, in 1953, when I won Wimbledon, he decided that his loss to me hadn't been so bad after all. He went into his closet, dug out his old rackets and began playing again.

A lot of older players don't relish the thought of losing to much younger players. (They forget that the opponent's youth is a wonderful built-in excuse for them if they lose.) Bobby Riggs, for one, hasn't any desire to play a good young player, let alone lose to him. "I don't even want to *play* a good young player, a young college kid,"

---

* In competitive tennis, by the way, I don't think it's bad for a qualified youngster to play in the men's or women's competition, if that's the only way he or she is going to get to play with someone better. I think that's far superior to staying in his own age group forever when he's head and shoulders above his peers. If, on the other hand, he's in an area where there is an abundance of good young players, then there's no need for him to be pushed ahead.

Bobby declares. "Al Bunis says he likes to play a good, strong, young player, but I don't know why. He couldn't win a game from him if the kid didn't want him to. Who's going to enjoy that? I'm honest about it. I hate playing good young players. I don't even want to get out on the court with a really good young tournament player. I just want to play old guys and women."

In competitive tennis, however, a player has to take whoever is matched against him in a tournament, whatever the opponent's age. An older player who's just interested in the exercise and the fun can have more of a choice in selecting an opponent. But keep in mind, there can be a good deal of enjoyment in playing someone younger and pitting your experience against his youth (providing he's not a sadist).

THE EXPERIENCE FACTOR

Whether it's playing someone younger in a tournament or a social game, or even when it's one of us playing a new over-forty-five "kid" who's just joined the Grand Masters, there are occasions when an older player finds himself or herself competing with a relative youngster. That needn't be all bad.

At Wimbledon in 1982, Billie Jean King, a mature thirty-eight-year-old, saved three match points and battled back to beat twenty-three-year-old Tanya Harford of South Africa in a third-round match. In the rain-interrupted contest, she lost the first set, 5–7, and was down 4–5 in the second and trailing love–40 on her serve. But she volleyed her way back to win that set in a tiebreaker, 7–6, and then took the third set, 6–3. "I can't recall the previous time I have been so close to defeat and won," she told a reporter. "When I was down 4–5 and love–40, I told myself, 'You have been here twenty-one years, so use that experience and hang on.' "

Billie Jean then beat Tracy Austin, who at nineteen was half her age, to win a berth in the semifinals. Thus, Billie Jean became the oldest women's semifinalist at Wimbledon since Dorothea Lambert Chambers made the semifinals at age forty-two in 1920.

It was the first in six meetings that Billie Jean had beaten Tracy and her ninetieth victory in 103 singles matches in 21 Wimbledon tournaments. Her reaching the semifinals there for the thirteenth time was described as "without parallel" by Ted Tinling, the tennis fashion designer who has followed women's tennis for more than half a century.

Billie Jean decided not to match Tracy stroke for stroke. "I just made up my mind I was going to dink the ball and give her garbage." Mrs. King won 3–6, 6–4, 6–2.

"She's had enough experience to know what to do at specific points," Tracy said of Billie Jean after the match. "She's a real smart lady because of her experience. She loves tennis and thinks about it twenty-three hours a day. That's why she's able to keep in it so long."

Billie Jean lost to Chris Evert Lloyd in the 1982 Wimbledon semi-finals and was upset later in the year in the first round of the U.S. Open by eighteen-year-old Susan Mascarin. Billie Jean, who'd played in her first national championship five years before Susan was born, said, "I was trying as hard as I could, nothing went right, I was exasperated."

Nevertheless, she has already firmly established herself as an out-standing competitor with a long record of excellence. Conqueror of Bobby Riggs in 1973, Billie Jean won her sixth Wimbledon singles title in 1975 and then, in 1979, teamed with Martina Navratilova, won the Wimbledon doubles for a record twentieth Wimbledon title. In 1980—at the age of thirty-seven—she was ranked fifth in the United States, a record seventeenth appearance in the top ten. She should be an inspiration to all prime-timers.

That experience factor is sometimes pivotal in defeating a younger opponent. "It definitely helps, especially now," says Alex Olmedo. "You realize you can't hit the ball as hard as they do, so you stay back and you push the ball back, and make them hit the ball. A lot of times young kids just kill themselves trying to overhit the ball, or they don't know when to stay back and when to come in. When you're older, you've already learned those things. My return of service is just a short chip shot, so a lot of college kids on the West Coast will come in so close that I lob over their heads. They say, 'I can't play against you because you don't hit the ball hard enough.' They don't realize that I can't pass through them, so I have to do something else—make them bend down and then go for the lob.

"So you learn to adjust. You use different shots. You start to depend more on getting it over the net one more time. It's still a fun game."

Of course, Alex is at a stage where he both knows what to do and can still do it, and so his experience offsets the advantage of youth. But eventually you reach a point where all your experience doesn't do any good because while you know what to do, you can't do it.

Younger opponents tend to just want to bash the ball and blow you off the court with volleys and overheads. We can't knock the ball by them anymore, so we're inclined to keep the ball low and just make them miss, or maybe fool them with lobs. On the other hand, they may play a whole match without ever thinking of hitting a lob to fool us. They might throw one up occasionally when they're in trouble, but they'll never think of the lob as an offensive shot. And they may not realize that every ball is landing at their feet and yet they're still trying to blast it.

I seem to be playing younger opponents all the time. Often, I've felt that even though I couldn't outrun or outhit them, I had an edge on them mentally, I could sense that they were in a bit of a quandary about where I was going to hit the ball or how I was going to play, and it worried them.

A nice young pro I was working with at a hotel could hit the ball and was an eager competitor, but in matches between us, he was completely at a loss most of the time; he didn't know where I was going to hit the ball. I fooled him constantly.

But unfortunately, you reach a level where that doesn't work anymore. No matter how much experience you have, it does no good if you don't have the equipment to back it up.

PRIME TIME GREATNESS

Unlike wine, few *good* tennis players improve with age, but some have sustained excellent tennis performance over a period of years. Billie Jean King is certainly an outstanding example. Her great showing at Wimbledon in the summer of 1982 is typical of her continuing excellence.

Among men, Ken Rosewall is the premier current example. While he can no longer win the big tournaments, he's still a mighty tough tennis player and at age forty-six or forty-seven he's still capable of beating a good many of the younger players or giving some of them who aren't at the top a good deal of trouble. At the age of forty-three, you'll remember, he made it to the Wimbledon men's finals.

Another outstanding prime-timer is Pancho Gonzales, who played some great matches after he was forty. Some competitors have playing longevity or reach their peaks later than others and so are able to carry on late in their lives. Much depends on how injury-free you are. Many top players have had their careers cut short because they developed a chronic problem with their back or arm. Lew Hoad is one example of that, and even Rod Laver has had some back problems.

EXTRA DIMENSIONS TO SENIOR TENNIS

A question often asked is whether there are dimensions in senior tennis that don't exist elsewhere. Basically, they're around the waistline. But, seriously, there are some differences. Al Bunis, speaking of the Grand Masters, comments, "They play with a different style than the modern player. They hit more flatly and are more accustomed to serving and volleying, while most of the modern players are baseliners.

"Because the senior game is slowed down a little bit, you can see what's happening out there. The tactics and strategy of senior play are far beyond what the young people do. The players have time to think, and these people are *willing* to think."

He also points out that for the most part, the Grand Masters are "great coaches"—present or former captains or coaches of Davis Cup teams. (Neale Fraser is captain of the Australian Davis Cup team.) "They're probably the best exposed and educated citizens in the world. They know everything there is to know about the game, and it shows up in their play. Their tactics are impeccable. The flesh may be weak sometimes, but in terms of what they're trying to do and how they analyze the situation, it's a much more cerebral game that's played at the senior level."

Another difference that Bunis sees is that while young players "basically react, the senior players do much more than react as required." Bobby Riggs, Bunis points out jokingly, was, from May

1973 when he defeated Margaret Court, to September 1973, when he lost to Billie Jean King, the "finest women's tennis player in the world." Bobby, says Bunis, "never hit a ball in his whole life that he didn't have some thought behind. I don't think one would say that about young people's tennis, though in a lot of cases it's there."

DOUBLE YOUR PLEASURE

■|■

A tennis player went to his physician for a checkup, and the doctor asked, "How old are you?"

"Forty," the man replied.

"I don't think you should play singles in your forties," the doctor said.

So the poor guy had to wait ten years before he could start playing singles again.

As a prime time tennis player, you're apt to find yourself playing doubles more frequently than singles. It makes sense not only from the standpoint of its being less demanding physically but also because it provides a different dimension of playing pleasure.

Doubles is a little more like a chess game than singles, and, if it follows that the mature player approaches things more cerebrally now than in years past, he or she should find doubles most enjoyable. Obviously, there's the added element of teamwork; you have to play with a partner and against two opponents, so there's more strategy and tactics involved. In singles, you're essentially just trying to keep the ball away from your opponent and get it over the net one more time. But in doubles, there are such components as hitting the ball down, moving wide, covering for your partner, and setting the stage for your partner to put the ball away. To be a good doubles player, you have to enjoy doubles play. Doubles is played primarily

60

at the net, so you should like to come to the net and attack. Many of the current crop of champions—Connors, Bjorn Borg, and Guillermo Vilas, to name just three—are not inclined to rush the net and consequently are not doubles-oriented, whereas McEnroe is. In my era, most of us were of the serve-and-volley persuasion and played the kind of game that lent itself to doubles. The baseline player is probably less enthusiastic about doubles than the serve-and-volleyer.

Some of today's better players avoid playing doubles because they feel it would detract from their concentration in singles. Many of them say they would rather not run the risk of getting into a doubles match that might hamper their singles match, which has so much more money involved. But I think that's just an excuse used to avoid playing doubles because they're not doubles-inclined. I don't buy the theory that doubles is detrimental to your singles game. In fact, I think it's helpful because it gives you the chance to play a different kind of game, get your mind off your singles, and get in some play on days when you're not scheduled for a match. It also gives you the opportunity to develop a more rounded game because you concentrate on shots tailored to doubles that you can incorporate occasionally into your singles play. In fact, John McEnroe, ranked first or second in the world as a singles player, *insists* on playing doubles. He's participated in doubles—and won—often just after an exhausting, late-round singles match.

I can't think of anyone in my generation who didn't play doubles. As Torben Ulrich points out, it was taken for granted by the people who invited you to participate in a tournament that you would play doubles as well as singles. In those days, he says, you wouldn't just come to town, play only in the singles, and leave when you were eliminated. If you were eliminated early, the tournament sponsors might say, "We'd like you to play in the mixed doubles because we'd really like to see you play," and the players would accommodate their hosts' request. Today the relationship is different. Players *enter* tournaments rather than get *invited*, and so it's their choice entirely about what they play. Economics often dictates which they focus on, Torben says.

DIFFERENT STROKES

Aside from the obvious fact that there are four players instead of two, doubles has some basic differences from singles. In singles, your aim is to hit deep shots toward the baseline, while in doubles your objective is to keep the ball at your opponent's feet when he or she is at the net or approaching it.

In doubles, rallies tend to be shorter than they are in singles because the ball is not hitting the ground as often. All the players, or at least two, are at the net, so the point is likely to come to a climax quicker in doubles.

From a recreational or social angle, doubles offers a lot more than singles and is especially attractive to older players who feel they should play singles less frequently or not at all. For spectators, too, doubles holds a special appeal: some of them relate more to doubles than singles. After some of our Grand Masters matches, people will ask why they can't see more doubles played everywhere. I think that would be a good thing for tennis, but as long as prize money is pro-rated the way it is—with the preponderance going to singles—the emphasis is going to be even more on singles.

QUALITIES OF A GOOD TEAM

What makes a good doubles *team*, first of all, is that the players enjoy playing with their particular partners. My most successful doubles play was with Tony Trabert and, in mixed doubles, with Doris Hart, and I enjoyed playing with both of them very much.

Ideally, partners should not only enjoy playing together but like each other as well. Yet, doubles teams have thrived where there was no love lost between the partners. For example, Frew McMillan and Bob Hewitt, who made up one of the best doubles teams ever, hardly, if ever, saw each other off the court. There were no positive feelings between them. There was no great love, either, between Sven Davidson and his first partner, Lennart Bergelin, or Sven and Ulf Schmitt, but the latter team won the Wimbledon doubles. There's a difference between fondness for your partner and respecting his or her playing ability. Even Tony Trabert, my good partner of many years' standing, and I were not bosom buddies. We got along fine and traveled together, but he had his close friends and I had mine (partly because of our age differences: I *used to* be older than Tony). Doris Hart and I got along splendidly; she's one of my all-time favorites as a player and a person. But, two people can play beautifully together without being a mutual-admiration society.

For your doubles chemistry to work well, at least one of you has to be willing to set up the point for the other. Both of you have to feel that setting up the winning shot and making it are of equal importance.

The best teams are those whose players complement each other, such as a big, powerful player teamed with someone a bit more agile and better at covering. This is a much better setup than having two players who share a weakness that can be exploited.

Ken McGregor was not a good singles player, but he had a great return of serve and when teamed with Sedgman, they made a great partnership. Alex Olmedo and Ham Richardson began teaming in 1958. Ham needed somebody like Alex who could dink the ball and run better than he could. Alex would chip and Ham would poach. Ham felt he could take chances and move closer to the net because he knew Alex was fast enough to cover if he got caught. Tony Trabert and I would do the same thing. I'd dink a little shot, and he'd move in and bludgeon the return. Occasionally he'd move too soon and get caught, but he knew he had someone who was prepared to cover for him and was fast enough to do it. (That wasn't necessarily true the other way around. Because it wasn't his way of playing, Tony had trouble covering shots over my head.)

Tony was a big, strong player who didn't run particularly well. He had a super backhand and return of serve, and his game was power. I was strong enough but didn't hit the same kind of heavy shot that he did. Still, I could move a lot better than he could and cover more court, so we had what each other needed. We complemented each other very well, and we learned to play together. We practiced tactics together. We knew, for example, who was going to take a ball hit down the middle. You have to learn where your partner's going to be, how he plays, and what shots he likes to hit. If it's to my backhand at a certain point on the court, I'll take it; otherwise, you take it. This sort of knowledge is gained through experience by playing together as much as possible.

In social play, of course, you want to make the teams as evenly balanced as possible because a doubles match is only as good as the weakest player on the court. If one team is slaughtering another in a nontournament match, it makes sense to change the composition of the teams.

At a social *or* professional level, however, you do need that complementary factor between partners if the team is to be successful. A player's great return of service doesn't mean much if his partner can't do anything to capitalize on it. "As soon as you see some weakness," Alex Olmedo says, talking about his partnership with Ham Richardson, "you attack it. That's what Ham would do. As soon as I'd return a shot, he'd get in, and I'd move to the other side. We'd move together."

That psychological factor I mentioned is equally important. Tony was a great left-court doubles player, but I feel he also needed someone like me as a partner. When he teamed with Ham or players like him, his effectiveness was reduced because they were too much alike —neither wanted to make the assist; they both wanted to score the winning goal.

SPECTACLES OF OURSELVES

Talk about togetherness between doubles partners. Gardnar Mulloy and I were teamed up years ago in a match against Art Larsen and Tony Vincent in St. Augustine, as part of the Florida circuit. We were all having vision problems (a subject I get into in more detail elsewhere), but Gardnar seemed to be having more trouble than anyone. To a nearsighted player, the ball can look like a great big pineapple. It so happened I had taken to wearing glasses at night, which was when this particular match was being played. The lights were no good, and Gardnar had forgotten his glasses. He was aiming at that big pineapple, thinking he was hitting it in the middle, but wasn't. It turned out that his eyeglass prescription was similar to mine, so on one changeover we decided we'd share the glasses. Whoever was serving would wear the glasses, on the theory that the server would get more balls to hit. We played out the rest of the match, sharing that one pair of specs—and won.

MIX AND MATCH

In the days when I was at the peak of my tennis game, most men's and women's tournaments were played at the same place, and it was only natural that mixed-doubles matches would be a component of those tournaments. With few exceptions today—notably Wimbledon and the U.S. Open—the men and women players are seldom competing in the same place at the same time, so mixed doubles is becoming an endangered species. While it could never assume the importance of singles, there is something about mixed doubles at Wimbledon that sets it apart from the same event held anywhere else. It gets its share of Centre Court exposure, the fans seem to love it, and the players always seem to try harder. Most of the top men players—and almost all the top women—played in mixed competition in my day, and some of the most enjoyable portions of my tennis career were the times spent teaming with Doris Hart.

Earlier in my career, I played with Bunny Vosters in Philadelphia and we had a pretty good record, retiring a couple of bowls at the Merion Cricket Club. But Bunny (who's still playing and has won many mother–daughter championships with her daughters, Nina and Gretchen) didn't play much on the national scene. Shirley Fry (who's now a tennis pro) and I won Wimbledon one year, and I occasionally played with Margaret duPont and Louise Brough, but they pretty much had steady partners. Maureen Connolly was probably the greatest woman player I've ever seen. Yet she wasn't a very good mixed-doubles player. (We were partners a few times in minor exhibitions, but I played against Little Mo quite a lot.)

My early teaming with Doris Hart took place on the South African tour in 1950. Then she teamed with Frank Sedgman and they won just about everything in sight. When Frank turned pro in 1952, Doris and I agreed that whenever there was a mixed-doubles tournament at a place we were both at, we would play together. Over the five-year span (beginning in 1950 and ending when Doris turned pro at the end of 1955), we lost only one match! We won almost every major title during this period—including Wimbledon three times, the U.S. Open (at Forest Hills) three times, as well as the French, the Italian, and the South African championships and many others. We never were together in Australia. Our only loss was to Shirley Fry and

Gardnar Mulloy in the finals of the Caribe Hilton Invitational in Puerto Rico after both of us had played singles and doubles finals. We lost to them, 6–4, in the third set.

In my opinion, Doris was the finest mixed doubles player of her time, and I deemed it a privilege to be her partner. I honestly felt at times that we could have given some of the better men's doubles teams a run for their money. (That's just an expression; remember, we were amateurs.)

By the way, Doris got into tennis through her brother, Bud, a fine player. She had had quite a bad accident when she was young and took up the game as therapy. Although she never was able to run very well (and walked with a slight limp), she got to be excellent at the game, winning singles at Forest Hills and Wimbledon, in addition to her doubles triumphs. In recent years, she has been a teaching pro at the Hillsboro Club at Pompano Beach, Florida. She lives in Coral Gables, where she grew up.

Above and beyond the results Doris and I achieved, I'll always remember the fun we had. Doris had a great sense of humor on the court (just as she does off), and many times during a match she would come over to me and say something like, "I'm going to lob more over the Mabel." To Doris, all our female opponents were Mabels.

I can't recall an unpleasant moment playing with her, a factor I think had much to do with our success. We had an understanding from the very beginning that she would take all the shots she could reach comfortably and leave those she couldn't for me to try to return. She knew that I would not take balls within her reach and attempt to hog the court, a mistake made by so many men playing mixed doubles.

MALE CHAUVINIST HOGS

Too often, men try to take over too much of the court in mixed doubles. To give you an extreme example, I was teamed with a good mixed-doubles player from California, Barbara Krase, against Bob Falkenburg and his sister, Jinx, who was a fair tennis player but better known as a TV personality. Before the match began, Jinx was instructed by her 6'4" stringbean brother that, when she wasn't in the act of serving or returning a serve, she should, in effect, get off the court. Which is what happened. She got out of the way, and he played the whole court. I told my partner that there was no way the two of us could lose to him, and, of course, we didn't. I don't think they could have won anyway, because Jinx wasn't that good a player, while Barbara was. (In my opinion, the abilities of the woman are essential in mixed-doubles success.) But they had absolutely *no* chance when she had to endure the unnerving presence of her partner, who was all arms and legs, all over the court. Those of you who enjoy playing mixed doubles, at club level or elsewhere, might do well to remember that overplaying by the man can only undermine the confidence of your partner and lead to confusion, probable loss of the game, and an unpleasant time. A much better approach is for the woman to be clearly responsible for returning the balls hit in her area, rather than expecting her partner to cover three-fourths of the court. With a sharing of responsibility, both partners will play better. It's no fun for a female player to go out on the court and then be told by her male partner to watch the action from the sidelines. Men players should either not play mixed doubles or, if they do, accept the fact that their partner plays her side of the court, as far as possible, and they play theirs. If the woman isn't good enough to get her share of the shots, they're not going to win anyway, so they might just as well let her play. Hogging the play is bound to come back to haunt you (especially if the partners are husband and wife). In general, the same principles apply to mixed as to unisex doubles—play with someone you enjoy and have fun playing with.

If the male partner is a much better player than the woman, he'll take more of the shots, especially the ones that are pretty close to both of them—just as the better player would on a team of the same sex. But where players have fairly equal ability, and anytime the objective is fun for all, the playing should be shared as equally as possible.

On the subject of playing *against* the woman in mixed doubles, many men are not aware of the fact that spin is usually more effective than sheer power. Most of the better women players are not as troubled by hard-hit balls as by excessive top spin or slice, especially on the serve. Good news for male club-level players, who feel reluctant to whale a drive at a female opponent: spin can be used even more effectively in a social game against the woman, without destroying the gentlemanly image we like to create and perpetuate.

YOUR PLACE OR MINE?

I remember playing in an exhibition match in Chicago with Althea Gibson as my partner. As we walked out to take our positions, Al, who was then in her prime, asked, "Which side do you want?"

Her question astounded me, because I had taken it for granted that, as the man playing in a mixed-doubles match, I would play the left, or ad, court.

She started me thinking about the subject; maybe I was wrong to make the assumption I did. But the more I thought about it, the more I was convinced that in 99 percent of the cases the woman should play the right, or deuce, court; and the man, the ad. The exception would be in the case of a woman who either was left-handed or had a strong, two-handed backhand. The main reason I feel this way is that the right-hander in the left court is usually served a high-kicking ball to the backhand, and most women have more trouble with that kind of shot than most men. It may be that Althea felt her backhand return of serve was better than mine—and who am I to say it wasn't— but I finally convinced her to play the right court by telling her it was the tougher side to play!

Another reason Mal Anderson, for one, thinks it's advantageous to have the woman play the deuce court is that it's easier to hit the traditional lob return of serve over the opposing woman's head without fear of a forehand smash by the male opponent—a more likely result if she's returning serve from the ad court.

When partners are of the same sex, I think generally it's the lefty who should play the left-hand court. One of the most difficult shots in tennis is hitting a backhand that's away from you, which is the serve a right-hander in the left court would most often get. The left-hander would have a better chance of returning that serve, since it would be his or her forehand. A serve aimed at the lefty's backhand, when the lefty is playing the ad court, would be down the middle and not as difficult to return. In general, you make it tougher to serve to you if you have the two forehands on the outside. By having the left-handed partner on your left, you may make the center weaker.

But if you can make your opponents keep the ball coming into the middle of the court rather than having them going wide all the time, you'll have a slight advantage.

Thus, I think a lefty, or the partner with the stronger righty backhand return, should be on the ad court, but if you disagree, you'll be in good company. You see a lot of lefties playing the deuce court and the righties in the ad court, mainly because they've become accustomed to it.

Don Budge, whose backhand was one of the best ever, strikes me as an ideal left-court player. His backhand return was as good as his forehand and possibly better than a forehand return from the right side. If they served to his backhand in the ad court, the ball would come back with plenty of pace, in contrast with my chip shot. If I were on the left side, they'd serve to my backhand all day. Yet Budge would argue that the best backhand should be in the deuce court because most of the balls during rallies come down the middle.

You can make a case for both arguments. Some social players like to have the extra reach with their forehand on a ball hit to the opposite corner, so a lefty might prefer being on the right side. But the competitive player is able to cover lobs or other types of shots to his backhand corner without any trouble, so that's not a factor.

Mal Anderson, a right-court player who thinks the first point of a game is very important, believes the stronger player should be on the backhand, or left court, because when you have the opportunity for a service break, the server then has a little more pressure on him as he is serving to the stronger player.

But Alex Olmedo points out that if there's a player with a great backhand in the ad court and a partner in the deuce court who can hardly make a point, the stronger player might not get a chance to hit an ad point. He might then be better off playing in the deuce court. In any case, according to Alex, such factors as which court a player prefers, where he's more comfortable, what his strengths are, and how much pressure he likes to face should be considered in deciding which player plays where.

Whenever I ask a partner in a pro-am tournament which side he or she wants to play, the answer inevitably is, "Oh, I'd better play the forehand side, because I'm the weaker player," or "The ad side's where the *important* points are. You better play it." But I respond,

"That's not so. Don't say that. If you feel more comfortable playing the ad court, then play it." In this context, *all* the points are important.

For me, it's not any easier to play one court or the other. In fact, in some ways I think it's tougher to play the deuce court. I've played both sides a lot, but when I was Tony Trabert's partner I played the deuce court exclusively. The one year I played with Rex Hartwig, we started out with him in the ad court and me in the deuce court. We lost our first two tournaments, both in the finals. I thought about our alignment. "Look," I told myself, "Rex is probably the best right-court player who ever lived, and we're giving up something when we put him in the left. I feel more comfortable in the right, but I can play either one." So we switched—and we won the next five tournaments in a row. So it really isn't a matter of who's a better player, but who plays the particular side of the court better.

At club-level tennis, go by what is most comfortable for you and your partner. (You'll often hear a social player tell a partner, "I'm just as bad on either side, so pick the one *you* want.") And if, after a set or two, you're looking to change your luck, change sides with your partner.

TRANSITION

As you make the transition from youth to middle age, some of the same changes take place in your doubles game as in singles. You don't hit the ball as hard on an overhead, serve, or ground stroke, so you have to take a more tactical approach to the game. You have to concentrate more on where you place the ball than on trying to blow it past somebody. Or you have to rely more on deception.

This knowledge can be helpful on defense against another aging tennis player. In the Grand Masters tournaments, for example, we know we don't have to return serve quite so hard because the server isn't going to be able to get to the net as quickly. Consequently, we can be a little more careful to make sure we get the serve back over the net, and we don't have to make quite as good a shot as we would against a young player who, half a second after he hits the ball, is on top of the net. Our return of serve would be duck soup for him because he's sitting up there, waiting for it. Against our own age group, however, we know the server is going to take a little longer getting to the net behind his serve. Age hasn't taken quite as much of a toll on return of service as it has on rushing the net. What at one time was not a very good return is now a better return, and this takes a little of the advantage away from the server. As a result, the game is more even, the rallies are longer-lasting and the competition more interesting.

The single volley that would often end a rally in matches in our younger days is no longer as effective, and so we tend to build the point a little, trying even harder to keep from making errors than we used to. Longer points make for more interesting watching.

SERVICE

The now deposed prince of an Asian nation had a simple rule when he served in tennis: he served until he got tired, then his opponent got the chance.

Serving is not only enjoyable but tremendously important, especially in doubles. But there are circumstances when, unlike that prince, it's to your advantage to let the other player or team serve first.

It's not widely known, but you actually have four options if you win the toss of the coin or twirl of the racket to determine serve. You can choose to serve first, in which case your opponent chooses which side of the net he will start. You have the right to decide to receive first, in which case your opponent serves and gets the choice of the side. You can choose the side, in which case your opponent has the option of whether or not to serve first. You can also elect to let your opponent make the decision.

Usually, the winner of the toss will make a decision about whether or not to serve first. Only in a rare case—say, where the sun is intense on one side of the court—will the winner of the toss pick a side rather than the option of whether or not to serve first.

(By the way, a team comprised of a righty and a lefty never has to be concerned about serving into the sun. The sun at one end of the court favors either the right-hander or left-hander, and they can arrange their own serving rotation accordingly. In other words, the righty can serve with the sun at his back at one end of the court, and then, after they've changed sides, the lefty can serve from the other end of the court with the sun at *his* back.)

In doubles the assumption is that servers are going to hold serve, so almost always a team will elect to serve first. If that team does hold its serve, it will be a game ahead every odd game beginning with the first, which is a nice psychological advantage. Frequently, singles players elect to receive, in the belief that their best chance to break service is in the first game, before their opponent is warmed up or before he loses his nervousness.

As to which doubles partner should serve first for his or her team, you might want to evaluate who has the better serve or who feels more warmed up. If you're playing outside, it might also depend on who serves better with the sun in his eyes. There are no hard-and-fast rules, especially in a friendly game.

The main difference between serving in doubles and serving in singles is that you should concentrate even more on getting your first serve in. You should do that even if it means taking something off that first serve and hitting at 75 to 80 percent of your potential velocity. It's essentially a psychological matter. Miss that first serve and the receiver will take a couple of steps in. He suddenly feels that, like the cripple pitch in baseball, the second serve is something you've got to lay in there. And so he moves in confidently, determined to get a better shot at it. Often, he does.

Aside from wanting to deny your opponents the psychological advantage of your missing with your first serve, there are some very practical reasons for getting it in. If you were to serve two balls exactly the same, you'd be much more effective with the one that's a first serve than with the one that's a second serve. Why? Because on the first serve, the receiver doesn't know what to expect and hasn't moved in. Also, if you get your first serve in four out of five times, your partner can be much more helpful at the net. The receiver is standing back expecting a harder serve; he's not aware of where the serve is going to land or how it's going to act, so he has a tougher return to make. On the second serve, however, this edge is removed, and your partner at the net has to be concerned about the receiver hitting one down the line or over his head. His movement is now more limited.

So while you may occasionally try for an ace in doubles, to keep your opponents honest, most times it's a lot wiser not to bash away at the ball but slow it down a bit—just spin it in, if need be, but get it in.

FOLLOW THE BOUNCING BALL

A lot of club players make the mistake of not following their serve to the net. This leaves a big hole on the court and allows the opposition to take control of the net and the point. In top-level doubles, the first team that gets to the net is usually going to win the point. You never see a top-level doubles player not follow his serve to the net. That's the right way to play, and you should force yourself to do it or you won't get past a certain point in your development. Even if you're not a good volleyer, you're going to win more points just by being up there than by hanging back and thus letting your opposition take the offensive. Your presence at the net may force the receiver into a hurried, weak shot. He may look at you instead of the ball and blow his return. He may hit a lob that's not high enough to elude your put-away. Sometimes you'll win a point on pure luck. But you've got to be up there to make it happen.

It helps for your partner to know where you intend to serve the ball. Assuming you're all right-handed and most of the time you'll be serving to your opponents' backhands, that means you'll be aiming your serve down the middle on the deuce court and far to the outside on the ad court. Occasionally you might decide that the ad-court receiver is standing so far over that you're going to swing one down the middle. It will help your partner to tell her or him what you intend to do. Then do it, and follow your serve to the net.

A basic axiom of good doubles play is that the partners move in tandem—they go to the net together whenever possible and retreat together when the enemy throws up a lob. Social players are sometimes a little timid about leaving the baseline in expectation of a lob. But having one player at the net and the other partner back leaves a gaping hole that invites an easy volley. Moving in tandem doesn't necessarily mean that you and your partner have to be exactly parallel; one can hang back slightly if a lob is indicated. But move together as much as possible, and you'll be pleasantly surprised at the punch it puts in your offense and the errors or setups it causes your opponents to make.

GEORGIA FOR FOUR

Of course, surprising the opposition is a key to winning points. This is often accomplished by poaching; that is, the player at the net suddenly dashes into his partner's side of the court to cut down a cross-court return. If the serve goes where it's supposed to, the net man can start his crossing earlier, with greater confidence and more success. Tony Trabert and I hardly ever crossed on second serve. Our poaching was done on a random basis so that our opponents could detect no pattern. It really doesn't matter how often or when you poach, just so that your opponents are aware of your poaching potential.

Surprisingly, when Tony and I started experimenting with a poaching system, we discovered that we were among the few teams to use it. Not that there was anything new about this interception maneuver. It just hadn't been used for some time. I think a lot of the great teams felt that it wasn't necessary, and the others hadn't played enough together to perfect it. In any event, Tony and I thought it might just come in handy once in a while against the tough Australian teams.

For poaching to work, it's important that the partners have a pre-arranged signal and that the net player go all the way to prevent a successful cross-court return. As the net player crosses, the server must come to the net on the side his partner just vacated to cover any return down the line. Theoretically, the worst that can happen is that the return is behind the crossing net man and volleyed by the server to keep the point in play. Many times, however, the poacher can put away a relatively easy volley right on top of the net.

Equally important in this whole operation is the fact that both players can fake the move, which we did far more often than actually executing it. We'd often entice the receiver into returning the ball right to the net man. Precision timing on the part of both partners is of the essence. If the poacher moves too soon or too late, you can kiss the point goodbye. Similarly, if the server moves into the open court too soon or too late, he either telegraphs the whole plan or may not be in position to make the first volley.

We got the play down quite well, mainly because we practiced it a lot and because we both understood the important part each of us played in making it work. Many teams use this ploy today, but I haven't seen one that could produce any better results than we did.

Because this poaching play is used only by the serving team, it can only be an aid half the time. But it can be most effective. Appreciating the importance of when the move is used and how partners communicate it to each other, we eventually decided that it was imperative that we keep from developing a pattern that might become obvious to our opponents. So our basic plan was to pay virtually no attention to the score. As mentioned, our net man seldom moved on second serves; he also seldom moved against serves to the forehand. Both these factors helped us increase our percentage of first serves in, and to the backhand, an important plus for the system.

What may come as a surprise is the fact that the poach was more valuable against the better returners because, if it were properly carried out, it nullified to a great extent the best return of serve. Against the weak return, it served little purpose since it was not nearly as necessary to ensure the point.

We experimented with several methods of communication. First, we left it to the net man to use hand signals to tell his partner when he was going. But this left the server no say in the matter, and, more important, the signals could be stolen. (At one time during the finals of the Pacific Southwest doubles, when we were playing Hoad and Rosewall, we noticed the Australian coach, Harry Hopman, hiding in a box behind the court, noting down our hand signals on a piece of paper.)

We then decided that the net man would turn before each serve to enable us to make a decision face-to-face about whether to use the poach on this point or not. This worked fairly well, but it proved a little cumbersome and disruptive to our natural playing rhythm.

Finally, we decided that before the game started, we would arbitrarily decide on certain points on which we'd use the poach—say the first and third, or second and third, or none at all. Naturally, whenever we didn't execute the play, we faked it in order to keep our opponents constantly wondering. We liked this system because it enabled us to make a mutual decision, unrelated to the point score, and without any discernible pattern.

We could, of course, amend our plan as the game progressed, using either of the other methods. In fact, we continued to use hand signals for some time after adopting the game-by-game version just to throw off would-be signal-stealers. In this case, our hand signals meant nothing.

One night in San Francisco, Tony and I were introduced to a rather intriguing game at the home of some friends. There were seven or eight of us present when one of the women sent her husband out of earshot. She then asked us to pick some famous person known to all of us, including her husband. The game consisted of her communicating to her husband the name of the person we picked by a code we were supposed to decipher. After a frustrating hour of wrong guesses, we finally prevailed on them to tell us the code. The best way to explain it is with an example. As it turned out, she hadn't communicated the name itself, but a distinguishing characteristic, which made the code even tougher to crack.

To help her husband guess President Eisenhower, she said: "Take a trip to Germany, then Roanoke for three days, and then to Newport." Her husband immediately came up with the answer. If you can figure it out now, you go to the head of the class! If not, read on.

The first letter of each of the places involved is a consonant in the clue; the number of days or nights is the vowel (one is "a," two is "e," three is "i," and so on). The clue spelled the word GRIN, which described President Eisenhower in those days and which she knew her husband would recognize. Sometimes it might take several "trips" to convey the message, but as the team worked together more and more at it, as in tennis, the partners became more expert at communicating the celebrity's identity.

Tony and I played this game often after that and, as in our tennis partnership, became proficient at it. Rocky Marciano, for example, became "Kansas for four days" (KO); Clara Bow, the "IT" girl, simply "three days in Tallahassee"; and Winston Churchill, "Vancouver for three days and three nights" (VEE being his famous sign for victory in World War II). To this day, we have never had anyone figure out how it was done. In fact, I feel a little guilty giving it away now.

What connection does all this have with doubles? You'll see in a moment. It was the 1953 Challenge Round in Melbourne, and Tony and I were to face Lew Hoad and Rex Hartwig, who, as I mentioned, was substituted for Ken Rosewall in the doubles at the last moment. It was Rex's first taste of Challenge Round pressure, and he was playing the left court, which was not his best side. The Aussie coach, Hopman, was confident, however, that Rex's great ability as a doubles player would help him overcome any possible problems.

Tony and I had talked about using our crossing system, but since we had not yet tried it in a big-match situation, we were a little skeptical about introducing it at this point. But during the warm-up both of us noticed that Rex seemed a bit nervous, so just as Tony was about to serve the first game of the match, he said, "Georgia for four" (Go!). I crossed on Hartwig's excellent return and almost took Hoad's head off with a volley right on top of the net. For all intents and purposes, that was the match. We crossed a few more times to keep Rex guessing, but mostly we faked crossing. Rex's usually fine return was neutralized, and I honestly think he never got over his case of nerves the whole match. We won 6–2, 6–2, 6–4, a surprisingly easy victory over a tough team.

Whenever I get set to play Rex in a Grand Masters singles match, I am hopeful that he won't be as "Honolulu for four days, then Texas" against me as he has been on occasions in the past.

Someone asked me years ago why I turned my head and watched my partner as he or she was serving. Until the question was asked, I had never realized that I was doing that. To this day, I've never seen another player with this habit. Of course, I wasn't looking at my partner, but at the ball as it left his or her hand. As I reflect on it, this seems perfectly consistent with my belief that the cardinal rule in any game involving a ball is to watch the ball at all times. If so, why should the player at the net not see the ball served by his partner until it passes the net or comes within his peripheral vision? I've asked this question of many of the world's leading players, and I have never received a satisfactory answer. Some say you waste a precious half-moment of anticipation when you turn to watch the server. Most players have told me they prefer to watch the receiver to see which way he moves in preparing for the return of serve. My response to that is that I know which way he'll move before the receiver does, for I know sooner than they do where the serve is headed. My conclusion is that, by knowing a fraction of a second earlier where the serve will land, I gain an advantage—albeit an ever so slight one—over everyone else. I think we'd all agree that even a fraction of a second can often mean the difference between making and missing a shot.

I've read somewhere that the reason you should never face your partner when he or she is serving is the possibility of being hit by the ball. Well, it would certainly seem that there's less chance of being hit by it when you are watching than if you are not. I'm firmly convinced that I'm right about my feelings, and, for the life of me, can't understand why no one else does what I do.

IN GOOD TIMES AND BAD

Your team is down 30–40 late in a set with the score in games very close. Your partner receives a second serve, starts to hit cross-court, changes his mind and decides to lob, and ends up popping the ball weakly to the player at the net, who puts it away with ease and dispatch. Do you: (a) Tell your partner, "I've seen better strokes in the hospital"? (b) Impale yourself on your racket handle? (c) Throw your racket at your partner's head? (d) Shrug it off with a smile and a reassuring, "Forget it. We'll get them next game"? (e) Vow to take up golf instead?

If you're smart, you'll know that your partner feels bad enough about the blown shot without your rubbing it in. There's nothing worse in doubles than to play your guts out for a point, then hit a poor shot, and have your partner give you a look that says, "How could anybody miss a shot like that?" A player should know that his partner didn't hit the bad shot on purpose; he didn't *try* to hit the ball into the net or right into that racket. But some partners give the impression of believing that, especially those who are, or think they are, superior players.

(Mal Anderson comments that he wouldn't want to be John McEnroe's partner and make any bad shots "because he's such a great player and he thinks you should be at the same level. I've seen him sometimes when Peter Fleming [his partner] makes a few errors. Not that he gets real nasty, but if you're a player, you can tell what's probably going through his mind. And Fleming probably knows it, too, and that adds more pressure.")

Shouting or muttering something like, "Come on, hit the damn ball. You're playing lousy," certainly isn't going to help matters. Instead, the partner should say something to relax the player who made the bad shot. Some players, like Mal and his partner, Neale Fraser, have a relationship where they'll kid each other with some good-natured sarcasm, such as, "Great shot," when it's a terrible one. Others will console with a comment along the lines of, "You learned that shot from me," or "Come on, we'll get 'em next time." And then they'll get off the subject, rather than dwell on it, so they don't mess up the next point.

A good example of a harmonious doubles team is that of Martina Navratilova and Pam Shriver. In the semifinals of the 1982 U.S. Women's doubles against Barbara Potter and Sharon Walsh, Shriver made some great shots on an early point, which she won with a volley, dropping her racket in the process. Martina retrieved the racket for her and handed it to Pam with a mock bow.

Then a few points later, Shriver made several great saves on a point, only to have Martina hit the ball into the net. Shriver comically dropped to her knees on the court. She got up, the partners smiled, exchanged some friendly pats and words of encouragement, and went on to win the game (though they lost the set and the match). Their looseness and conviviality on points won and lost are good examples to emulate.

So give your partner a little encouragement. Assume that he or she is trying and doesn't like missing and being the goat any more than you do.

If you're saddled with a partner who gives you a look that says, "What a crummy partner I have," when you miss a shot, remind him that it's only a game. And if he keeps it up, change partners.

When You're the Offender

There are some tennis players who believe that tennis is one activity where "love means never having to say you're sorry." In other words, the partner who blows the easy shot or makes a bonehead play needn't apologize because, what the heck, we all make mistakes. That's a benevolent and proper attitude if you're the one whose partner erred. But if you're the offender, the right thing to do is to apologize the way you would—or should—to a spouse or business partner you've accidentally hurt or upset. No need to overdo the apology—you don't have to beat your chest, genuflect, and beg forgiveness—but offering a simple, "I'm sorry, I'll get the next one," is perfectly in order. Don't say you're sorry every time you err even slightly on the court, or, if you're a chronic hacker, you'll sound like a fugitive from a confessional. Besides, what would be left for you to say when you *really* goofed? And even though it's probably a defense mechanism to mask embarrassment, try not to look happy that you blew a point.

It's only a game, but the rules of common courtesy apply.

Honor Your Partner with Positive Stroking

As much as you shouldn't place a guilt trip on your partner when he misses a shot (even after you've kept a rally going for a dozen shots and he nets the first chance he gets), you should let him know you appreciate his good shots. Really congratulate him on a good play. "Great shot" isn't a bad phrase to use when he or she has, in fact, hit one. Don't overdo your compliments to your partner to the point that your praise seems insincere. But everybody likes positive stroking, including tennis players, and those who receive it tend to play better on succeeding points. Successful doubles teams are those who not only complement but *compliment* their partners too.

Follow the Bouncing Ball II

One helpful word you can say to a partner on a ball he's chasing that appears to be about to land outside the court (but may not) is "Bounce!" This tells him to let the ball bounce before he hits it. If he takes your advice, he won't save a ball that's headed out, but he remains alert to the possibility that it may land in. If so, he still won't have given up on it.

If you're positive the ball is going out, then yell, "Out!" so in his zeal he won't save it for your opponents. But be sure it is indeed going out. It's awfully embarrassing to call your partner off a ball that lands in.

Advice with Consent

There's nothing wrong with making a suggestion to your partner, provided that you don't do it in a know-it-all way or so constantly that he thinks he's taking a tennis lesson. We've all known people who lecture their partner throughout the match. They may be right most of the time, but it's still an irritant to hear constant admonitions to "Stand here," "Aim there," "Stroke like this," and "Stop trying to go down the line." Often, the player being told already realizes what he or she should be doing, and sometimes, knowing it or not, prefers to do it the way he or she finds comfortable. In a social game, that's certainly no crime.

With all this in mind, you *should* offer a suggestion that could be helpful. For instance, if you notice that one of your opponents is getting a little close to the net, you might suggest—I emphasize *suggest*—that your partner throw up a lob. But remember, if you bug your partner, he or she can also bug you.

If you're teamed with your spouse, making suggestions can be a little more delicate than usual. A good guideline as to whether or not you make them might be how well he or she takes to suggestions about driving when you're in a car together.

My wife and I have played some doubles together. As a teaching pro, she knows the value of suggestions on the court. As a good husband, I know the value of listening! We've gotten along fine. Seriously, we do enjoy playing together.

All of this is really a part of communicating, such a vital element in successful doubles. Obviously, it's essential when it comes to poaching, or letting a partner know about another aspect of strategy. It has another value, too. Mal Anderson teamed with John Newcombe in Davis Cup competition for a year. "He's always communicating," Mal says, "and it helps you to relax if you're in a tense situation, as well as letting you know exactly what he's going to do."

Anderson's doubles partner is usually Neale Fraser. "Neale and I chat all the time. He tells me what to do, basically, because he's the dominant one of the pair," Mal comments with a smile. "But if I want to do something, I'll let him know.

"I might say, 'If you hit a good return, I'm going in, you cover.' Or, 'If I get a good serve, I'm going to lob it. The guy is moving a lot and he's close in.' Same thing with serving. Basically, you serve to a pattern, and if you're going to swing one differently where he might have to watch his side, you say, 'Wide.' He won't change his position, but he'll keep a stricter eye on that particular sideline."

LOB IS A MANY-SPLENDORED THING

It seems to me that the lob isn't used enough in doubles. It doesn't win a point very often, but it serves to let your opponents know that if they get too close to the net, you have a very good antidote —the lob over their head. It may not win the point at hand, but can help you win future ones. Usually used as a defensive shot when you're in trouble, the lob can be as effective as an offensive shot, but the current players don't use it as much as they should.

In mixed doubles, the traditional response by a player receiving the man's serve is to lob over the woman player at the net. If you're successful in lobbing over her head, then her team, which was on the offense, has to go back to defense.

Of course, for every offense there's a defense, and if the woman at the net knows she's going to be lobbed over, all she has to do is stand back a little and the lob is a lot tougher to make successfully.

CONSORTING WITH THE ENEMY

In world-class tennis, there's little conversation between opponents, mainly because most of the time they're too far away to talk to each other and there's almost constant action. In a team sport like baseball, there's considerably more free time, and so it's perfectly natural for a runner to speak to an opposing first baseman while a new pitcher is warming up.

In competitive tennis, you obviously would not talk to an opponent during play, though you might say, "Great shot," (if it's deserved) or offer some comment after the point. On changeovers, there's seldom any conversational exchange because that rest period is too precious. We Grand Masters talk quite a bit. After all, we've all known each other for at least thirty years, so we have a greater camaraderie than we did when we were younger and greater than the younger players have today. Basically, though, today's players are friendly to one another. They fight like mad when they're on the court, but it doesn't prevent them from being civil otherwise.

At any level of play, you really shouldn't go out of your way to talk to an opponent too much during a match because it might disturb him and upset his concentration, something you wouldn't want to do. There really is no hard and fast rule, though. If your group of social players enjoys or at least tolerates chatter, then chatter away. If it's the norm, you can even "ride" the enemy a little—but remember it's a two-way street.

DOUBLES AND REDOUBLES

Let me summarize some points I've made about the essentials of good doubles.

I've often been asked what you have to do to be successful in doubles, and my immediate response is "Get a good partner." That's more than a flip remark. First of all, you should do your best to team with someone who, as nearly as possible, complements your game. If you're a bit slow on your feet, seek out someone who's better at covering the court. If you're the steady, "backboard" type of player, find a partner with a variety of shots and who plays with greater deceptiveness. In other words, try to find someone whose strengths and weaknesses are different from your own. This way, you'll produce a more balanced attack and a stronger defense.

Second, communicate with your partner. Congratulate him after a good play and let him know you sympathize when he misses. Let words of encouragement flow constantly. Make him aware that you are trying all the time and that you know he is, too. After all, everyone can't be a super player, but everyone can try.

Third, move with your partner at all times. You should never be in a one-up, one-back position in doubles after the ball is put into play. If your opponent throws up a lob when you're at the net, retreat as quickly as possible. When you are both in the back court and one of you lobs over your opponent's head, go to the net together.

Fourth, don't be a hog on the court, especially in mixed doubles. Take all the shots that are yours, and leave the rest for your partner. As you gain experience together, you will gradually learn when a ball is yours and when it is not. Teamwork, like everything else, takes practice.

Last, try to keep the ball at your opponent's feet at all times. The secret of success in doubles is to make your opponents hit up so that you can hit down. And remember, the shot before the put-away often wins the point, so let your partner know you appreciated the fact that he made the assist.

A lot more goes into being successful in doubles, but keeping these few suggestions in mind will almost surely lead to improvement and greater enjoyment.

Doubles can be a lot of fun, and, as you get older and reach the point where you're playing doubles more than singles, it can become a real challenge to keep improving. Since good doubles play requires more mental and less physical ability than singles, age becomes less of a factor. This in itself is comforting to those of us who, like the forty-year-old mentioned at the beginning of this chapter, is waiting a decade to resume playing singles.

Members of the Marlyn Tennis Club in Philadelphia, circa 1932, where Vic began to play. The youngster in the photo is Vic and the gentleman standing third from the right is Vic Seixas, Sr.

———•———

Big Bill Tilden was forty-seven in 1941 when he was paired with Alice Marble, twenty years his junior, for her professional tennis debut at Madison Square Garden. Photo by Acme Newspictures

Don Budge (right), whom Vic ranks as the number-one male player of the past fifty years, congratulates Bobby Riggs in 1946 after he was defeated by Bobby for the world professional indoor tennis title. Don had won tennis's grand slam in 1938. Photo by Acme Newspictures

Frank Sedgman (right) and Vic just before the finals of the U.S. Singles Championships at Forest Hills, New York, in 1951, in which Frank defeated Vic.

———•———

According to Vic, Maureen "Little Mo" Connolly was probably the greatest women's tennis player. Photo courtesy of the U.S. Tennis Association

———•———

*Vic and Kurt Nielsen (left) before the
finals of the Wimbledon singles in 1953.*

*Vic was victorious over Kurt and was
presented the Wimbledon trophy by the
Duchess of Kent.*

——— • ———

The 1954 Challenge Round between the United States and Australia was held in Sydney and drew the largest crowd ever (25,587) to a tennis match, with the exception of the Riggs-King match in the Houston Astrodome. The U.S. team of Vic and Tony Trabert defeated Australians Ken Rosewall and Lew Hoad, 3–2.

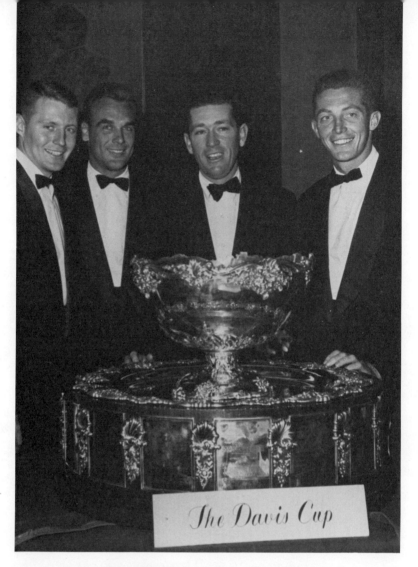

The 1954 U.S. Davis Cup team at their victory dinner in Sydney. From left to right: Ham Richardson, Vic, Bill Talbert (captain of the team), and Tony Trabert.

RACKETS, BALLS, AND SURFACES

∎▮∎

RACKETS

The World's Best Nonwinner

Frank Kovacs was often described as "the best player in the world who never won anything major" because he was always defeated by Bobby Riggs wherever he went. He could beat everybody but Riggs, and while he was a super player, he never won a really major title because Riggs got in his way.

On my seventeenth birthday in 1940, I played my first match at Forest Hills against Kovacs, who was seeded number two in the U.S. Championships tournament behind (who else?) Riggs. I was just a second-year junior player out of Philadelphia with a name that nobody could pronounce, and so our match on the grandstand court was played before a crowd of about two dozen people (most of them my relatives, including my parents). Everyone else was in the stadium watching Riggs play somebody.

That year I was on the Junior Davis Cup team. We'd been practicing a lot in the rain, and I had broken the strings in my rackets (three or four Wilson Squires). The day I was to play Kovacs, I didn't have a racket with strings in it, and Elwood Cooke, a player working for Wilson, brought me a racket about an hour before the 1 P.M. start of the match. It was a Don Budge frame, which I had never used, but at least it had all its strings intact, and since I had nothing else, I had to use it.

Meanwhile, Kovacs, who was known as "the clown prince of tennis," had come out on the court with a ballboy carrying about a dozen of his Canadian-made rackets, a model which at the time was the only one in the world with the design it had. While the ballboy carried his rackets, Kovacs carried a case of Pepsi Cola on his shoulder. Before the day was over, he would consume all but one bottle of soda from that case; I'd drink the other one.

The match began, and that unfamiliar Don Budge frame was like a magic wand to me. I'd never played as well as I did those first two sets, defeating Kovacs, 8–6 and 9–7. I played out of my head. Unfortunately, it was a best-of-five-set match, and since I'd had no hope of winning, I had no idea how to pace myself. After those first two sets, I felt I was near death. I could hardly stand up. A crowd, hearing there was a possible upset in the making, had gathered to watch.

In the third set, Frank led by 2–love when a string broke in my miraculous new racket. I had to borrow one of his to finish the set. Big player that I was, I decided to throw that third set and take advantage of the upcoming intermission to rest and have my racket repaired. Then when play resumed, I promptly dropped the last two sets, 6–4 and 6–2.

But I'd scared the daylights out of Kovacs. The next day I got quite a writeup in the newspapers. Al Laney wrote a human interest story (in the *Herald Tribune*) about this kid with an unpronounceable name from Philadelphia. Didn't the kid know, Laney said, that he was good enough to get more than one racket, and get them free?

The fact was, though I never was on their payroll, I'd been getting rackets free from Wilson since I was thirteen or fourteen years old and went on to use that Budge-frame model into the 1970s, for more than thirty years.

Just because the racket bore Don Budge's name didn't mean that it enabled me to play like Don Budge. It just happened to be a fine racket, suited to my needs. Interestingly, that same racket had many different names on it over the years. It had Budge's name originally, but when he parted company with Wilson, it became the Tony Trabert frame, then Barry MacKay's, then Alex Olmedo's, and, finally, Stan Smith's. But it was the same frame. So if this racket model did possess magical powers, a player who used it would logically expect to have his playing style change to conform with each succeeding player whose name was put on the racket. Obviously, this isn't so, or I would have played, first like Budge, then like Trabert, then MacKay, Olmedo, and Smith.

Depending on the terms of a player's contract with a manufacturer, he may or may not have to actually use the racket he endorses. Some agreements call for the player to use the racket just in the United States or Europe. If a player really can't comfortably use a model that bears his name, he may doctor the racket. One top player had been using the Dunlop Max-ply, one of the more popular wooden rackets. At the same time, though, he was endorsing another manu-facturer's metal racket but found he couldn't play with it. So the manufacturer made a regular wooden racket for him and painted it to resemble their metal model. If he were ever pinned down, he could claim that he had said only that he had *endorsed* the racket, not *played* with it. That was an exceptional case.

Most good players can play with almost any racket if they use it for a while. But don't buy a racket just for the player's name that's on it. A racket endorsed by John McEnroe isn't going to help you play like him.

How should you choose a racket? Basically, you should choose one that feels right to you and has the right weight, balance, and handle size. There are a lot of well-made rackets around, but what feels good to you may not feel good to me or someone else. For instance, I don't like the feel of the big-headed racket and only recently succumbed to a midsized one. Until then I played with only a normal-sized racket.

You should probably start out with a racket that's as heavy as you can hold and yet feels comfortable. The handle should be as big as you can manage without it being too big. Don't start out with a small one. A good guide to what size handle is right for you is the distance from the second line of your palm to the tip of the finger next to the pinky. This will give you the handle measurement you need within an eighth or sixteenth of an inch. There's some scientific basis to it, having to do with the tendons and how they fold to give you the least feeling of discomfort or fatigue.

As far as racket balance is concerned, your racket should not be head-heavy. In fact, you should start—and maybe stay with—one that's a little bit light-headed. You can determine how light your racket is in the head by balancing it on one or two fingers. The farther down on the handle you have to hold it to balance it, the lighter it is in the head. It should not be difficult to find a light-headed racket, since many are made today to accommodate modern flick-hitting styles. Most are being made either light or medium weight, with about a half-ounce weight difference.

In summary, it's better to have a racket that's too light than too heavy, one that's lighter in the head, and a handle that's big without being too big.

Wood versus Metal

For a young male player, the wooden racket is probably the best to use, and if I were a young player, I'd play with one (unless I was being paid a lot of money to use a different type).

The weight of a wooden racket can be the same as that of a metal one, but its density makes it harder to swing through the air. So as you get older, it would be wise to switch to either a lighter wooden racket or to a metal one, which seems to go through the air with less resistance and is therefore easier to swing. Thus, metal, or any racket other than wood, gives you more power with less effort, and you can use this help, especially with your serve.

With rackets other than wood, it seems you do give up some control. So when you reach the point in the development of your game where you need power more than control, switch to metal or composition. This applies especially to a good player, but players of any caliber can benefit from more power with less effort.

I would suggest the same for women players of any age. Chris Evert Lloyd and a few of the other top women have used wooden rackets, but, by and large, like the older men players, women cannot swing the racket as hard as they'd like, and so, if they think they can get some extra help, they should use metal.

I felt this way when I started using the T–2000 when it first came out and was the only metal racket. It felt the way it was made to feel—like metal, complete with a sort of trampoline effect.

Now there's an abundance of metal available, along with graphites and composites, some of which give the extra power with less effort, and some that don't. I don't believe a solid graphite racket gives you any more help on this score than a wooden racket—but it has properties that will help it last ten times longer than wood, so perhaps that consideration is enough to make someone want to buy one.

The T–2000

The T–2000 was invented by René Lacoste, the French tennis player who is probably best known for the shirts that bear his name. As the first metal racket on the market, it was designed to feel and play quite differently from a wooden racket. It was designed to have a lot of flexibility, with a slight trampoline effect. It wasn't meant to be a metal racket that played like wood. But then metal caught on and all the companies started bringing out metal rackets, many of which are intended to play like a wooden racket. Very few succeeded because there are fundamental differences between metal and wood.

Lacoste introduced the racket in France and hoped to market it in the United States. Tony Trabert happened to be in Paris, running the Jack Kramer tour over there. Lacoste asked Tony to show the racket to Wilson, for whom he was working, and Tony did. Wilson marketed the Lacoste racket as the T–2000, and I think Tony still gets a royalty on each one sold. One year he received something like sixty thousand dollars in royalties just from this racket!

Jimmy Connors, by the way, uses the T–2000 but doctors it up a little by putting some weight on one side of it, which is perfectly legal. He's one of the very few top players still using this racket, but he's surely had some fine results with it.

Fantasizing

Part of the club player's racket-buying fantasy, I think, is to buy the latest model, one that nobody else has, regardless of cost.

Tennis should be inexpensive to play. But if the trend in pricing rackets and clothing continues, you're going to have to be fairly well-to-do to play. The price of rackets has gotten out of line, and it's ridiculous. When my three-year-old starts playing, she's going to start with a regular little old wooden racket. A no-frills model is fine.

PLAYERS WITH BIG HEADS

There are days you look around the courts and you think anything but an oversized racket is abnormal. Big-headed rackets have become that popular.

For people just starting out in the game, I think the big-headed type is fine because it gives them a bigger hitting area. They're more likely to hit the ball with the strings of an oversized racket than with a normal-sized one. But once a player gets to the point where he or she is hitting the ball in or near the middle of the racket most of the time, I don't think there's any advantage to the big-headed racket. I can't see much difference in the playing qualities between the oversized and normal-sized racket, although the big one might help a little bit at the net because you don't have to move the racket as quickly to cover the area. Still, if it feels good to you, by all means use it.

There are those who tout the big rackets because, they claim, they have a bigger sweet spot. I've always believed a sweet spot is a spot, and it doesn't get any bigger with a bigger racket. If you cross your arms at the wrist or at the elbow, they still intersect at one spot. I think the same thing applies to the strings of a racket. The spot of the intersection doesn't get any larger.

The large racket might be helpful to someone bothered by tennis elbow. (I go into this malady at length elsewhere.) If you have a tennis elbow, it's a good idea, first of all, to change the weight and balance of the racket, to change where the fulcrum is. If you're playing with wood, switch to metal, and if you're playing with metal, change to a big-headed racket. Just keep changing.

RACKETINI

I once played with the so-called spaghetti-string racket, which supposedly allowed you to do all kinds of strange things with the ball, but I'm not convinced that it would help anybody. When I hit a few balls with the "spaghetti stringy," I found that it does enable you to put a lot more spin on the ball, but many players do that now with a regular racket. Putting spin on the ball doesn't necessarily give you an advantage. You might do better to hit with a baseball bat. Anyway, the spaghetti-string racket kind of died in its own strainer.

I suppose people will always be trying to come out with rackets to "revolutionize" the game. We don't have to worry about a racket that's too big (personally, I'd like them to increase the length of the handle rather than the diameter of the head). Not only the rules of tennis, but the laws of physics, would prevent the use of a racket that was too big. A racket head reaches the point where if it is made any larger, it isn't strong enough to withstand the strain. If you reduce the density to keep the weight down, then you don't have a substance strong enough to withstand the tension of the strings pulling.

Win One for the Gripper

If you are subject to blisters or a comparable problem, you might want to wear a glove on your racket hand, but otherwise I don't particularly advise it. Wearing a glove causes you to lose a little feel of the racket. Torben Ulrich, though, has worn a glove for years; he's mystical enough that maybe it doesn't bother him.

I used to be grip-happy. I could never get a handle grip that felt right to me. Then in the early 1950s while we were playing in Australia I finally came up with an idea. I turned the racket grip inside out and found it to be perfect for me. My hand didn't slip, and I felt comfortable grasping it. Even though the reverse side of the grip is a rough felt, it presents no particular problems to me because I don't alter the way I grip the racket when I change from forehand to backhand. The roughness might make the hand of someone who does change a little raw. I think I was the first player to reverse the grip; others have done it since.

Stringing

The modern synthetics used in stringing rackets nowadays are so good that 90 percent of the people who play tennis, from the rawest hackers to the best pros, could not tell you the difference between some of the synthetics and gut. The ten percent who could tell the difference are topflight older players, who played a lot with both types of strings. Today, you don't really need gut—it's much more expensive, much harder to string, less durable, and very much affected by dampness. Many of the top players, especially those using big-headed rackets, are using nylon or some other synthetic, which is what I recommend for you.

TENSION

How tightly your racket should be strung is a matter of personal preference. The best tension for you is something you'll pick up with experimentation. When you start playing tennis, you're probably not aware of whether the strings are tight or loose. If you have the kind of strokes that tend to keep the racket on the ball a little longer (which is more likely the stroking style of the older players, rather than the flicky type of wristy strokes you see today), you probably won't want your racket as tightly strung. You get a little more feel with a loosely strung racket. On the big-headed racket, the tension has to be a lot higher to get the same feel from the strings. The more you flick the ball, the more you spin with your wrist, and the shorter the time you have the ball on the racket, so you would probably use tighter stringing.

The *way* you hit the ball, not how hard you hit it, will determine how tight your stringing should be. For example, Bjorn Borg, who probably doesn't ever hit a flat ball, has his racket strung at about eighty pounds of tension. By contrast, a player with a more fluid, traditional, old-fashioned type of stroke would have a racket strung at about fifty-five to fifty-eight pounds.

I haven't found that I want to reduce the string tension as I get older. I like tight stringing, about sixty pounds, in my normal-sized racket, which is the equivalent of about seventy to eighty pounds in the larger-headed racket. A few players prefer loosely strung rackets, but I think most of the players today are using tighter strings, with sixty to sixty-five pounds of pressure, because most of them hit the ball with more spin than players used to.

BALLS

NEW PSYCHEDELIC

It's funny. For 90 percent of your career, you play tennis with a white ball, then suddenly you're playing with yellow—and white looks strange. Psychedelic colors are around, too, and multicolored balls are gaining popularity—and white looks stranger than ever.

Manufacturers started to produce yellow balls to go along with the tennis boom and the growth of indoor facilities. No question, yellow is easier to see indoors, and even outdoors when you don't have good lighting or against certain backgrounds.

White balls still exist, however. A grass-court ball made in the United States is white and has less fuzz on it than the usual tennis ball. That's because a ball played on grass tends to get heavier as it picks up moisture.

At Wimbledon they still use white Slazenger grass balls specially made for the tournament, but they are actually no different from others except that special care is exercised to make sure all the balls shipped are good. The balls they export to the United States are probably different from what they play with over there because we don't play very much on grass and we want the ball to last a little longer.

Changing Balls

How frequently balls should be changed depends on several factors: whether you're playing competitive or social tennis; whether special tournament rules are in effect; the type of surface you're playing on; and who's paying for the balls.

Each tournament will indicate how often balls will be changed. Generally, it's after the first nine games (since warm-up is considered the equivalent of two games), and then after every succeeding eleven games. If weather conditions change so that the balls get very heavy, they are changed more often. This probably happened at Wimbledon in 1982 because of all the rain that fell. The referee has the discretion to order the change.

Among social once-a-week players, the custom is to introduce a new can of balls every week (whether they need to or not. You really should have two sets, and wash one while you play with the other). When we're practicing we'll play three or four sets with the same balls, and when we're teaching we'll use balls possibly for months until they get soft. Eventually, though, a ball will lose some of its pressure and that changes the way it bounces.

On hard courts (cement or composition) the balls wear out pretty quickly. It stands to reason that the rougher the surface, the more it wears out the ball. As nap wears off the ball, the ball starts to get lighter and harder to control, so you change. The ball reacts just the opposite on grass. There, you start with a lighter cover, but then the ball gets heavy, especially if dampness makes it soggy. On grass, you have to change balls more often. You try to keep them at a reasonable, constant weight, but on grass it's almost impossible to do that.

With new balls, the server has a tremendous advantage—everything else being equal—on grass more than on any other surface, for the new balls go like bullets until they pick up the green and become heavier. So serving on grass with new balls is great. In a crucial game, you'd want to point to having new balls, if possible.

SURFACE IMPRESSIONS

The surface you play on makes a big difference not only on how balls wear but also on how they react—and, for that matter, on how *you* wear and react.

When you talk about a tennis court's being fast or slow, what you are referring to is how the ball bounces on it—not, as some uninformed people think, the flight of the ball through the air. Generally speaking, the smoother the surface, the more the ball skids when it hits, without coming straight up. The grittier the surface, the more bite it has, and so the ball tends to bounce up straighter. Consequently, you have more time to get to the ball. If you hit a ball on a smooth wooden floor, where there's no friction to grab the ball and make it stand up, it stays low when it hits and scoots along. On a very fast court like that, the ball gets by you quicker. You have less time to recover. Even on a relatively fast surface like grass, the ball gets by too quickly for rallies to last very long, while on a slow, dirt court, the rallies can go on forever.

In the United States we tend to speak of *hard* surfaces, meaning such materials as cement and asphalt, and *soft* surfaces, such as clay and Har-Tru. But you have to be careful because to a European, a hard court means clay or dirt. They have hard courts and grass courts. A safe way is to differentiate between "gritty" and "nongritty" surfaces.

COMPENSATION

You can compensate for the speed of a hard, or nongritty, court by shortening your backswing because you have less time to swing and you have to move a little quicker to prevent the ball from getting past you. On a slower court, you have time to get set, so you can lengthen your backswing.

Depending on the surface, you hit the ball a little differently. On a gritty surface like Har-Tru, you have to slide into the shot a little, so you must adjust your stroke and footwork accordingly. If you're running for the shot, you try, if possible, to hit the ball as you finish your slide. On a hard court, where the footing is secure and you don't slide, you would run right to the ball to hit it. There, you don't have to slide, so you hit the ball without allowing for a slide. But on a gritty surface, you know you're going to have to slide, so you prepare for that little give in your feet as you're moving toward the ball.

It may surprise you to know that you don't slide on grass very much. If it's not wet, it's not slippery, and so you don't play with the idea of sliding. Grass plays more like a hard court, but it's easier on your body. If a grass court gets a little wet, however, it can be treacherous because you might slip. A slide is planned and you know what you're doing but a slip is a surprise, and you don't have control. Someone who depends a lot on making quick stops and starts is not going to enjoy playing under slippery conditions. I know when I lost my footing, I lost my confidence.

PLAYING FAVORITES

Until the end of my junior years, I don't think I ever played on grass. Grass courts were strictly at cricket clubs and similar places, and unless you were brought up belonging to those clubs (I was not), you didn't get to play on grass that much. I was raised playing on clay courts, but, as it turned out, my style was better suited to the grass courts than to clay and other slow surfaces.

The reason was that, from the beginning, I was a pretty aggressive player who liked to serve-and-volley and come to the net. I played that way even on slow surfaces, where it's difficult to attack all the time. (This is one of the reasons I had a rather erratic career for a while, playing a great match one day, then losing to someone I should have beaten the next.) When I got into the men's division and started playing more on grass, I found it to my liking because an attacking style pays off more on that kind of surface. Then, we started traveling and playing on cement and other hard courts, and I found them even more to my liking.

For example, until recently, the Pacific Southwest Championships were always played at the Los Angeles Tennis Club on cement courts. I won that tournament three times, twice without losing a set, and this was against the top competition of the time. I felt that when I got on that court—which was a fun place to play— I could run down every ball. And I just about did.

Of course, cement courts are hard on a player's system, primarily the legs. Because you don't slide, the joints take a beating on your stops and starts. We were particularly aware of it when we came to the Pacific Southwest on cement after having just played the Nationals at Forest Hills on grass. Many of the players would suffer from shin splints and comparable discomforts.

In the Grand Masters tournaments, we play on whatever surface is used at the site of our match. Ironically, the hard surface, which I always preferred from a pure tennis perspective, is the surface I least prefer from the standpoint of physical comfort because it's the hardest on the knees. Now, in my later years, I'd rather play on clay or Har-Tru, which allows you to slide a bit and is therefore easier on the knees. The very thing I liked about a court is what hurts me now. (I never thought I'd have any problems with my legs, which, by the way, I don't think are the first things to go. But the wear and tear from the pounding I gave them finally caught up with me.)

I think that most competitive senior players will reach the same conclusion I have. If you go all-out in your play, you'll find that the grittier surface is easier on you. Your knees, ankles, calves, and hips don't take the beating on the softer surface that they do on the hard. Also, the grittier material may make you more confident about hustling after balls far to your side because you feel there's less chance of twisting an ankle than on a hard surface.

Not everyone agrees, but I feel the speed of the hard court is probably a little better for a senior player. If the court gets too slow, you have a hard time winning the point. So while I like the slower surface for the good of my legs, I prefer the faster court when I'm hitting the ball because I feel I have a better chance to win the point. The ball doesn't come back as often.

STANDARDIZE THE COURTS

It's really difficult to say which type of court is more difficult to play on. It depends very much on your style. On the slow court, you have to do more with the ball to win the point. The ball is easier to get to, so your opponent has a better chance of returning your shot. Consequently, you have to hit a better shot to win the point. By the same token, because it's easier for your opponent to get to the ball on a slow court, he can pass you more readily. Slow-bounce courts tend to favor the back-court players. Since they have more time to reach the ball, they're not forced into errors as easily, and they have time to develop ground strokes that give them passing-shot ability.

The beauty of a hard-surface court is that you can make it fast or slow by how much you rough up the surface. Leave the cement surface slick and you have a very fast court; rough up the cement a lot, and you can make it quite slow.

The typical hard court is a little faster than the gritty-type surface and possibly a little slower than grass. Because it's in the middle, I think it's the best playing surface from the standpoint of not favoring one style of play over the other. That's why I preferred to play on it. If the court was just the right speed and the bounce was just right, I felt I could play aggressively but also defend.

A grass court on which the ball skips too much, leading to bad bounces, favors the aggressive, net-rushing volleyer who doesn't wait for the ball to bounce. A very slow court, on the other hand, favors the less-aggressive, baseline player. On that type of surface, the ball stands up and you have endless rallies because you can't hit the ball beyond your opponent's relatively easy reach. You have to keep your errors down. I watched a little of the 1982 French championships on TV. In the finals, Guillermo Vilas and Mats Wilander hit the ball back and forth, back and forth, until it almost put me to sleep; it was like watching grass grow. I went to brush my teeth, came back, and they were still playing the same point. Neither would miss and neither could do enough with the ball to hurt the other one. So it became an endurance contest.

That's one extreme; the one-two-three net-rushing, volleying end to a point you get on a fast grass court is the other. They're equally bad.

Most of the players in my era. myself included, were net-rushers. In those days, we played a lot more on grass, a surface on which you couldn't stay back. You had to force or your opponent came in on you and you were in trouble. In the United States and in Australia, therefore, where there were grass courts, we played a much more aggressive style. But in Europe, where they didn't have grass courts, they developed a different style of play, building their game around the slow courts. Their style was much more defensive. When the Europeans came to play on grass, they were hopeless; very few could adapt. And when we went to play on their slow courts, we had trouble against them. We had to learn to stay back and wait for a good opportunity to come to the net, and most of us weren't patient enough to play that way.

So surfaces play a tremendous part in the game, and the ability to play well on all surfaces is an important criterion of greatness. On this theme, I think Jimmy Connors plays pretty much the same on all surfaces, though he's probably best on a hard court. I believe he has won three U.S. Opens on three different surfaces. Forest Hills originally had grass courts, but then switched to Har-tru, a synthetic clay, which was going from one extreme to the other. When the Open moved to Flushing Meadow, the courts used in the tournament had a solid hard surface, combining cement and some other substance. (It's called DecoTurf II.) Purely from the tennis standpoint, it's the best surface because it doesn't favor a particular style. To win on that surface, a player has to have the ability both to attack and defend better than anyone else, and that should produce the best tennis.

A long time ago I advocated having a standardized surface for Davis Cup competition, which involves players from all over the world. If Italy were to come to play the U.S. team in this country on grass, the Italians would have no chance. If we played them in Italy, unless we completely outclassed them, our team would have no chance. Competition should be held on a neutral stage and not a surface that gives one player or style a built-in advantage over the other.

Standardization may be a very idealistic concept, but it is feasible. When the pro circuit plays indoors, one surface is put down everywhere. Obviously, you can't have courts all over the world converted to the same type of surface, but for international competition you could require either a standardized surface or one that falls within a certain range of conditions. Then there wouldn't be any "home-court advantage" due to surface.

DOWN TO THE NITTY GRITTY

For reasons of economy, mainly the cost of maintenance, hard courts are the wave of the future. Consequently, your choice of surface may be more and more limited as time goes on. But as prime-timers, when you have a choice, for the good of your aging knees and other joints, choose the court with a gritty surface.

DEM BONES,
DEM BONES

Someone once said, "It's hell to get old, but it sure beats the alternative." I guess that's about the way all of us feel about the relentless process of aging. We have to accept it, even though we don't like the idea. I do think, however, that we should fight it every bit of the way, taking advantage of every available tactic or device that helps us delay the inevitable. Thus, keeping as fit as possible as we grow older should be uppermost in everyone's mind.

We all know workaholics who haven't the time for exercise. How many have succumbed to heart attacks or strokes at an age we now consider young? How about those (especially men) who have stressful jobs all week long, get little or no exercise, and then overdo the athletic bit on the weekend? Invariably, they come up injured, which prevents further athletic activity for awhile and drives them even deeper into the hole they've been digging for themselves for so long. It takes careful planning, along with a steely desire to break through this syndrome, but we all know deep down it's worth it. Many companies now actually instruct their key employees to get some type of regular exercise, knowing that it will not only keep them healthier but will result in a higher degree of efficiency and productivity at work.

IN SHAPE TO PLAY

Most people who are not competitive players use tennis as a means of exercise to get in shape. At the recreational level, however, it's a good idea to start getting into shape *before* you begin to participate in sports activity. When the tennis boom started, one of the problems was that a lot of people went out and immediately started playing on a pretty hectic basis. Men and women who hadn't been exercising started using muscles they didn't know they had, and pain and sometimes injury resulted. What they should have done, of course, was to make sure that they weren't starting off in this vigorous sport without their heart and other vital organs and parts of their body in shape to take this activity. This is especially important for seniors. But common-sense caution applies to all ages.

Therefore, while I would be the first to advocate the game of tennis, I think it is imperative that proper precautions be taken by anyone first starting to play, especially someone who has not been exercising on a regular basis. Tennis is a vigorous activity, and when played outdoors in the sun, can be a little more than the sedentary body is ready for all at once. That is why a checkup by your doctor is always a good idea before starting any serious fitness campaign.

PREPARING FOR TENNIS

The average recreational tennis player gets out on the court one, two, or at best three times a week and leads a fairly sedentary existence the rest of the time. How can he or she best stay in shape?

The answer, I think, lies in a combination of what you do and don't do before you even come to the court, plus what you do before you start a game and what you do during the game.

For example, although I was never much on weight lifting or a lot of calisthenics, there are various exercises that are good for you and that I recommend.

In preparation for playing tennis, exercises that help strengthen your stomach muscles, especially sit-ups, are beneficial, and jumping rope is a good way to help increase your speed. If you're playing a good bit of tennis, you're probably getting as much running as you need. If you're not playing a lot, some running is advisable. I advocate running rather than jogging, since jogging doesn't do enough to prepare you for competition. But build up to it, eventually running hard for awhile, doing sprints and other kinds of running that are more closely related to what you do on the tennis court.

If you are overweight, start your getting-in-shape program with one of the best of all exercises, pushing away from the dinner table. You want to be a Pancho, not *Pauncho*, Gonzales or Segura.

I never had a weight problem, but if I put on a few pounds, they trickle down to my waist, so I feel the additional pounds very quickly. There are ways to keep the waistline under control.

For example, in 1982, Chris Evert Lloyd managed to lose seventeen pounds by cutting chocolate, doughnuts, and other desserts from her diet. She found water to be "a wonderful appetite-suppressor" and began drinking between six and eight glasses of water a day.

Chris recently said that she considered her most important meal the one she ate the night before a match; it might include steak, vegetables, a salad, and spaghetti. Chrissie said that she supplements the meals with iron and vitamin C and gets at least nine hours of sleep a night. "Also, by cutting out junk food," she said, "I have more energy. Proteins and carbohydrates give more long-term strength."

John McEnroe supposedly has a blended concoction of bananas, strawberries, and orange juice on every morning of the U.S. Open, along with pancakes or an omelet, and maybe both.

In recent years, some players have taken to having a high-carbohydrate meal before they play for energy. I never subscribed to that theory, although there might be something to it. I agree with Sven Davidson, who says it's better to eat too early and too little before a match than too late and too much. I always tried to eat fairly normally, without making myself feel full. I wouldn't eat closer than an hour to a match, and certainly not something like a big steak even two hours before.

In England several years after World War II, I had a rather unusual pretournament meal. On the Sunday before Wimbledon starts, there is traditionally a large outing at the Hurlingham Club just on the outskirts of London. It starts with luncheon and continues through the afternoon, with friendly doubles matches on the grass courts of the club. Most of the players attend, as it's a chance to visit with old friends and get a short workout.

At the luncheon in 1952, I happened to be seated next to Lord

Templewood, then the president of the English Lawn Tennis Association. He was a white-haired, somewhat stern-looking Englishman, with a command of the language that seems to be the special province of the British. The luncheon was pathetic, representing the times. It consisted of some tired-looking lettuce on which there were a paper-thin slice of ham, some potato salad, and a small wedge of tomato. As I brought my fork to my mouth about midway through the meal, I noticed a little green worm squirming on the piece of lettuce. My first concern was how many of the little fellows had already made the trip, but I managed to remain relatively calm. Not knowing just how to handle the situation, I suddenly got the bright idea that I could shake up Lord Templewood, and perhaps create a little excitement during what was a rather dismal affair.

Gently nudging him, I said, "Look what I found in my salad." Without so much as batting an eyelash, he replied, "Oh, lucky fellow, you got meat with your salad." I think I realized at that moment why the English could never have lost the war.

By the way, whether or not you're winning the war of the waistline —whatever the shape of your upper body—you should keep it under wraps until you're warmed up. In all but the hottest weather—weather in which you, as a prime time, part-time player, should go to an air-conditioned movie instead—most good players wear a jacket until they feel they're properly warmed up. You might want to consider doing the same.

ON THE COURT

Once you get out on the court, the main thing is to avoid doing anything quickly, and that applies to both moving and stroking.

If you are middle-aged and out of shape, you must be prepared to hurt a little if you want to get fit. Playing tennis uses almost all the muscles of the body, and chances are a good many of them haven't been subjected to any abuse for some time. Starting slowly and warming up thoroughly, therefore, are essential to prevent injuries. So, even before you hit a ball, you should do some stretching and turning, little exercises that consume very little time but are important as precautionary measures.

Among suggested prehitting activities: slowly jog around the court once or twice; loosen the neck muscles by rotating your head slowly half a dozen times or so in each direction; loosen the shoulders by rotating your arms past your head, windmill fashion, several times from front to back and then back to front (as if you're swimming); stretch the hamstrings by putting one leg at a time up on a bench and slowly bending your upper body toward it several times; put one leg out straight behind you and the other in front of you, knee bent, and bend your upper body toward the knee (then reverse the legs, and repeat). Stand up straight and bend from the waist very slowly to one side as far as you can go about five times, then do it to the other side. Next, go up on the balls of your feet and come back down on your heels very slowly.

All these or comparable exercises should be done very slowly, gently, and deliberately, without bobbing up and down, so that you slightly strain these muscles and more or less test them before you start playing. In any event, don't do anything herky-jerky right off the bat.

And remember, even after you've reached the stage when the newly activated muscles stop hurting, it's a good idea to do some preliminary stretching before vigorous playing.

WARMING UP THE STROKES

As far as warming up your strokes is concerned, you should swing very slowly and easily at first and then gradually increase your pace. Major league baseball players will often start batting practice by just bunting the ball a few times—merely meeting the ball with the bat—to activate their eye-hand coordination comfortably. You might do the equivalent in tennis, at first just meeting the ball with your racket and then swinging harder and harder.

The pros generally start a warm-up by hitting a few from the baseline. Then one player will go to the net and volley a few. His opponent will then give him a few lobs to hit overheads. This will help him locate the light, shadows, and sun, and adjust to the wind. Then the second player will go to the net to hit volleys, after which he's fed some lobs.

Next, the pros practice serving. It's interesting—and unfortunate—that many club players will often go out and hit a hundred or more ground strokes in the warm-up but never a serve or an overhead.

They may think the motion is the same with these strokes as with ground strokes, but that isn't so. Ground strokes give you no opportunity to extend your arm above your shoulder or your head.

At a club or public courts, one of the players will ask, "You ready?" The other will nod yes, and after a couple of practice serves by the first server, the game begins. His opponent will also take a couple of practice serves when he's set to serve for the first time, but those will be the only practice serves they've taken. In some games, it's a matter of the match beginning with "the first one in," so if, by luck or skill, the *first* serve comes in, that server has *no* serving practice.

Not only is this detrimental to your serving game, but it is potentially dangerous to your health. Serves and overheads can have a more drastic effect on your arm and shoulder than ground strokes, so make sure during the warm-up that you hit serves and overheads to get yourself warmed up overhead as well as to the side.

Don't Get Hustled into Starting

In match play there's a time limit (usually three to five minutes) for warm-ups. In major tournaments, they're quite strict about enforcing it. In other competitions, depending on where they're held, the umpire may be more lenient and wait until both players or teams indicate they feel properly warmed up.

With or without a time limit, the players will usually give each other the shots they request, although some, like Torben Ulrich, warm up so deliberately, they don't hit the ball with pace for quite a while. You'll hit a solid warm-up ground stroke at Torben, and he'll just block it back. This can be a little irritating because you don't get to hit with the pace you want. But then, he's not getting any practice either. If a player carries that to an extreme, he'll acquire a bad reputation and have what he's doing returned to him, in spades.

At the other end of the warm-up spectrum are players who either are ready to play almost immediately, or who start bombarding the ball on their first warm-up shots. There's nothing in the rules, as far as I know, that says that you *must* warm up. Still, the supreme act of gamesmanship would be to walk out on the court and announce to your opponent, "I'm ready." (Of course, you would already have warmed up with someone on another court.) I don't think anyone has ever done this, except maybe jokingly.

Extremism aside, we've all known players who come out on the court with their rackets smoking, ready to start playing long before you are. If you're facing someone like that, you can't let him hurry you into accelerating your warm-up pace or starting the game before you feel you're properly warmed up. When he says, "Ready?" simply say, "Just a few more," and keep hitting (within reason) until you feel your body is as ready to play as his.

THE COLDER, THE GRADUAL-ER

The necessity of warming up slowly before you extend yourself is most pressing in cooler climates, especially for the prime time player. As we get older the muscles become more susceptible to a pull or strain, and if you're playing before your blood is circulating the way it should, the vulnerability to these problems is great.

When you're young, you might be able to get away with just walking out and swinging away. I tended to do that as a young player, but, although I haven't had any real problems, I'm much more aware of the importance of warming up slowly and not hitting the ball too hard right off the bat. It's when you first start hitting that you're most susceptible to injury. Our group has had some muscle pulls and strains, only a few of which have resulted in a player's having to leave a match, but they probably wouldn't have happened if we had warmed up a little more.

You should try to avoid injury at all costs not only because of the pain and expense and the fact that it will keep you from playing tennis for a protracted period of time—all compelling reasons—but also because of what happens to your body during the lay-off period. Especially at a later age, when you don't play tennis for a month or two, you lose tone all over your body, and you have to recondition everything before you can start again.

Sometimes everything goes sour while you're waiting around for the injury to heal. Once you are well enough to play again, something else can go bad. It's a chain reaction. So it's essential to do some stretching exercises and keep your warm-up sufficiently gradual over a long enough time to prevent injury.

WARMING UP DURING A MATCH

Once you warm up and you're perspiring, your body is functioning at a normal rate so you shouldn't have to do anything special to keep yourself warmed up during a match. However, if you find a little tightness or soreness in your leg or neck during a match, you might do a bit of stretching or rotating during a momentary lull in the action. If rain should interrupt your match and you find yourself standing around for half an hour, it's critical that you warm up once more. If you've cooled off and start right in, you run the same risks of injury all over again.

A good way to stay limber and avoid muscle pulls in your legs during a game is to grab an ankle with your hand behind you and pull your heel up toward your buttock. Do this with both legs (but not simultaneously).

WARM-DOWN

It's probably a good idea not to come to a complete halt after a match is over. Just as a runner keeps moving after a race, you should stay in motion or even do a little bending and stretching when a match is over. I don't think people pay much attention to this warming-down, which is all right, because although you might get a little stiff or chilly, you're not likely to incur an injury from failing to do it.

What *is* important after a match, in my opinion, is that you get out of your wet clothes fairly soon because if you stay wet you'll stiffen up very quickly. I don't buy the idea that catching cold is the result of going from hot to cold or being in a draft. I just think the "cold bugs" are around and if your resistance is low, you're susceptible. However, you should change promptly.

DRINK DURING A MATCH? NO SWEAT

An old theory was that you shouldn't drink much while you were playing. There's nothing wrong, however, with quenching your thirst during a match. In fact, it's desirable. You should drink a little bit on a regular basis during a game—say, every time you change courts. This is a lot better than waiting until you've built up a tremendous thirst and then, when you can't stand it any longer, gulping down about five glasses of water or some other liquid. This leaves you bloated and very uncomfortable.

I like to drink plain water when I'm playing. Many prefer tea or something with a little sugar to get quick energy, particularly if the match is long. Gatorade and drinks of that sort probably have their good qualities, but I'd rather have water.

I have never been in favor of taking salt pills either. I happen to like salt, so I have a lot on my food (contrary to what doctors advise people) and that probably compensates for the loss of salt from perspiring during play. Whether you should take some salt supplement depends (in addition to what your doctor says) on whether you're someone who perspires a lot or not. Incidentally, being a heavy sweater has nothing to do with what kind of physical shape you're in. Some who perspire profusely are in much better condition than others who perspire a lot less.

The questions surrounding salt loss and thirst quenching are intensified, of course, in particularly hot and humid weather. It would be ridiculous for a prime-timer to go out on a hot summer weekend and play for four or five hours, especially if it's an intense brand of singles. Yet I've seen competitors seventy or older playing in the noontime July sun. But they weren't running like young kids and they were sensible enough to wear hats, refrain from running very much, take long breaks, and stop before they got overtired.

Assuming you're in reasonably good physical condition, it comes down to a question of how often you play, rather than how old you are or how hot it is. If your system is conditioned to playing almost every day, then you can get out in the heat and, provided you're sensible, play without worry. But if you're a weekend player, you should head for that air-conditioned movie and otherwise keep a close watch on yourself *whenever* you play, even on cool, low-humidity days.

WEIGHT

If you're overweight, running around in the hot sun is very risky. You're asking for trouble playing under almost any conditions. When we speak of getting in shape to play tennis, girth is almost as much of a consideration as overall condition.

As a rule, you don't see many heavy tennis players among the good ones. Playing tennis most of their lives in itself has helped them keep their midsections pretty trim.

ALCOHOL'S THE RUB

Cutting down on cigarettes and alcohol is not a bad idea, with moderation being the key here. I've never believed one had to lead a Spartan life to be fit, but I would suggest a sensible approach to the various temptations we all encounter.

It's really not a good idea to have anything alcoholic before you play. It can have a very serious, adverse effect on your play—and on your health.

A social-level, prime time, tennis-playing acquaintance of mine once brought some wine to share with friends at a swim club he belonged to. They disparaged his selection, and kidded him about his lack of taste. One friend promised to bring "good" wine the following Sunday. Well, my friend thought *that* wine was worse than what he had brought, and so he said he'd bring something "really good" the next weekend.

As promised, he brought yet another brand (ironically that of the company that sponsors the Grand Masters) and proceeded to share it. The bottle was large, the wine chilled and delicious; the day was warm, the number of people sharing the wine was fewer than anticipated. Before long, my friend, who is not much of a drinker, was feeling as high as the proverbial kite.

Then came a fateful invitation. "I've got a court signed up at four. Want to play?"

"Sure," my friend said. "As soon as I finish this game of Boggle" (a word game, in which he was having difficulty spelling words like *cat*). The word game over, he went into the pool for a dip to clear his head. Then he laced up his sneakers, probably not tight enough (certainly not as tight as he was), and went to the court.

Figuring that in time he'd feel okay and that he'd play all right by putting extra concentration on the ball, he began warming up with his opponent. He took what he considered were textbook, level swings, but found that his shots were going as high as a major leaguer's pop fly, a phenomenon that sent this fifty-year-old into giggles. His opponent hit a ball to his forehand corner and he moved to retrieve it. My friend got his racket back well in advance and rotated his body to get in position to hit the ball. The next thing he knew he was crumpled in a heap against the fence, his weight on one ankle.

"You looked like you were doing an umbrella step," his sympathetic opponent said (referring to the game, Giant Steps), as he helped him to a comfortable resting place.

It turned out that my friend's ankle was severly sprained, and he had to be on crutches for four weeks. He was in pain and away from tennis for months. Two years after the accident, he still wraps his bad ankle with an elastic bandage as a precautionary measure before he plays (and wraps his other ankle, too). "I guess," he says, "Boggle and tennis don't mix." But, just to be on the safe side, he doesn't even sniff the cork of a wine bottle within days of when he expects to play tennis.

He learned a painful lesson that really should be obvious to everyone. Even if it doesn't lead to injury, as it did in this case, drinking alcoholic beverages can only be hazardous to your game. It's bound to weaken your coordination and otherwise affect the skills basic to tennis. (Remember the grinning Frank Sedgman serving into the stands?)

As a rule, professional players don't drink much at all. If they're not going to play for three or four days, they might have a few beers, but never any close to a match. I never drank on the eve of a match because I felt it would have a bad effect on my system.

SEX GOETH BEFORE A MATCH

You'll get varying opinions on whether prematch sex can be harmful to your game. Boxers go into hibernation for months, while some football players have lived a jet-set life up to the opening gun.

Among tennis players, you'll find some who abstain before a match from midnight on, others who observe no such self-imposed rule.

I think there's a happy medium between Spartanism and hedonism. You have to find out what suits you. A good standard is moderation in all things, including moderation.

MARATHON

I've lost my share of matches, but rarely if ever because I was not in sufficiently good shape or because my opponent was in better condition than I was. If you can approach tennis or any other sport feeling that way, you've got something extra going for you.

At the age of thirty-five, Stan Smith was one of the oldest pros in the draw at the 1982 U.S. Open. After winning his opening-round match from twenty-two-year-old Mike Leach, 4–6, 6–4, 6–3, 7–5, Stan recalled an opening-round match he had played against me in the 1966 Nationals, when I was forty-three. I beat him in five long sets. "I got cramps in the match against Vic," Stan told a reporter, "and he was older than I was."

I always felt the longer the match, the better chance I had.

I was already forty-three and hadn't been playing full-time for eight years when I met Bill Bowrey in 1966 in a Penn State tournament match at Merion Cricket Club. Bill was fifteen years younger and a Davis Cup player for Australia. I was still playing enough competitively—the Nationals, Penn State, and maybe one or two others—so I could still be a factor.

We started playing at 4:00 in the afternoon and didn't finish until five minutes to 8:00 that night. A couple of women spectators told me the next day that they had gone home to fix dinner for their families at 6:30, fixed their dinners, and came back in time to see the end of the match.

The marathon was memorable not only for the elapsed time but also because of the first-set score and my age. The first set comprised sixty-six games! I lost it 32–34, and I don't think anyone could blame me if, after that set, I had decided there wasn't much point in hanging in there and trying any more, especially at my age. But I did hang in—and won. I took the second set, 6–4, and struggled through the third and final set for a 10–8 victory.

The match was played on grass, and there were virtually no service breaks, which is why it went on so long. I don't think it could be characterized as a particularly well-played match because there weren't many rallies, but it was long enough to get into the record book as one of the longest ever.

If that match with Bowrey had been played under the rules in effect today, which allow thirty seconds between points and ninety seconds on changeovers, it would have gone on for seven hours! (Ironically, those rules were put in to keep players from taking too long, but the effect has been that most players take longer than they customarily would if there were no such time limits.)

My victory entitled me to play Clark Graebner, one of the top players of that era, the next day, and, to my surprise, I played pretty well. I won the first set, then started to remember how tired I was, and lost the next two sets and the match.

NEVER DEFAULTED

I'm proud of the fact that I never defaulted a match in my entire career. And, as I will go into in more detail later, I never sat down while changing sides, other than during Davis Cup matches.

If you sit down, your body relaxes, and suddenly when you have to get up, as in the case of turning a light on and off, it takes more energy than if you'd been standing up continuously. So I'd suggest that if you're not too tired, you keep standing rather than sit for a break. Possibly stop and towel off, have a little drink, and just keep walking around. It's a matter of self-discipline, too; it gives me the feeling that I'm doing what nobody else is. But this is just my opinion. Others say to take every opportunity to get off your feet.

FULL MEASURE

Speaking of feet, when we were playing in Australia in the 1950s, the most popular tennis shoe there was called the sand shoe. Developed by Dunlop for play on grass, it was a very lightweight shoe that would have been ideal, except that it was made in full sizes only. I happen to wear a half size (10½ in the United States and a 9½ in Australia); the Australian 9 was too small and the 10 too big. I persuaded Dunlop to start producing half-size shoes.

I convinced Dunlop of something else, too. An American company named Hood manufactured a very lightweight shoe for yachting. It had a sole with a herringbone-type weave that made it very effective on the deck of a ship or boat. We also found that it gripped very well on grass in this country. It was the best shoe I'd found. So I told

Dunlop about that, too, and they began producing a tennis shoe with a herringbone-weave sole, a style that's become very popular.

Anyone who plays tennis, at a competitive or club level, should baby his feet. Someone once told me, "You should never skimp on shoes or a mattress because you spend most of your life in one or the other." I follow that advice. I always buy good shoes and make sure my feet are well taken care of. Everybody's feet are a little different, so you have to find the shoe that fits your foot best. But there is such a wide selection of good tennis footwear around now, that's not really a problem.

HATS

Take care of your head, too, and if you're not accustomed to playing in intense heat, you might want to consider a hat. One of my idiosyncracies is that I don't like hats and, except when I was in the service, I've never owned a hat. But, I certainly don't suggest not wearing one.

INJURIES? DEFAULT'S NOT OURS

As a group, the Grand Masters have been remarkably injury-free. The most serious injury was Frank Sedgman's snapped Achilles tendon, for which he needed surgery. His injury didn't happen in one of our tournaments, but in a senior tournament at Pebble Beach, California. And Sven Davidson broke a tiny bone in his foot and missed a season.

But other than those and an occasional muscle pull, we have had very few injuries and very few defaults, which is pretty remarkable for the age group. I attribute it to two basic factors. First, we're in pretty good shape because we've been playing all these years, and second, perhaps even more important, we know what to watch out for and how to be careful about some of the pitfalls involved in growing older. Because you are more injury-prone as you get older, you have to learn to warm up properly and stretch and do some of the other things you never thought about doing when you were younger.

There are certain muscles and tendons that come under heavy

attack from tennis and therefore need more attention when warming up. The Achilles tendon is one. Many tennis players have experienced varying degrees of injury to this large tendon, which connects the calf muscle to the heel.

Nobody knows exactly what causes a snapped Achilles tendon. It's believed that the tendon has been strained over a long period of time and then, suddenly, it gives. The victim thinks he's been hit in the back of the leg with a racket or ball. Many players have experienced a similar feeling and injury with at least one other tendon, often in the calf.

When you play without benefit of a ballboy, you have to be on the alert to danger from an unexpected source. It may look harmless, but one of the great potential injury-causing hazards is a ball on the court—whether it's rolling or just lying there. Pick it up at once, or warn the player it's near to get the ball out of the way. If a point is in progress when this happens, just play it over as a let. No point is worth a sprained ankle.

Obviously, tennis players, like all athletes, are subject to a variety of injuries, such as sprains, strains, and breaks. Quite often, these problems will occur to even the most finely trained player because, although tennis is not a contact sport, it is demanding with regard to the body's joints and muscles. Quick starts and stops, abrupt change of direction, and frequent slippery playing conditions can all lead to occasional injuries. Needless to say, the older you get, the more prone to injury you become, and the more precautions you must take to avoid these physical setbacks. Since it also takes longer for the older body to heal, the problem is aggravated. As an older player, the one fear I have is a serious injury that would keep me out of action for a lengthy period of time. While recovery is at a slower rate, the rest of the body declines more rapidly, thus creating the climate for further problems.

A few years before Sedgman snapped his Achilles tendon in one leg, he had suffered the same injury to his other leg while playing squash in Australia. In each case, surgery was required to reattach the tendon, and he was out of action for about eight months. Since Frank was in excellent physical condition, it's obvious that this particular injury can occur at any time to anyone. The fact remains, however, that it is less likely to happen if you are properly warmed up and do a little preliminary stretching of this tendon.

Another area of concern to tennis players is the hamstring muscle. An injury relatively common to runners as well as tennis players, a pulled hamstring seems to occur most often when the weather is cool and the athlete has not warmed up sufficiently. The pull or tear causes pain high up in the thigh, and, if severe enough, can put you out of action for a month or so. Again, proper warming up and stretching prior to play is the best way to prevent this annoying injury.

I suffered a pulled hamstring while playing at Wimbledon in 1967, ten years after I'd retired from full-time tennis. It was a second-round singles match on an outside court that had been soaked by several days of rain. It was also quite cold and damp as it sometimes can be in England. Early in the fifth set, I ran hard for a drop shot, stretching at the last moment a little farther than I should have. I felt only a slight twinge, but it caused me to come up lame. I could no longer run and merely played out the few remaining games at half speed.

Not knowing at the time that I had actually ruptured some blood vessels, I made a huge mistake by having heat and massage after the match. Several days later, I discovered that hemorrhaging had turned a large portion of my thigh purple. It was frightening. Needless to say, the heat treatment was the worst thing I could have had, since it served only to increase the internal bleeding. That scary experience taught me one lesson I will never forget: *always use ice first*. In almost every type of injury, cold is better than heat at the outset, and ice is one of nature's great gifts to man when it comes to treating athletic injuries. You can't ever go wrong in applying ice to any kind of pull, strain, or bruise. It can reduce pain, swelling, and bleeding, and never do any harm. Heat may *subsequently* prove helpful in increasing the rate of healing for many injuries, but ice should always be used first.

BYPASSING SHOTS

Of course, some physical problems on the court are not of our own making.

In 1980 Sven Davidson was coming back to the United States from Sweden when he collapsed in the airport terminal in Malmö. Four times his heart stopped beating—he was literally dead—and four times he was revived. At first, his collapse was attributed to a heart attack, but he had none of the other symptoms usually associated with one, so his problem was attributed to a virus in the heart. He resumed playing tennis soon after.

About six months later, Sven was playing in a match in California, when, during a rally, he came to the net, hoping to make a winning volley, but the ball passed him. He motioned his opponent to the net, and said, "That was a very nice shot; now please call an ambulance."

With that, he fell to the ground. At the hospital, he was found to have roughly 90 to 95 percent blockage in five coronary arteries. To save his life, Sven underwent quintuple bypass heart surgery. Today, he competes regularly—and well—in the Grand Masters competition. He's still the (streamlined) bull he used to be. His great condition and complete recovery are a tribute to the way he's always taken care of himself. The fact that he's played tennis continually over the years hasn't hurt either.

People have died on a tennis court; others have been saved. One avid player, then in her forties, was in a social match at a private club when she suddenly fell to the ground, lifeless. Fortunately, an oral surgeon and an ophthalmologist, playing in a doubles game nearby, hurried over and administered heart massage and mouth-to-mouth resuscitation, finally reviving her. Again, the woman's heart stopped beating, and they repeated their lifesaving technique. Yet again she died, and yet again they brought her back to life. In the ambulance taking her to the hospital, her heart stopped beating at least once more, and she had to be revived again.

Finally, at the hospital the woman was thoroughly examined and tested, and her condition diagnosed. She had suffered a potentially fatal bursting of an aneurysm in an artery of the brain. (An aneurysm can be compared to a worn-out section of hose that has bubbled out.) She underwent surgery and, after tortuous months of learning to speak and write and walk again, began to live a normal life. In a year she was back on the tennis courts, and today plays as intensively as ever.

It could be said that, in a sense, tennis saved her life. Had the bursting occurred while she was at home, in a car, or any place else where no one had been around to revive her—rather than on that tennis court—she would not have survived. And her excellent general physical condition, because of her continuous tennis playing over many years, was an essential part of her astounding recovery.

I can't overstress how imperative it is for tennis clubs to have oxygen readily available and people trained in lifesaving techniques always on the premises.

EYESIGHT

A far less serious problem, also not of our own making, is related to changes in vision.

People growing older usually become farsighted, but my only vision problem is that I continue to be slightly nearsighted. Because I'm myopic, I need glasses for distance, especially indoors when the light's not good. From about 1950 to 1960, I was very much aware of light conditions. I preferred to play outdoors at the time of day when the sun was at its brightest and I used to request playing then. If I ever got a match indoors or late in the afternoon, I sweated it out.

About 1960 I began wearing glasses to play, but they gave me the feeling of being caged in. They steamed up, and they disturbed my concentration. I had never worn glasses off the court, so whenever I put them on to play tennis, they felt as unfamiliar to me as a hat. But I needed them because my depth perception wasn't that good.

Contact lenses really solved my problem, enabling me to see perfectly without being cumbersome. I wore hard contacts for about ten years, both on and off the court. Then I began having difficulty seeing close with the contacts in, so I decided to wear them just for playing tennis, and I could tolerate them easily for three or four hours. When I'm playing tennis and concentrating intently, I'm not even aware of them. If I'm just going to hit some balls, I wear glasses because it's too much trouble installing and removing the contacts. I wear glasses, too, for watching TV, driving, and similar activities, but I don't really need anything for up close.

I think contacts are ideal for playing tennis and the greatest boon for players with eye problems. Now I can play—make that *see*— as well as anyone on an indoor court.

COMMON SIGHT

Strangely, quite a few tennis players seem to have the same vision problem. I know because I've looked through their glasses. In fact, looking through a fellow player's glasses was how I discovered I needed them. During my tour in South Africa, Eric Sturgess and I went to the movies one night. Sitting well up in the balcony, I could hardly see the screen. "There's a lot of smoke in here," I said to Eric. He said he didn't think there was that much. I looked through his glasses, and it was as if someone had turned the lights on. I had never realized just how bad my eyesight was.

It's just a theory of mine, but I think playing in the sun so much must have an effect on a player's eyesight. Maybe it doesn't damage the eyes per se, but it must have an effect. Gardnar Mulloy has the same kind of eyesight problems that I do—which is why he could use my glasses and shared them with me in one match. Frankie Parker, Herbie Flam, and Eric Sturgess, of course, were among other players of my day who had almost identical degrees of nearsightedness.

I don't think my theory applies to players who get farsighted as they get older, which is usual with advancing age. My vision stayed the same for more than twenty years, which I think means my nearsightedness has played the farsightedness tendency to a draw.

If, like most people, your eyes are changing so that your arms—and your time to react—seem too short, consider contact lenses. If you prefer glasses, make sure they're shatterproof plastic.

THE MALADY LINGERS ON

All kinds of maladies can strike. In the 1982 U.S. Open, Chris Evert Lloyd had such a bad case of food poisoning that she couldn't keep food down, and defaulting was a possibility. She played, though, and went on to win the championship. Martina Navratilova, in that same tournament, suffered from a viral condition often transmitted by cats. Her doctor gave her the option of not playing, but she did compete, and was upset by her friend and doubles partner, Pam Shriver, in the quarterfinals.

The pros have pride and money on the line, but if you're feeling sick, it's usually wise to skip your club-level match in order to hasten your recovery and play another day.

TENNIS ELBOW

Of all the physical ailments confronted by the tennis player, the most vexing and probably most common is tennis elbow. While usually thought of in connection with tennis, this painful condition can also be caused by other activities. Painting and window washing come immediately to mind, and no doubt you can think of many similar types of continuous action involving the wrist and forearm. Baseball pitchers and golfers are often victims of tendinitis of the elbow of one type or another, but there is no doubt that tennis players are the most likely to suffer this nagging problem.

There are basically two types of tennis elbow, one that hurts when you hit backhands (the worse, I think), and the other, which hurts on the forehand and serve. Among beginners and less experienced players, the backhand causes most of the elbow problems. In this case, the pain is on the outside of the joint and hurts mainly on contact. Quite often, a person experiencing this common type of tennis elbow can hit all the other shots without feeling much pain, but the backhand produces an effect much like being hit on the funny bone with a hammer. With this type of tennis elbow, it also hurts, in varying degrees, to shake hands or to even lift a cup from its saucer. Pressing the lever of a shaving cream spray can becomes a painful experience if the problem is serious enough.

Most of the time, the cause of this type of tennis elbow is improper technique in hitting the backhand. Whenever you see someone hitting a backhand with the elbow ahead of the racket head, you can virtually predict tennis elbow sooner or later because of the bad stroke. If the elbow is ahead of the racket head before contact, the upper arm has finished its swing and you end up hitting the ball with just your wrist and forearm. The elbow point was not designed to take this kind of abuse, and eventually tendinitis (inflammation of the tendon) will occur.

To avoid strain on the elbow joint, the whole arm, held straight, should be hitting the ball. The best way to accomplish this is to keep your elbow tucked into your body as you start to swing. Then, when you meet the ball parallel to your front foot, your whole arm is in line and the strain is minimized. If this is done properly, there is the synchronization of the racket head, elbow, and upper arm, which is vital to the correct backhand swing.

Stan Smith had a really bad elbow for a long time because he had started trying to hit over the ball instead of under, and began to put his elbow out a little too far in his attempt to flick it. He fought that problem for several years before he corrected it.

At times, many of the better players will find that the inside of the elbow joint hurts when they hit serves and forehands. While this can be a serious type of elbow problem, it usually isn't, and it ordinarily goes away merely by easing up a bit on the serve or slightly altering the forehand swing, which might have been improper.

Essentially, I think that the only way to get rid of a tennis elbow is to *stop doing what hurts*. If your backhand causes you pain, hit everything forehand, or change the way you hit backhand. The elbow condition is not going to get better as long as you're doing things that cause it to hurt. I'm not a doctor but that's exactly what they'll tell you. Often, if it's only the backhand that hurts, you can continue to play, running around your backhand whenever you can. Some of us do that anyway, preferring to hit the forehand whenever possible. In this way, you can keep playing and prevent the rest of your body from atrophying while you wait for your elbow to heal. It's also a good idea to warm up your elbow before playing, using hot water and/or a hot salve of some kind. After playing, ice applied on the joint for a few minutes is helpful.

One thing to remember if you have a tennis elbow is that with proper care and treatment, it will get better. Think of it as an injury rather than a permanent disorder, and although it seems at times that it will never go away, be assured that it will. Once you rid yourself of the problem, take steps to avoid its recurrence by improving your technique and doing some exercises specifically designed to strengthen your forearm. If you feel it coming back, take the necessary steps early to prevent it from becoming serious.

The only time I had tennis elbow was in 1959, and it lasted about four months. It was the classic backhand elbow caused, I feel certain, by my more sporadic play after semiretirement in 1957. I had never had the problem before and didn't recognize the symptoms until it was too late. I just thought I had a sore forearm muscle that wouldn't get better. By the time it moved up into the tendon, I had an "elbow." I played a long five-set match at Forest Hills against Tut Bartzen in the Nationals and we were interrupted twice by rain. Each time we resumed, my elbow hurt more, until finally I could hardly hold my racket. Fortunately, I lost in the fifth set. I say *fortunately* because I could never have played the next day. In fact, I couldn't hit a backhand for four months. Since then, on several occasions when I've noticed some slight symptoms of the problem, I've taken precautions immediately to prevent its recurrence. Never again will I suffer as I did in 1959.

Medical people who have studied the problem of tennis elbow and specialized in its treatment have found success with a variety of treatment approaches. Depending on the severity of the case and the healing abilities of the sufferer, inflammation and pain have been relieved with rest, ice, and antiinflammatory medications. These medications, while they help ease pain, do not promote healing by themselves, and you shouldn't rush back into action prematurely. Nevertheless, progressively increasing exercise programs often help stimulate healing, according to Dr. Robert P. Nirschl, assistant professor of orthopedic surgery at Georgetown University School of Medicine, and Janet Sobel, director of rehabilitation at the Virginia Sports Medicine Institute in Arlington, as stated in an article in the June 1981 issue of *The Physician and Sports Medicine Magazine*. Some of the medications, such as Butazolidin, must be taken with proper precautions relating to dosage and duration because of adverse effects they can have on blood.

Braces can be helpful, once you're recovered, in preventing a recurrence. Mal Anderson says he's had all sorts of remedies suggested to him for his elbow problems. If any of them worked as well as their proponents suggest, his elbow would be completely pain-free. But it isn't, so when he plays he often wears a protective splintlike brace device, which has bands at the wrist and at the upper forearm, with a connecting piece down the middle of the inside of the arm. This takes up some of the pressure from the impact of the racket's hitting the ball and dissipates the force before it reaches the elbow.

Many tennis players find it helpful to wear some sort of bandage to support joints that are weak or sore. At a prime time age, there are so many parts that ache, you often wish you had an ace bandage body stocking.

All-important, of course, is modifying your stroking technique so that you don't perpetuate the strain that caused the tendinitis. And you might think seriously of changing the court surface you play on, the design and stringing of the racket you play with, and even the balls you use. Dead balls or those that have soaked up moisture tend to produce overload forces that contribute to tennis elbow.

If your elbow problem persists after you've tried in your own way to cure it, you should consult a good orthopedic specialist. I, for one, reject the idea of repeated shots of cortisone, although there is often an almost miraculous cure experienced after one or two injections. Cortisone is a powerful drug, and too much of it can have devastating effects on the joints. Most of the leading orthopedists recommend that it be used sparingly, some not at all.

A last resort is surgery, but few cases require it. Of more than three thousand cases of tennis elbow seen by Dr. Nirschl, 92 percent responded to nonsurgical treatment. Among those who eventually had surgery, symptoms were improved in 97 percent, and 85 percent were able to return to the activities they engaged in before the symptoms.

CUSHIONS

In the words of Gilda Radner's comic newscaster, Roseanne Roseannadanna, "It's always somethin'. If it's not one thing, it's another." Hence, if it isn't the elbow joint, it's the knee.

When I was in my "prime," I relished playing on hard courts. I'm referring to asphalt-type surfaces, where you didn't slide when making your shots. I loved that kind of surface because the footing was good and you knew you could stop and start without slipping. Since I depended greatly on running and changing direction abruptly, I wanted and needed the security of sound footing. It occurred to me only a couple of years ago that I was putting extra strain on my knees by playing on this surface. As a matter of fact, I was always of the opinion that my legs would last forever! I never believed the theory that the legs went first on a tennis player and still feel that in most cases it is the back that gives out before any other part of the body. However, I have finally found that after fifty years of stops, starts, and pounding, my knees have started to complain. Arthritis has developed in both knee joints, and while I have no difficulty with normal movement, I am rudely reminded of it by sharp pain when I try to make a quick move or change of direction. The cartilage has lost its elasticity, I am told, and any abrupt movement that used to be properly cushioned by cartilage is now producing the feeling of bone against bone.

The fact that arthritis seems to settle in the joints that are used the most by an athlete seems to me to be one of nature's ironies. It's likely to settle in the site of old injuries, but in my case, arthritis has moved in not because of an injury but because of wear and tear. It's not something that can be operated on, and, essentially, it's something I have to live with.

Arthritis itself is a real enigma, and it is surprising to me how little is known about this troublesome disease. The dictionary defines arthritis merely as "inflammation of a joint or joints." There have been many cures and remedies promoted, including copper bracelets, none of which seem to have any sound medical proof behind them. There are conflicting beliefs with regard to the part diet plays in dealing with arthritis. A variety of special types of foods have been suggested as having almost miraculous curing powers, while most medical people claim diet has no effect whatsoever on the disease. In my case, I have discovered what works best for me through the old-fashioned trial-and-error method.

I've been given exercises to strengthen the muscles in the upper legs, which help take the pressure off the knees so that they don't take as much of a beating when I land hard. You don't have to have my problem to benefit from exercises to strengthen your knees and upper legs. They're also good if you're recovering from an injury or surgery, and they're valuable as a means of preventing injury.

Exercise is not only good but it is absolutely necessary. If I go more than several days without sufficient exercise, I hurt just as much as when I overdo athletic activity. There is a definite range within which I must remain in order to minimize the arthritic pain. For any of you suffering from osteoarthritis (referred to as the wear-and-tear disease), I'd suggest you experiment with various amounts of exercise until you are able to determine your proper range of activity. It's bound to vary among sufferers, and no one can better judge his particular requirements than the person himself.

Contrary to a widely held belief and my problem, I think that the loss in flexibility that most tennis players experience is essentially a back, rather than a leg, problem. As people get older, they get stiffer and lose their bending flexibility. This is especially true of men who put on weight around the middle as they get older, and their backs become stiffer and stiffer. I think that tennis helps delay the stiffness a little bit.

Flexibility in tennis is related not only to the back but to the hamstrings as well. Without thinking about it, most people, just through the walking they do in their everyday activities, exercise their legs—but they don't exercise their stomach and back muscles unless they make a point of doing so. You really should, if you want to slow the aging process.

With regard to medication, nothing beats good old aspirin. I take two buffered aspirin every four hours on days when I plan to play tennis and have found it eases my aches and pains while I play and helps ease them after the game, too. While I've tried many other antiinflammatory medicines, I've always returned to aspirin. It's the least expensive, does not require a prescription, and does the job as well for me as anything. It's gotten to the point now where I refer to aspirin tablets as my "knee pills." Before you take any drugs, however, be sure to consult a medical authority you trust and respect.

Once I feel the pain when I'm playing, my mind tells my bones, "Don't do it," and I try to avoid making a quick turn or sharp change in direction. I compensate by starting after a ball sooner because I know I won't get there otherwise. It's taken away what was probably the best part of my game, which is why it's difficult for me to win now.

It's also changed my strategy, to the extent that I might try to do more with a specific shot than before. I realize that I don't have the wherewithal to make a return, dig in, and get back to the center of the court when out of position.

To give an example, if I'm attempting a passing shot, I'm more likely now to try to hit a better one because I don't want to take a chance on having my opponent hit a volley that I'm not going to get to. Basically, it's the same motivation that has made Mal Anderson play more aggressively. The net result, unfortunately, is that I don't play as well; whatever I'm doing to compensate now is not going to be better than what I was doing before.

As an average senior tennis player, you're not going to run into this problem, unless you've played tennis all your life and as hard as I did. But you are going to have to think about compensating in some aspects of your game, since the aging process is going to slow you down. In years gone by, you might just have been content to keep a particular ball in play. But today you will want to make a better shot of it because if it stays in play, you may not catch up to it.

There are obviously various stages of arthritis, and we know it only gets worse, not better. There is no known cure, only treatment. With that in mind, the aging athlete must reconcile himself to living with it. This is almost as much a mental or psychological adjustment as a physical one. You must learn and respect your limitations brought on by this condition. Once you are able to do this, you begin to realize osteoarthritis is not as bad as it sounds. It won't kill you and you can live with it. As a matter of fact, according to the Arthritis Foundation, thirty-seven out of every one hundred adults have osteoarthritis and 97 percent of all people over age sixty show signs of the disease. Aging athletes are particularly vulnerable, but they say if we live long enough, every one of us will develop the disease to some degree. My suggestion to those of you who have this problem, as I do, is to hang in there and keep playing tennis. Find your range and limitations and stay within them. You can continue to enjoy the game indefinitely.

The highly trained athlete should be less injury-prone than the weekend jock. He or she has worked hard for long hours to tone the muscles and joints and is more accustomed to the vigorous activity. In tennis, the social player must become more aware of the possibilities of injuries. Playing once a week or less is not enough to keep your body in the mint condition needed to ward off injuries. If you are an occasional player, take extra precautions to warm up sufficiently and try not to overextend your physical capabilities. As you get older, all of the above becomes increasingly more important.

Tennis can be the sport for a lifetime, provided you make the necessary changes along the way. I can still remember a cliché my Dad used when I was young and had boundless energy: "Youth is a wonderful thing; too bad it's wasted on young people."

PSYCHOLOGY

The old expression in poker "The winners count their money while the losers yell, 'Deal, dammit, deal' " can sometimes be applied to tennis, at least at club level. You can often tell who's winning and who's losing without seeing them play, but not always.

Some players are so intent about playing and winning that it's as if their lives depend on the outcome; others play as if they couldn't care less. Either approach is okay, I suppose, if everyone in the game shares it. Otherwise, the happy medium is probably best.

Tennis ought to provide relaxation, recreation, and a release of tension, as well as pleasant competitive exercise. Therefore, you don't want to play the game in a way that creates more of the very tensions and concerns you're trying to escape. On the other hand, for the sake of the other players, if not for yourself, you shouldn't take such a lighthearted, noncaring view of the game that you spoil the fun.

Having said that, however, I want to add that playing with something of a laid-back attitude can be the cause, as well as the result, of winning. And you may be shocked to hear an old competitor say this, but, with the right attitude, there can be a lot of pleasure in a good-natured, hard-fought match, *even if you don't win!*

But winning is more fun than losing, and the more everyone does to try to come out on top contributes to the quality of play and heightened enjoyment. This means using all the resources of mind and psyche, as well as body, in an optimum way.

126

At any level of play, psychology plays an important role, in both obvious and subtle ways. For example . . .

MIND AND HEART

A lot of the game of tennis is mental, especially after you've mastered the mechanics. It's like learning how to drive. Once you've learned how to start a car, steer, shift, and brake it to a halt, you can start planning itineraries. Similarly, in tennis, once you've learned how to make the different strokes and cover the court, you can start planning your strategy: what you're trying to accomplish and what strokes to choose to make it happen. The better your level of tennis—at any age—the more it becomes a mental game. The mind plays tricks, though, or if it doesn't, the heart does. Your mind tells you not to go for the low-percentage shot—say, the attempted pass of the netman in a foot-wide space down the line—but your heart reminds you that the lower the percentage, the deeper the satisfaction—if you make it.

The practical player, the person ruled by the mind, overcomes this temptation and lobs or hits cross-court. But the romantic tries the passing shot, and—you look sheepishly at your partner, who wasn't too happy the last three times you tried, and failed with, that same shot. At least now you'll know whether he's really your friend.

TAKING IT TO HEART

At any age or playing level, there are players who take a loss more to heart or express their disappointment more dramatically than others.

In the 1941 National Juniors Tournament (at Culver Military Academy in Culver, Indiana), for eighteen-year-olds and under, Gardner Larned, then the country's best junior player by far, was playing Budge Patty in the quarterfinals. Patty, who had been down match point against two earlier-round opponents but had survived, now appeared to be finished. Larned had taken the first set, 6–love, and had Patty in the second, 5–love. One more game and the match was his. So confident was Larned that he turned around at one point and commented to a few of us sitting behind the fence, "Hey, this guy can't play tennis at all. How'd he get into the tournament?" He soon found out.

The score went to match point, but Patty hung in. Again, match point, and again Patty brought it to deuce. After Larned lost a few more match points, Patty took the set, 7–5, and then won the third and deciding set by the same score.

Larned, who already had a reputation as a bit of an eccentric, gathered up his rackets and sweater and walked right into the big lake next to the tennis courts. Someone had to go in and pull him out. I can understand disappointment, but there are better ways to drown your sorrow. Especially in a social game, it's foolish to take a loss that much to heart.

Later that week I met Budge Patty in the finals, which observers say was one of the best junior matches ever played. I'll go into more detail about this match later in the book. Suffice to say, for the moment, I lost 10–8 in the fifth set.

I didn't walk into the lake. Instead I caught a train from Indiana back to Rhode Island, to play in the Newport Invitational the following Monday. It took a night and a day to get there, and I sat up in coach the whole distance. Patty, who'd collapsed after our match, didn't get up for three days, and showed up on Wednesday. At least I had the satisfaction of recovering sooner.

I was never too happy when I lost, but I tried not to be morose or dwell on it too much and take the after-effects home with me. There wasn't money involved when we were playing in amateur competition, so if we were eliminated early in a tournament, say a Monday or a Tuesday, that was it for the week. We had nothing to show for our loss except grief and a long wait until the next tournament. It irks me to hear people say that we didn't try too hard because there was no money riding on the outcome. On the contrary, we may have tried harder.

MENTAL TOUGHNESS

"Mental toughness is about 80 percent of the battle in the majors," Steve Denton told *New York Times* writer Neil Amdur. "That's why the top guys have an edge. If you start beating those guys, you start believing in yourself. You don't panic in pressure situations and you start relaxing. A lot of tennis matches are won on just a couple of points. The better players don't put pressure on themselves."

"The mental aspect is so important, particularly confidence," according to Tracy Austin. "How much you want to win, how much desire you have, how much you put in, and how much you're willing to work."

Wendy Turnbull, who has been a runner-up in the U.S. and French Opens, makes a different point. "When a player who hasn't won those tournaments gets in a position to win, they seldom come through. They want to win, but mentally, it's such a big thing that they can't handle it. It's all psychological."

"EYE OF THE TIGER"

I'm completely convinced that you've got to be hungry to win, no matter what endeavor you're engaged in. I'm sure today's top tennis players, with as much money as they're making, aren't thinking about the purse while they're playing. They're concentrating on winning the point. They're *hungry* to win the point. Otherwise, they wouldn't be out there. I'm talking as much about the hunger to prove themselves, as the craving for money.

To a degree, even in social tennis that hunger is desirable, provided it doesn't become all-consuming. I believe some of this competitiveness is an inborn quality, as is the talent for a given endeavor. I began taking piano lessons when I was about six. I could have kept taking them from then until now, and I never would have been a great piano player. It's just not in me, and yet I had a certain gift of ball-to-hand-to-eye coordination that I was able to pursue, develop, and capitalize on. And so, just as I marvel at the ability of someone to sit down and play a piano concerto, that person may think the same thing about a gifted tennis player. You can call it Quality X, but whatever that inborn special element of desire and talent is, you should develop it and use it to advantage.

PSYCHOLOGICAL CYCLE

In tennis, as in life, mind and body continually affect each other. If physically you're able to perform a certain task, this gives you a confidence in your ability; and because of this confidence, you are able to perform even better.

A case in point: I used to feel, rightly or wrongly, that when I walked out on the court, the longer the match went, the better chance

I had to win. It didn't necessarily follow that I won, but I never felt I was going to get tired. After my experiences at Wimbledon in 1950, I had become determined that I would never again lose a tennis match because of a lack of stamina, and I worked on keeping myself in excellent condition. The knowledge that I had the stamina helped me convince myself that, during a long match on a hot day, I was in better shape than my opponent, and therefore would probably win. I might not have been in better shape than Sedgman or whoever else I might be playing, but I convinced myself that I was.

I never tried to stretch a match to three or four hours (I wanted to win as quickly as I could), but if it came to that, I was emotionally ready. When it got to five–all in the fifth set, this confidence helped me. We were obviously evenly matched, so my feeling that I was as tough as anybody under those conditions sometimes was enough to give me the winning edge. I didn't win them all, but I think I won more than my share because of this self-confidence.

CONCENTRATION

When I'm playing I try to keep my mind from wandering away from tennis. I try to think of what I'm going to do or how I'm going to try to hit the next shot if I get a chance. I try to keep my basic game plan in mind—perhaps play one side more, or stay back more, for example.

In the Grand Masters, because we all know each other's game so well and how to play against each other, most of the time it's just a question of whether we're able to carry out our plans. The more you play with the same group—as you who've been playing regularly with the same foursome for years know—the tougher it is to come up with something that will fool them.

I still have the same problems with the same guys I had trouble with in the old days. By now, I think, I've tried everything under the sun at one time or another to beat Frank Sedgman, but he still beats me more than I beat him. I'd have to say he's a better player than I am. His biggest asset was his speed on the court. When you depend on your speed to win and you come up against someone who is faster, you're in trouble. Frank is still an extremely consistent player and, for our age group, a very good aggressive player. He's been the most consistent winner of the Grand Masters, but I think Mal

Anderson, Alex Olmedo, and Gene Scott are young enough and good enough to beat Frank more often than Frank beats them now.

If you're not nervous going out to play a Davis Cup match or an event on the Centre Court at Wimbledon, there's something wrong with you. It's also natural to feel nervous at the prospect of a match that's out of the limelight, even one at your club. There isn't much you can do to overcome your nervousness except to forget everything else by shutting out everything around you and just concentrating on hitting the ball. The better you are at doing that, the quicker you'll get over your nervousness, the more settled down you'll become, and the better you'll play.

Unfortunately, however, I think everyone has trouble with concentration, to a certain degree. Yet it's probably one of the most important elements of successful tennis. Some people can lose themselves in a game of tennis to the point where their business, domestic, or health problems are blocked out during playing time, while with others, those same problems intrude on the game. It depends a lot on how severe the problems are and what kind of person you are. All I can suggest is that you view the tennis ball coming toward you as a target for unleashing your frustrations and concentrate on making solid contact, as you would like to with the villains in your life. Think of tennis as a vehicle for striking without fear of punishment.

BIG POINTS

Confidence is intimately related to the ability to play under pressure and win the big points. This is what makes one player better than another. I think when Connors played McEnroe at Wimbledon in 1982, Jimmy had the feeling that when a big point was being contested, he was going to win it. Thinking that way often helps make it happen. If you're more confident than your opponent, you're going to win more. But don't get overly confident or you could end up like Gardner Larned—all wet!

Knowing you're about to play a crucial point isn't likely to help you play it. In fact, dwelling on the fact that the set or match is now in your (sweaty) hands can easily panic you. So when you or your team is down 3–4 and 30–40, with the serve coming to you, treat the point as ordinary, or you're likely to tighten up and blow it. Beyond determining not to try any of your pet wild shots, try not to think of the point's significance as you play it. And if the serve is coming to your partner, resist the temptation to say something like, "It's all up to you, so don't screw up."

WHEN YOU LOSE THE FIRST SET

Some players get so downcast after losing the first few games that they're pretty much out of the set. And some who lose the first set effectively count themselves out of the match. Don't let this happen to you. At a level and on a surface where service breaks are common occurrences, the game, set, and match aren't over until the last point is lost.

Certainly, losing the first set of a best-of-three match is more serious than losing the first of best-of-five, but turnarounds are always possible. You can help it happen if you stay optimistic—and make some alterations in your game.

Some players start hot and cool off, and believe it or not, there are others who feel uneasy if they get off to a lead. They try harder, and play better, if they're down a set. But even if you're a slow starter, don't let down in the first set and subconsciously try to lose. Despite what I've said about turning the match around, having to win just one of the remaining two sets is a lot easier than having to win both.

PLAYING AGAINST YOURSELF

Does this describe you? You anticipate that the serve is coming to your backhand, so you cheat a little in that direction. But the server notices and takes advantage, serving a sharply angled ball to your forehand. You lunge to hit the ball, barely making contact, and the net man puts it away. Through the next point, you can't forget what happened and you're determined not to repeat it. So when he serves next to you, you're ready. You concentrate so hard on making good contact and on returning the ball cross-court that you fail to notice the net man is on the move. The poacher disposes of your return with ease. By the next time you're going to receive the serve, you're a mess—the victim of your past history. You're talking to yourself (as we all do), and you're making the mistake of dwelling on what happened. Don't do it. Don't let the last point or the last game become an obsession, or you'll be doomed to repeat your mistake or create a new one.

Fortunately, the action of tennis usually doesn't allow you to linger that much over an error of judgment, a poor choice of shot, poor execution, or whatever. Being a continuous-action sport, tennis really doesn't allow you to stew in the juices of your misfortunes. If your boo-boo took place right before a changeover, you'll have time to dwell on it a little more. But if you're smart, you'll forget it and concentrate on the next shot.

Unfortunately, the same action element that prevents you from dwelling on your bad shots also leaves you with little opportunity to gloat over your good ones. But as you step up to serve, get set to receive, or change sides of the court, it's a nice idea to reinforce your confidence with a thought along the lines of, "I did pretty well with that one, maybe I'll hit this one a little better."

Inner pep talks go on all the time, and they're helpful. Telling yourself, "Hang in there," or, if you're getting tired, "I'm not *that* tired," is a nice way to convey positive thoughts to yourself.

Saying the same sort of positive things out loud to your partner can also be beneficial. But different people react differently. Telling a partner, "Let's get this one" after *you've* bungled a series of points could well prove counterproductive. And telling him or her, "Come on, we need this one. Don't choke." is a good way to make it happen.

NEMESES

As much as you can help yourself psychologically, you can also defeat yourself that way. For example, for one reason or another you may have convinced yourself that you can't beat a given opponent. If you really believe this—even if you're as good as, or better than, he is—you're defeated before you go out on the court.

By the same token, you may find that you can beat a particular player regularly but then lose consistently to someone he always defeats. Why is he your "nemesis?" Often, it's as much a matter of playing style as self-psyching, but whatever the reason a player constantly defeats you, eventually it's going to be established in your mind as the way it's supposed to be.

Everyone used to think Ken Rosewall had my number, that he was my nemesis. I used to lose most of the time, and people would say,

"You never played well against Rosewall." On the contrary, I played great tennis against him, but he just played better. His style of play was especially difficult for me. Yet Lew Hoad, who, according to statistics, was as good a player as Rosewall if not better, didn't bother me as much. Rosewall's shots were deep and penetrating and difficult for me to handle. Hoad's shots, while they were hard hit, were shorter and had a lot of spin on them. He played a little more like I did than Rosewall.

For several years when we were frequent opponents, I would fare well against Hoad while having trouble with Rosewall, and Trabert would do well against Rosewall and find Hoad difficult. For awhile Hoad dominated Rosewall, which I could never quite understand. Eventually, Rosewall gained the edge on all of us, but for quite some time we presented an interesting study in contrasting styles.

I had a similar playing relationship with Rex Hartwig, my final-round opponent in the 1954 U.S. Championships. He had eliminated Trabert and Rosewall, both of whom proved quite difficult for me, but I was slightly more comfortable against Hartwig.

Rex, who always stimulates pleasant memories when we meet in the Grand Masters competition, was always a shotmaker who could handle the racket well, and when he was hot, he was hot. Winners would streak off his racket, and no shot seemed too difficult for him. Fortunately for the rest of us, he couldn't keep it up forever. He was the best doubles player of all the Aussies, and many place him high on the list of all-time great doubles players. A natural volleyer, he returned serve from deuce court about as well as it could be done.

In singles, while he always did well against Trabert and Rosewall, he had his troubles with Hoad and me. I think this points out what an important part style or type of game plays in the outcome of a match. I always found it difficult to play against the heavy hitters with penetrating ground strokes, especially on a medium fast surface, but I felt I could serve-and-volley with most players when I was playing well.

Coming out to play Rosewall, I didn't have a defeatist attitude, yet I never approached any match feeling I would win it easily. Against Rosewall, I knew I was in for a rough time. To win, I knew I was going to have to play very well and work hard, because he was the kind of player who never gave points. Not that he was a pusher, but he didn't give many away, and you had to win the points from him. Against another player, you'd win your serve pretty easily and then concentrate on trying to break his serve. But Rosewall, no matter who his opponent was, was in every point, no matter who was serving. He didn't have an overpowering serve, but he played so that you had to win the point. That style made it difficult for most people, especially me.

Ken and I played a lot and had some great matches. I won a few but he took most of the big ones. He just outplayed me. His aggressive net-rushing style, supported by a beautiful backhand, was too much for my chipped, underspin backhand.

TENNIS TENSION

The biggest problem I experienced when building up to a big tournament was the mental tension, which translated into physical tension. A tennis player, like a golfer, can't let out tension the way a football player or boxer can, but we all have to find some way of relieving it. I'd feel the tension in my neck, and all I could do was try to involve myself in activities to take my mind off what was causing the pain in the neck. I'd often do crossword puzzles or play bridge as a way of diverting myself.

A lot of the cramps players get are due to tension. When you're tense and tight, your muscles behave as if you're using them in a game. Although most leg cramps are caused by tension, some do have a physiological basis, but taking salt or sodium during the match is after the fact. You have to take those supplements in advance, if they're to accomplish what you want them to. But don't take anything anytime without first consulting your physician.

PSYCHING AN OPPONENT

The points mentioned in the past few pages amount, in essence, to psyching yourself. What about psyching your opponent?

Harry Hopman, captain of the 1951 Australian Davis Cup team, was a crafty guy who would use every bit of guile to undermine our tactics. Sometimes he outsmarted himself.

In our day, there was a foot-fault rule that required the server to maintain contact with the ground at all times. When you served, you were not even permitted to swing your back foot over an imaginary line above the baseline or a foot fault would be called. The foot-fault judge would listen for the sound of the ball and watch your feet when determining whether you had swung over the line before the ball was hit. Because we always rushed the net, we all came close to swinging our foot over that imaginary line, but up until then I had never had a problem with foot-fault calls.

Hopman was writing for some Australian newspapers at the time, and he launched a propaganda campaign in his columns against my serve, claiming I constantly foot-faulted. We went to the trouble of having pictures taken of my serve, and it appeared that when I stood close to the line, it really could not be determined conclusively whether or not I was foot-faulting. To eliminate any possible controversy, I began standing about three inches behind the baseline (which I still do out of habit, though the rule has been changed). That way, I couldn't possibly swing my other foot over the line without feeling uncomfortable.

Hopman wasn't convinced, however, and he asked the foot-fault judge to be especially attentive to the possibility of my swinging over. The Australian foot-fault judge told Hopman where to go. "We'll call foot faults; we don't need your help." The upshot of the whole squabble was that when I played Rose in the first match, there were two foot faults called—both against Rose! Topping it off, they were both called on second serves with the score at ad-out. In each case it probably cost them the set.

Ironically, we all served pretty much the same way and swung our foot the same, but the judge never called a foot fault on me because I stood back a little farther. So Hopman's propaganda campaign backfired. In a sense, he outpsyched himself.

The master of gamesmanship is probably Bobby Riggs, who could probably outpsyche Sigmund Freud. I've never really been a practitioner, although accidentally or subconsciously, I've probably been guilty.

As I mentioned earlier, I was the head ballboy for the 1939 Davis Cup Match between the United States and Australia. John Bromwich, then twenty, was playing for the Aussies. Eleven years later Brom and I were to compete at Wimbledon. Before we went out that day (to play a match I would win), I reminded him that I had ballboyed for him eleven years earlier. I didn't do it deliberately to psyche him, but it may have had that effect. (Incidentally, I've since played—and lost to—many a top player who had at one time been ballboy for me, Fred Stolle and Manuel Santana among them.)

A similar, and possibly worse, feeling must have been experienced by Billie Jean King each time she lost to Tracy Austin. When Tracy was in fifth grade, she chose Billie Jean as the subject for a composition on a famous person and received an A plus. For years (until the 1982 Wimbledon quarterfinals), Tracy taught her elder some lessons on the tennis court, defeating her in five of their first five tournament matches.

I enjoyed playing fast, and sometimes I played too fast to suit other players. I didn't do it to upset them; it was just my preferred style. There's no problem slowing down an opponent whose playing pace is too fast. Just put your hand up to motion that you're not ready, or step out of the court. But if someone plays too slowly, there's no way you can speed him up. There is now a thirty-second rule, which requires the server to get off the serve for the next point in just half a minute, but there are some players who take the full interval. Before the rule came into being, a player could slow down, methodically wipe his glasses, walk around a little bit, take the Great Circle Route to get the ball, and, to my dismay, there was nothing I could do about it. I'm sure there were opponents who deliberately played extra slowly, knowing that I liked a much faster tempo. It always bugged me that the fellow playing too fast could be slowed down but that the one taking too long could not be speeded up. Of course, it's the server who controls the tempo, so if you like playing slowly, there's no problem doing it (within reason).

Other than in Davis Cup matches, where players must sit down with their captains on changeovers, I have never sat down when changing sides of the court. I'm not sure why. In the earlier years, they didn't have chairs and I got used to standing up. Then, when chairs were available, I felt I'd rather keep standing. I may have been more tired than my opponent, but I chose not to sit. This was another thing I didn't intend as a psychological ploy against my opponent, but it may have turned out that way, and maybe subconsciously I was trying to communicate the idea that I had plenty of stamina left.

A timely comment directed to an opponent can plant a seed in his mind, and do wonders for your game. "Gee," you might say as your opponent walks out on the court, "I never noticed that limp of yours." He'll start concentrating a little on that imaginary limp and maybe favor the foot or leg in which his alleged malady supposedly resides. Or ask him, "Do you always string your rackets so loose?" and he may convince himself he's not going to be able to hit as hard as he usually does. You can also contribute some tension during a match with a compliment, "You always play the big points so well."

At the club or social level, where the game is played for fun, you can get away with a certain amount of psyching, whether it takes the form of good-natured riding or seemingly innocent comments. In some games the banter is expected and even encouraged. But remember, sauce for the goose is sauce for the gander. Psyching tactics work both ways, and whatever you do to your opponents, they can do to you.

REFLECTIONS

Just as you can get a good picture of a person's character when he or she is driving or drinking, I think you can get a fairly good idea of a person's temperament from his behavior and attitude on the tennis court. Without getting too psychoanalytical about it, it seems to me that the "real" person emerges during tennis competition, and you can tell how he feels about himself and others, how he reacts to adversity, whether or not he's a good sport, whether he's inclined to be ruthless or principled, hard-driving or easygoing, and whether or not he's someone you'd like to have as a partner off the court. Assuming that tennis playing does provide an accurate reflection of personality, you might want to take a look at yourself (but preferably not during the match).

Grand Master E. Victor Seixas, Jr.:
Wimbledon singles champ (1953), Wim-
bledon mixed doubles champ (1953–56),
U.S. singles champ (1954), U.S. doubles
champ (1952, 1954), U.S. mixed doubles
champ (1953–55), member of the U.S.
Davis Cup team (1951–57), captain of
the U.S. Davis Cup team (1952, 1964),
member of the International Tennis Hall
of Fame . . . Photo courtesy of the U.S.
Tennis Association

——•——

Australian Lew Hoad, Vic's number-six pick of all-time great men's players, with the Wimbledon singles trophy in 1957. He had also won the title the previous year, along with the Wimbledon and U.S. men's doubles championships with Ken Rosewall. Photo courtesy of the U.S. Tennis Association

Following Lew Hoad on Vic's list is Ken
Rosewall in the number-seven spot. Two-
time U.S. singles champ (1956, 1970),
Ken also played Jimmy Connors for the
title in 1974 when he was past the age of
forty. Photo by David Levin, courtesy of
the U.S. Tennis Association/Russ Adams

Rod Laver, Vic's number-four pick for
great men's players, won the grand slam
of tennis twice (1962, 1969) and is a four-
time Wimbledon singles champ (1961,
1962, 1968, and 1969). Photo courtesy of
the U.S. Tennis Association

At the age of thirty-five in 1982, Stan Smith was one of the oldest pros in the draw at the U.S. Open. He won that title in 1971 and was a stalwart on the U.S. Davis Cup team for ten years between 1968 and 1979. Photo courtesy of the U.S. Tennis Association

———•———

*Francisco "Pancho" Segura joined the
Grand Masters when it began in 1973.
His two-handed forehand was one of the
best shots in the game.* Photo courtesy of
the U.S. Tennis Association

On the one-hundredth anniversary of Wimbledon in 1977, the Duke and Duchess of Kent posed with past singles champions. Vic is in the back row, seventh from the right.

———•———

*The Tennis Grand Masters, circa 1980.
From left to right: Torben Ulrich, Rex
Hartwig, Sven Davidson, Giuseppe
"Beppe" Merlo, Neale Fraser, Whitney
Reed, Bobby Perez (assistant to Al Bunis),
Vic Seixas, Al Bunis (founder of the
Grand Masters), and Frank Sedgman.*

———•———

COURTLY BEHAVIOR

Imagine an important tournament match in which a smashing rally ends when a player drills a backhand past his opponent at the net. The shot hits the baseline for a winner—or so the player who made the shot thinks. The linesman calls it out.

In a gesture of disbelief, the shotmaker hits himself in the forehead with the palm of his hand. Then he stands for a moment in silence with his hands on his hips, staring at the linesman. He looks to the umpire to overrule the linesman, but the umpire indicates that the call was correct and will stand. "How stupid can you get?" the player shouts to the umpire. Then, turning to the linesman, he mutters, loud enough for all to hear, "Who the hell ever told you you could officiate?" Spectators start whistling and catcalling, and the player responds with an obscene gesture.

While this example is made up, it is not far from what happens all too often in major events by some of the world's top players.

I don't think competitive spirit is synonymous with the rudeness and crudeness we often see in tennis. And I don't think bratty behavior can be excused on the grounds of youthfulness or a player's having been brought up to "fight for his rights." I think the only way of policing it effectively is to penalize disruptive players early with loss of points or worse.

Jack Kramer tells in his book *The Game* how as a youngster he had started to think of himself as a "big deal" and in one match carried on a continuing argument with the umpire. When the official called him for a foot fault, Jack threw his racket over the fence.

As Jack recounts it, his father walked over to the umpire's chair, and he felt confident his dad was supporting him. But the official waved his arms to signal that the match was going to Kramer's opponent by default. Jack's father had called off the contest.

Then his father warned him, "You ever do that again, you'll never go back on the tennis court as long as you live in my house." Jack comments that he never lost his temper that badly again.

I can't recall in my day that any of the players in my age group behaved badly on the court. I don't remember any incidents of bad sportsmanship comparable to what we see on the courts today.

Examples are legion.

At the 1982 U.S. Open, Ilie Nastase was charged with an "audible obscenity" and assessed a penalty point after he abused the chair umpire for having not allowed him two serves on a disputed play in a losing match with Jimmy Connors. The penalty cost "Nasty" the game. He was also fined a thousand dollars after the match for "verbal abuse of an official." But he wasn't finished yet. When rain started falling later in the set and an official ordered the umpire, Don Wiley, to suspend play, Nastase threw a towel at Wiley. Then, defying the order, he strode onto the court. Connors followed and play continued.

Earlier, Connors had been charged with a "code misconduct" violation when the umpire misinterpreted Connors's signal to a linesman that his call on a serve was okay. The umpire rescinded his charge.

"We tried to have fun out there," Connors said after the match, "but we weren't even allowed to do that. Nastase's been great for the game, whether you like him or not."

No comment.

In that same Open, during a thrilling four-hour, twenty-five-minute match that went to five sets and included two tiebreakers, winner Chip Hooper irritated his opponent, Roscoe Tanner, by staring at officials on close calls and by aiming at Tanner when he approached the net. "I don't care to play a guy who stares at the official on every call that doesn't go his way," Tanner said. "I just like to play the game, not the other stuff, especially when he has the full court open. Maybe he doesn't like me."

Hooper told reporters that he was surprised by Tanner's comments but did not deny that on some shots he did intend to hit him.

As hard-fought as tennis matches often are, certain rules of etiquette govern the game. They may be a little hard to detect, what with the way some of these players approach the game. In fact, sometimes they seem to be conducting a clinic in how *not* to behave. That doesn't mean you should follow suit.

I can't figure out how players like John McEnroe can think that the way they conduct themselves in relationship to officials and spectators is a plus. If anything, the official-baiting has to detract from their game. It's okay to be a little angry with yourself and urge yourself on to play better, but I can't see how exploding against a linesman or umpire can help you accomplish this. I disagree with anyone who claims to play better when he's angry or upset with someone else. Players who do this complain that everyone's against them. If so, they've brought it on themselves.

(Players sometimes complain about the noise of a cameraman during a point. However, as Don Budge, among others, has said, "They don't hear the camera when they *win* the point.")

There's nothing wrong with being competitive and griping at a call now and then, or even stamping or throwing the racket down on the ground. I don't think that people object to an occasional complaint about a line call. Quite often, they're in agreement with the complaining player. But when the player calls the umpire a "son of a bitch," mutters something sarcastic to humiliate him, or is otherwise abusive to the official, the crowds turn against him.

It certainly doesn't do the player any good, since it's self-defeating. It makes the umpire angrier at him, so he's not going to get a break from the official later. The worst thing about this kind of behavior is that it sets a bad example for the younger players, who see this kind of carrying on and figure, "If he's the best player in the world, and he can do it, why can't I?" It does a disservice to the game.

If you accept the fact that officiating has gotten better over the years—and I believe that it has—chances are that we older players got more bad calls than today's crybabies do. When I got a bad call, I complained to the linesman because I wanted him to know that I didn't agree. Also, it relieved a little of the anger and disappointment I felt. But I tried to do it in a nice way so that he wouldn't take it out on me later. I didn't want to incur his wrath so that he'd say to himself, "I'll get that bugger. When there's another close one, I'll give him another bad call." But I did want him to know that he missed a call, especially when I'd seen chalk fly and he'd called the ball out. Since we didn't have the overrule rule, we had more legitimate reasons to complain.

The most irritating thing about bad calls is that they come most often on your best shots. Let's say I hit a ball past you at the net and it lands right on the baseline. Not only have I won the point, but I've also hit the best shot I can. When the linesman calls the ball out, he has not only taken away the point I deserve, but a super shot as well. It's not as if he made the mistake on a ball I'd popped up to you that you would have easily put away. In that case, you probably would have won the point anyway, and the bad call doesn't matter to me. But on the excellent shot, the bad call is devastating. Most often, it's the call on that kind of a shot (or one called in that they've let go, convinced that it was going out), that gets players most upset.

In fairness, the difference between an ace and a fault can be the width of the fuzz on a new ball, and you can't really be sure, from where you're standing, that it wasn't exactly as the linesman called it. Part of the problem, of course, is that players *want* the ball, and the call, to be a certain way, and the wish becomes father to the scream. McEnroe, for example, may think or say he's objective about it, but he's being subjective. In his mind, he sees the ball land where he wants it to, which is why I think he's so often wrong, for the ball frequently doesn't land where he imagined it. That's not to say the linesman can't be wrong some of the time, too.

STICKING TO A BAD DECISION

The worst thing a linesman can do, in my opinion, is stick to a bad decision. As soon as he realizes he's made a mistake—sometimes it comes from calling too quickly—he should change his call. "I'm sorry; good," is what he should say on a ball he incorrectly called out. Most players, even McEnroe, would not get angry if the linesman did that (and the player agreed with the call).

Ivan Lendl was once serving in a final and hit the chalk. Too quickly, the linesman ruled the ball out but corrected his call and said, "I'm sorry, it was good." It was for the umpire to decide whether the original "out" call had caused Lendl's opponent (Jimmy

Connors) not to go after the ball. That particular serve was clearly one on which Connors had no chance to lay a racket, so Lendl got his ace. Usually the players know, and if they're fair, they'll acknowledge that if it's an ace, it should stand as an ace. They'd rather not leave themselves open to losing an ace on a similar situation when the roles are reversed.

The rule used to be that anytime a call was reversed from "out" to "good," it was a let and played over, while a change from "good" to "out" stood as an out. But that rule was changed on the assumption that a good-enough shot should stand as a winner, since it would be unfair to give the receiver another shot. But it's up to the umpire to decide whether the player could have returned the shot, had it not been for the wrong call.

BETTER OFFICIATING

If anything, officiating is improving. Officials are concentrating more and becoming more conscientious, if for no other reason than, what with TV coverage and the game's growing popularity, they know there are more eyes on them.

In this country especially, there is more of an effort now than there used to be to train people to be good officials. They're taught to understand that when they make a mistake they should change it. They're taught the proper way to watch the line or the ball. Thus, on the serve they should always watch the service line, but the rest of the time they should watch the ball because if they just watch the lines they'll go buggy. Watching the service line on the serve, though, they know the ball is coming once or, at most, twice and they're finished. They're also taught to call loudly and promptly.

Most officials are volunteers who do their calling as a part-time activity for love of the game (or masochism, or both). I don't think tennis is ready to have only professional officials. If the game ever got as big and popular as baseball, then that would happen. There is some similarity to baseball in that, just as you assign your better umpires to work the World Series, the more experienced tennis officials are chosen for the major tournaments.

OFFICIATING MACHINES

Machines have been used as an officiating aid for some years now. They use them on the service lines at Flushing Meadow and Wimbledon to call faults. (The linesman is always watching when the machine operates.) Jimmy Connors had some unkind words for their performance at Wimbledon in 1982. I once played in a Hall of Fame doubles match on the center court at Flushing Meadow, in which the machine was used, and I swear the machine made a mistake. The bad call and, for that matter, the match, wasn't significant, but if the machine can be wrong—as it clearly seemed to have been that day—I don't see the point in having it.

POINT THROWING

To watch some of today's players in action, you'd get the impression that bad calls are a new phenomenon that is deliberate and directed only against them. But bad calls have been in existence for as long as there's been tennis. They're never intended to be bad, and sometimes, believe it or not, a bad call can be in your favor rather than your opponent's. What should you do in a case like that?

Years ago a player who was the beneficiary of a flagrantly bad call might throw the next point. That is done very seldom now, except by some of the European players, who have the old-fashioned notion that tennis is a gentleman's sport. Today, by allowing the umpire to overrule an obviously bad call by a linesman, much of the need for equalizing an official's mistake has been eliminated. It's rare that a point is given away now, and it was not very common in years gone by.

When I was playing world-class tennis, the overrule rule was not in effect, so under certain circumstances I'd throw a point. First of all, I had to be satisfied that my opponent had not only received a bad call, but also had suffered from it—say, he had hit a winner that I knew I couldn't have returned but that was mistakenly called out. In a case like that, I'd throw the point if I knew my opponent would do the same for me, or if I was playing him for the first time and didn't know whether or not he'd reciprocate under the same conditions. If I was playing someone I knew would *not* do the same for me, then I might not do it.

The Australians—I played against hundreds—would never throw a point not because they weren't being sportsmanlike but because they were brought up to play every call, good or bad, and whether or not it was in their favor. By the same token, they never griped about the calls. So, if I was playing an Australian, I wouldn't throw a point.

My decision to give one away had nothing to do with whether or not I liked my opponent, nor was it the result of any streak of generosity. I was really just trying to forestall any guilt feelings on my part. I knew if I got a point I didn't deserve, it would bug me longer than it did anyone else and adversely affect my game. (Stan Smith, by the way, feels the same way.) If, however, I knew my opponent wouldn't do the same for me, the guilt feeling wasn't there; he was playing by the call, so I would, too.

Don Budge stopped throwing points on bad calls in his favor, he says, after he met Baron Gottfried von Cramm, who told him that throwing a point embarrassed the linesman. The best of players make mistakes, von Cramm told Budge, and so do linesmen. "We're not out there to be linesmen, so let's just play." Budge agreed, and from that point on, played the calls. When von Cramm got a bad decision in his favor, he'd nod to Budge to let him know, and Budge would do the same when the situation was reversed. But they'd do nothing to equalize the bad call.

Whenever I gave a point away, I did it discreetly, not in an obvious way that would embarrass the linesman. I was in the minority, but I felt better for giving the point away. An argument can be made that there are times when you'd have to throw *two* points to really equalize. For example, suppose it's fifteen–all and your opponent serves a clean ace on his serve, but it's called a fault. The score is 15–30 when it really should be 30–15. But my guilt feelings weren't ever deep enough for me to throw two points to even it up. I'd give back the one because I didn't feel I was entitled to it. Then I'd feel better and could play the next point with a clear conscience.

What's the right thing to do in a social game? Some friendly players go by the rule that if you don't see the ball clearly out, then it's presumed to be in. Others play that if nobody had a clear view of it, you play the point over—and no one can get too angry about that. Often the big problem in friendly games is not so much that opposing teams call a given shot differently, but that partners do. You should either decide between you ("Maybe I was wrong, let's call it good") or play a let and do it over, which is probably the best solution. But it's not always that simple. What happens, for instance, when your partner served what he's sure was an ace, your opponents either didn't see it or disagree whether it was an ace or a fault, and you, standing at the net, feel pretty sure it was a fault? No matter what you do, someone is going to be unhappy. Honor dictates that you call it as you saw it, but there are going to be other factors to weigh. Were you closest to the ball? Is your pronouncement going to convince your partner he's playing with Benedict Arnold? Did your partner buy the can of balls today? If you remain quiet or are overruled, you still have recourse—you can throw the next point (but discreetly, discreetly).

WHO CALLS?

In making calls, you don't want to cheat anyone, including yourself. If you're continually making bad calls, deliberately or accidentally, sooner or later it's going to come back to haunt you. Two of the most beautiful words you can utter on a tennis court are "Just out," but you want to be sure that the ball was indeed out. Don't let your hopes color your judgment, and if there's any doubt in your mind, just say, "I'm not sure, let's play it over."

If you think you or your partner has been wronged by a call but don't want to make too big a deal about it, offer a polite, "I thought I heard tape," or "You sure?" On clay or Har-Tru, you can look for the mark where the ball landed, being careful that the mark you look at was made by the shot in question. On surfaces where no mark is left, it's difficult. On any surface, however, too much quibbling over calls, even when you're right, can spoil the enjoyment of the game. So sometimes you might decide you'd rather swallow your protest and vent it on your next overhead.

In general, the person closest to the ball, or with the best view of it, should make the call. The serve in doubles should usually be called by the receiver's partner, because he's likely to be in the best position to see it, and the receiver is—or should be—concentrating intently on the ball.

One situation that often leads to quibbling is when the ball is either double-hit (struck twice by the racket) or carried (held an extra moment on the racket before it's returned). These used to be lost points, but the current rule provides that, unless it's *deliberate*, the shot is good and the ball is in play.

An obscure situation that can lead to disputes is the case in which a player hits the ball so that it bounces on his opponent's side of the court and, due to backspin, comes back over to his side of the net before the opponent can hit it. Bobby Riggs makes that kind of shot quite a lot. If you're the opponent, what are your rights? You may not invade the other side of the net or put your racket over the net before the ball clears the net. But once the ball does clear the net, you can lean over and, provided you don't touch the net with your body or your racket you can legally hit the ball on *his* side of the net before it bounces a second time. If your racket touches the net, or the ball bounces for the second time, you lose the point.

WAIT TO CALL

You should always wait for a ball to hit the ground before you call it in or out—even on the most obvious shots. Sure, lots of times the ball is headed out by ten or fifteen feet, and you're tempted to stop it and get on with the next point. But who's to know for sure when a ball that looks as if it will drop a couple of feet out won't drop very close to the line? Eventually you're going to catch one that's so close that there's doubt about whether it would have landed in or out. So, even though it involves extra steps—and we prime-timers want to conserve our energy—get into the habit of letting balls hit the ground before you call them out.

A little-known technicality that ties in with this is that if a receiver's partner is hit by the serve, the server's team gets the point. This is so, even if he's far from the service box being aimed at, because a ball is considered in play until it hits the ground out of bounds (or bounces twice on one side of the net). Similarly, on a shot other than a serve, you can be back against the fence, but if the ball hits any part of you or your racket before it hits the ground, it's considered in play.

The fact that the point isn't over until the ball has bounced a second time on one side leads to some interesting situations. In a 1982 tournament in Newport, Rhode Island, a player hit a winning volley, but on his follow-through his racket went over the net. This made it a judgment call on the part of the umpire to determine whether the ball had bounced a second time before his racket crossed the net. If it had, the player would win the point; if it hadn't bounced that second time, his opponent would get it, even though he was nowhere near where the volley landed. The rule is very specific. In this case, the umpire ruled that the racket had crossed the net before the ball bounced twice and so the volley-ee not the volleyer, won the point. The player complained bitterly, but the call stood. Just like the ball you catch outside the court, the ball on the court that hasn't bounced twice is still in play.

THAT'S YOUR FAULT

Social players tend to overlook some of the technicalities that competitive players cannot or will not overlook, which is probably as it should be. But sometimes the loose atmosphere surrounding a friendly game contributes to some delicate situations. For example, how do you deal with one of the players in your regular game (which has been going on for years) who constantly foot-faults.

You might like to know how Frank Sedgman dealt with that problem. In a friendly match, where there were no linesmen, his opponent kept foot-faulting by a good twelve inches into the court. Perplexed as to how to deal with the problem, Frank finally decided on a plan. When they next changed sides and it was his turn to serve, Frank walked to the service line and let go with a sizzler into the service box. "What are you doing?" his astonished opponent yelled.

"Well," said Sedgman, "you're foot-faulting and I'm foot-faulting." His opponent got the message.

Foot-faulting is something you should be aware of and control, or call on yourself, rather than have your friend have to call it to your attention. If the foot-faulter isn't you, but your friend, you can try the Sedgman plan. Or you can wait until he calls you on something like your racket's touching the net, and respond, "Oh, yeah, what about all your foot faults?" Actually, if it's a friendly match, you're probably better off avoiding the issue, but if it's a ladder match at a club or something comparable, you're perfectly within your rights to say, "I'd appreciate it if you'd watch your foot-faulting." Then if he continues, I'd serve from the service line.

CHANGING SIDES

It's customary for individuals or teams to change ends of the court after every odd game. Some friendly prime-timers feel they're better off staying put for a full set and then changing, saving the energy they'd use up in frequent court changes for the competition itself. If you play indoors, there's nothing wrong with that because conditions are pretty much the same on either end of the court. But outdoors, there's too much variation in wind direction, intensity of the sun, and background, so it's fairer to change ends as frequently as the pros do.

THY NEIGHBOR'S COURT

When courts are close together and there are no ballboys or ballgirls to help out, errant balls are a constant source of potential irritation. Never go onto a neighbor's court to retrieve one of your balls—unless you're hustling after a ball still in play. And don't even ask for your ball when the players on the next court are in the middle of a rally or one of them is preparing to serve. When there's a break in the action on their court, just politely say, "Thank you," the age-old tennis code phrase for "Please hurry up and throw me the ball that my opponent hit wildly." Don't say "Thank you" in an imperious or impatient tone. And, when the situation is reversed, quickly and good-naturedly return their balls.

DON'T WATCH
THE BALL, FANS

■|■

While there's no substitute for being a participant in the game, some of your greatest tennis enjoyment as a prime-timer can be derived from being a spectator. Witnessing firsthand two high-quality players or teams compete on a tennis court can provide not only a (well-deserved) rest from your own playing but also a good learning experience for improving your game.

As a spectator, how well you enjoy the competition and how much you learn from it hinges, in part, on where you sit and what you look at.

Undoubtedly, you've seen the classic photographic or cartoon takeoff of people watching a tennis match: hundreds of expressionless faces endlessly turning from one side to the other like so many metronomes as they watch the ball go back and forth. If you're like most fans, you'll want to be among that sea of faces, and, if money and availability permit, you'll choose as your vantage point a courtside seat as close to the net as possible.

But the best place to watch a tennis match, in fact, is not from "the fifty-yard line" but from the "end zone," and not right at court level but some fifteen or twenty feet up so that you can see the angle of the shots as well as the far end of the court. Position yourself so that you have an overview of all the action along with a good feeling of depth. If you can't get a seat high enough to see the other end of the court from directly behind, then sit in the corner. In any event, don't get so far up that you lose the perspective of the height of the ball clearing the net. The worst view is probably from the net cord judge's position. The best view is probably the TV camera's—usually right behind the center service line and high enough so that audiences are looking down on the court.

With all the drilling we do about constantly watching the ball, what I'm about to say may sound like heresy. But I suggest that when you're a spectator at a tennis match you spend a portion of the time watching a given player in action rather than the ball. Doing this will give you a different slant on the game.

Watch how the player prepares to hit the ball, how he or she gets the racket back early, especially on the backhand side, how the player contacts the ball in front of his front foot. Observe the player's footwork and constant movement. Many a mediocre player will, say, go to his right to hit a ball and then just stay there watching his shot go across the net; consequently, he will be out of position to cover his opponent's return. Watching someone who moves properly may remind you of how you should move on the court.

After watching one player for awhile, concentrate on the opponent and how he or she executes the fundamentals and the more sophisticated elements of the game. If you're watching a doubles match, alternate your attention between the teams. You might want to take special note of how partners operate together and cover for each other.

I think this is a great way to learn. As a youngster in Philadelphia, I'd watch Davis Cup matches and then go out to play, trying to put into my game some of what I had seen the good players doing. I always felt that I played better after watching good players compete. Of course, you have to find out in practice whether what you're copying suits you and your game.

By merely watching the ball as a spectator, you're just being entertained. But by occasionally focusing on each of the players, you're also learning.

AWARENESS OF THE FANS

Players are generally aware of the spectators, especially in Davis Cup matches, which are characterized by a lot of partisan rooting along nationalistic lines. Four-time U.S. Open winner Jimmy Connors says, "I really do like playing in New York. The people scream and cheer and get behind you and root—that's my kind of crowd."

Tennis players are often accused of being prima donnas when it comes to crowd noise. Why is it, people ask, that it's taboo for a tennis spectator to give vent to his emotions vocally while a point is being played, when, at a baseball game, tens of thousands of fans lustily yell and clap at the tensest moments? Surely, they say, the batter up with two outs, the bases loaded, and a 3–2 count in the bottom of the ninth, has to concentrate at least as hard as a tennis player does to hit the ball, and yet he's not bothered by the noise.

Well, what *would* bother that baseball player would be for the crowd to fall absolutely silent just as the pitcher threw the ball. He'd miss it by a mile. The same thing would happen if everyone were silent until the pitcher released the ball and then suddenly screamed. The point I'm trying to bring out is that it's the abrupt change in sound, not the noise itself, that's disturbing.

In such sports as baseball, football, basketball, and hockey, the noise is continuous and fades into the background, whereas in tennis relative silence is the norm. You can yell your head off *after* a great shot in tennis, but not while the ball's in play, anymore than you'd think of doing it while a golfer prepared to hit a tee shot.

Many years ago, we experimented in an exhibition match, the outcome of which meant nothing, by encouraging spectators to make noise throughout. After awhile, we found that the noise just faded into the background. With good concentration, the steady sound never bothered us. Still, the custom of respectful silence while a point is being played persists in tennis. It's one of the elements that has given tennis a bad image—the idea that you have to sit quietly. But that isn't so. You can make all the noise you want, providing it's at the right time. Believe me, we welcome your applause.

FANS' AWARENESS

What tennis fans applaud often isn't what tennis players would applaud. There's a tendency on the part of those who watch the game, but don't understand it well, to applaud the relatively easy winners while giving the truly skillful shots just passing attention. Often, of course, the easy winner they cheer is the culmination of a great exchange of shots. Or they may be showing their pleasure at the fact that the point was won by the player they're rooting for.

But these motivations aside, what shots or development of strategy really deserve your plaudits? One category is the passing shot, which requires skill and talent since it's almost always made by a player who's under pressure at the moment. A passing shot made on the run is particularly difficult since it's probably made in desperation by a player very much on the defensive. To make a winner or good shot on that is ten times more difficult than making the easy overhead, which usually wins a great deal of applause even though—like a slam dunk in basketball—it's often more spectacular than skillful.

A good drop shot or a lob over the head of an opponent who comes too close to the net may not be particularly thrilling, but it reflects the player's ability to outthink and deceive his opponent and often requires a delicate touch.

The more you play the game, the better you're likely to understand its complexities and the plays that merit your cheers.

THE BITTER TASTE OF BOOS

As to the boos, I think any player who incurs the wrath of the spectators in any way—intentionally or unintentionally—is doing himself a disservice. I just don't believe it's more fun playing with the crowd against you than rooting for you, and I don't think anybody plays better when he gets angry on the court. In tennis, you can't permit your emotions to take over; you have to remain in control. If a player can do something to get the fans on his side, to urge him on and support him, that has to be a plus; behaving so that they boo him and root for his opponent can only detract from his game.

Some players are natural crowd-pleasers. Torben Ulrich, the sometimes inscrutable, long-haired, Danish mainstay of our Grand Masters group, was playing Frank Sedgman, the incomparable Australian. Torben went wide to his right to return a volley and then, as *Newsweek* magazine recalled it, "instantly realized he had hit the ball back too softly. So he simply kept running, ended up in the spectator section, plopped himself into a seat—and applauded Sedgman's overhead smash along with everybody else. 'He's a very classy Bobby Riggs,' said one fan. 'He's the kind of guy young tennis fans could identify with.'" Unfortunately, many young tennis fans identify instead with the talented brats who bait the officials and spectators with abusive language and gestures.

Of course, a player doesn't have to be a comedian or perform comical antics to be a crowd-pleaser. Solid play, all-out effort, and good sportsmanship are, and should be, a popular combination for the fans.

POINTING TO THE WIN

Good guys don't always win, but then neither do villains. More often than not, it's the player who jumps off to the commanding lead who's going to triumph. That's not to say that you can predict with certainty that the player who wins the first set is going to take the match. But if you watch carefully, you may be able to detect that the player leading is serving better or that the other player is making a lot more unforced errors. You might notice the player who's trailing make an adjustment in his game plan, for example, coming to the net more or trying an occasional offensive lob, and he or she may be able to turn things around. Conversely, if those changes aren't made, the early leader is going to stay on top.

Not every point or game is equally important in a given match (which is why I object to the Van Alen scoring system, which has sets going to the first player to win 31 points). A 30–40 point has considerably more significance than a 40–love point. Losing a game when you're in the lead 4–love isn't as meaningful as winning one at 4–3. You might say that all points are important but that some are more important than others.

Most competitive players can tell you about particular points they won or lost in matches that took place years ago. One I'll never forget was in the National Juniors against Budge Patty, sometime back in the Dark Ages (1941). We had split the first four sets and were tied in the fifth at five–all when I broke his service to go ahead for the first time in our match of more than three hours. Now, serving with a 6–5 lead, I had him, 40–30, match point.

As I'd been doing for over three hours, I hit a high bouncing serve to his backhand, Patty's weak side. He always had a great forehand, and consequently he'd often run around his backhand, even when he was playing against topflight competitors. Patty ran around this serve, too, and hit a forehand down the line. The momentum of his run and swing was such that it carried him almost to the next court and down to the ground. All I had to do was return his shot almost anywhere in the court, and the match—and the national junior title—would have been mine. But his shot went a little past me, at about the service line, and while I got my racket on it, I sort of half-stopped the ball instead of stroking it. The ball didn't make it over the net.

I never got another match point, except to be on the losing side of one, as Patty took the set and match, 10–8. Talk about unforgettable moments, that point is one I'll always remember.

Sometimes a point is memorable because it helps you establish something important in your opponent's mind early in the match. One of that type took place in the Davis Cup match between Australia and the United States in 1954, which we won. I was playing Ken Rosewall, who always seemed to be at his peak against me and usually defeated me. In this match, he was obviously going to employ a game plan that had always worked against me—hit to my backhand, come in to the net, and cover down the line. He could do this with confidence because I was weak in hitting cross-court shots off my backhand.

On one of his earliest serves—the second or third of the match—we rallied, and then, true to form, Rosewall hit an approach shot to my backhand and rushed to the net, covering down the line. Seizing the opportunity, I unleashed a backhand passing shot cross-court and won the point. It was a critical moment because I suddenly established in his mind that I *could* hit that shot. I might not hit another one in the match, but he could no longer be sure I wouldn't. Accordingly, he could not safely camp at one side of the court and await the ball.

Making that cross-court shot was partially luck, but it also was part of my own game plan. I had wanted to try it early, because I knew if I made it, it would give me a bit of a psychological lift and at the same time, plant some seeds of doubt and concern in Ken's mind. For all he knew, I might have been practicing that cross-court backhand for a year and perfected it! Whatever he thought, I managed to beat him in four sets, and the United States won the Davis Cup that year.

Can a match be closer than the score indicates? Absolutely. Perhaps the prime example of this was the 1939 Davis Cup final between two of the steadiest players the game has produced—

Australia's John Bromwich and the U.S. team's Frankie Parker. They struggled for three hours, with exchanges that seemed endless and every point close and hard-fought. It was a match that had to be seen to be believed; those who see only the score will never know how close it really was. Bromwich won 6–0, 6–3, 6–1.

Close-fought matches often revolve around a few crucial points. Those who play better on the important points almost always win; those who play those points poorly, lose. In the 1982 Wimbledon final between Jimmy Connors and John McEnroe, John did not seem to be playing the important points well, and it was clear to a lot of us that he was destined to defeat. Most players can identify the big points on which they won or lost a match. "I lost it in the second set when I had him 30–40 at three-all and blew the return."

It would be interesting if a statistic could be devised that showed how a player did on crucial points or games, such as the seventh of a set when the score is 3–3 or 4–2.

There's a tendency to get too involved in statistics, but one of the most meaningful is the percentage of first serves in. This has a much greater bearing on the match than a player's number of aces and double-faults. It's interesting to know that someone served only four aces during the match, but that doesn't tell you about the points he won on serves that his opponent barely managed to get a racket on; they weren't aces but they won the point. Unless the number is excessive, like thirty-five, how many double-faults a player has had isn't especially meaningful. A player can be ahead 40–love and serve two successive double-faults but win the next point and the game. If he's won the game, his double-faults don't mean a thing. If he double-faults on something as important as game point, that's important, but in and of themselves double-fault statistics aren't vital, anymore than strikeouts are for the leading home-run hitter in baseball.

More significant are the numbers of forced and unforced errors, which are usually excellent indicators of performance. These stats can usually tell you who won the match. Chances are the player with a high number of unforced errors (in relation to his opponent, or to winning shots) lost the match.

One item that gets a lot of attention—and frequently gets my goat—is the "break point." TV screens are forever flashing those words to indicate that the receiver has a chance of breaking serve, that is, to win the game an opponent is serving. Television commentators make a big deal of its being "break point," "double break point" (two chances to win the game), or "triple break point" (three chances). Yet often it doesn't mean a thing.

This is not to put down the significance of break points entirely. If they occur against a man with a high-powered, booming serve on grass (where it's difficult to break), or in doubles, then they're significant. But TV commentators don't differentiate, and I think they should.

TIEBREAKERS

As a spectator you may disagree, but I like the 12–point tiebreaker as a way to decide all sets but the third of a three-set match or the fifth of a five-setter.

I never liked the 9–point "sudden death" tiebreaker, in which the first player to win 5 points was the winner, even if he or she won by 1 point. Too often a given point can be decided by something unforeseen, like luck or a bad call. Even though it's exciting to the people in the stands, it's a pity for a player to lose a hard-fought match on a fluke point. We used it for awhile in our Grand Masters matches, and in one tournament Sedgman and Ulrich met in the finals in Los Angeles. It got to six games each in the third set, and they played a tiebreaker. It reached four-all in that, and now the whole tournament hinged on one point. Unquestionably, it was exciting from the spectator's point of view, but it would have spoiled the whole tournament had the point been won on something like a net-cord shot or a ball that grazed the line but was called out. Fortunately, the point on which Ulrich won was a good one.

The U.S. Open used the sudden-death tiebreaker for quite a long time, but I never thought it was good for the game.

The best solution to ending sets is the 12–point tiebreaker put into play at Wimbledon. The first player to get 7 points in the tie-breaker, with a margin of at least 2 points, is the winner. In the tiebreaker, the first player serves one point from the deuce court, and thereafter serves alternate between them two at a time, starting from the ad court. This is similar in form to the court-changing pattern after games in regular matches.

Having the 12–point tiebreaker in effect in all but the last set of a three- or five-set match (which, once again, Wimbledon came up with) prevents having an early set overly drawn out. I think the match becomes less entertaining if the first set goes to, say, 14–12, and the players and spectators know there's a long match to follow. Yet no one will leave the stadium if the fifth set goes that many games. So I agree that it's important for the last set to be allowed to run its course, without a tiebreaker. If a tiebreaker were in effect in all sets, it would enable the players to pace themselves better and thus remove some of the suspense that results from a player's not knowing whether he's going to be out there for a long or short time. How a player adapts is an interesting extra element for the spectator to watch.

Having said all this, I have to confess to a conversation I had with Jimmy Van Alen, the "father" of the sudden-death tiebreaker. In the 1966 Penn State tournament at Merion, I played one of the longest sets ever with Bill Bowrey, losing it 32–34 but winning the next two. We were playing on a bad grass court, where it was very difficult to break serve. Years later, Van Alen commented that if we had been using his system, we wouldn't have had to play all that time. "But then," I said, "I wouldn't be in the record books."

As a social player, you might want to cling to the traditional—and, may I say, old-fashioned—method of letting sets go on and on until somebody wins by at least two games. There is some pleasure, granted, in being able to tell the spouse or the neighbors, "Boy, did we have a set today—it went to 83–81!" But preferably, you should use the tiebreaker currently in force among the pros—the Wimbledon-style, 12–point tiebreaker in all but the third set of a best of three set match.

LET'S GET PHYSICAL . . .

Okay, enough sitting in the stands. Let's get out and hit that ball and improve our game.

NEVER TOO OLD FOR LESSONS

If you're never too old to take up tennis, it follows that you're never too old to take lessons either. If you've been playing all your life, you're probably not going to learn as much from a lesson as someone just beginning in the game because you're not inclined to change your style. For instance, at the age of sixty you're not going to learn to become a net-rusher, but you might want to take a lesson, however, to help you with another aspect of your game.

For someone just starting in tennis, I think lessons are essential. Learn how to do things right, before the wrong way becomes ingrained. Then it's a matter of practicing what you've learned, occasionally going back to your pro for a checkup and a refresher. After you've taken lessons for awhile their value decreases (except for the pro you're paying to teach you).

While a beginner taking lessons should start from scratch and cover everything, the competitive player may want to concentrate on one aspect at a time. He may be having trouble with his serve, for example, or have fallen into a slump, as all players do occasionally. Therefore, he'll seek help for what is wrong with his game. A knowl-

159

edgeable observer—it needn't be a teacher, maybe just a fellow player—can usually help with that.

PICKING A PRO

Chances are you'll take your lessons from someone located nearby, probably the pro at the club where you play. Whether you take your lessons there or elsewhere, the question remains, how do you select an instructor?

It doesn't necessarily follow that a good player makes a good instructor. In fact, most of the best teaching pros have not necessarily been very good players. There are exceptions, of course. It also doesn't automatically follow that a poor player makes a good teacher, or a good player makes a bad one, but, by and large, the better teachers are people who have concentrated on teaching. In my own case, I think I'd soon get tired of doing it and the students would realize I wasn't enthusiastic enough. I have done some teaching, but I have to admit that I didn't look forward to doing it six or eight hours a day. A lot depends on the playing level of the students. Working with rank beginners requires an extra degree of patience, which I'm not sure I have.

Among the exceptions are Pancho Segura, who has a reputation as a good teacher, and Dennis Ralston. Alex Olmedo would be a good teacher if he devoted himself to it. Vic Braden is quite knowledgeable about the game. He's as much an actor and comedian as he is a teacher, but he knows tennis very well. Vic, against whom I played in college, was never a *great* player, but he's been around the game. I don't always agree with what he teaches, but he's come up with some good principles. He's very innovative and has a unique approach to getting his point across.

There are many lesser-known instructors who have been teaching for years and years and who I would approach for help with a problem in my game rather than someone who happens to be a good player. They're trained to look for things that are wrong. Among them are names you probably don't know—George Toley, a pretty good former player who coached at Southern California, and Bob Harmon, another pretty good player.

ONE LESSON

One of the greatest teachers was Ed Faulkner. The one lesson I had in my life I took from Ed when I was eight years old and he was teaching at a little club in Drexel Hill, Pennsylvania.

My parents thought I should have a lesson so they took me to him. I think he mentioned something about grips, which I promptly forgot, but he was a wonderful instructor and analyst. For years after, whenever I wanted someone to analyze my game or to discuss tennis with, I would always go to Ed. He was the one person I listened to. In my opinion, he has the greatest tennis brain I've ever known. I base that conclusion on the fact that we always agreed on everything. Seriously, when I had lost a match, for instance, he'd point out what I needed to correct, and I would agree with his analysis.

Ed was the coach at Penn Charter School, a prep school I attended on half-scholarship after a professor who was a tennis buff convinced my parents to send me there. They had a very good tennis team, and when I was a senior there in 1941, they hadn't lost a team match in twenty-eight years to any other school in their league.

Ed had also worked with the Davis Cup team years earlier, and in 1964, when I was the nonplaying captain of the U.S. team, I persuaded the USLTA to hire Ed for a short time to work with our players. He helped Charley Pasarell and Arthur Ashe a lot. Ed, who in 1980 won the USTA Tennis Educational Merit Award, worked all his life in the instruction end of the game.

WORK ON WEAKNESSES

When you take a series of lessons, you should work on every aspect of the game, but concentrate on areas of weakness. If your backhand is the bane of your tennis life, keep working on that rather than, say, your forehand volley, which you enjoy a lot more.

DURATION

Lessons usually run a half hour or an hour, but I found in the little bit of teaching I did that, depending on the age of the student, sometimes an hour is too long. Your attention can't remain high for that period of time. On the other hand, a half hour is not really enough.

I think a forty-five-minute lesson, in which the student is worked real hard for almost the entire time, is ideal. That's about the maximum time that the students can go all-out. In an hour-long lesson, they're struggling during the last fifteen minutes. Maybe the lesson can last an hour, but no more than forty-five minutes should consist of real tough working.

Group lessons are cheaper for the individual, and some people prefer players of equal level out there with them, but you can learn a lot more in a one-on-one lesson. There is an increasing number of group programs just for older Americans in most communities. The USTA has compiled a directory of some of these programs. See page 218 on how to obtain this directory.

Many players tend to keep taking lessons for too long. They'll take a lesson every week for four or five years, whether they need it or not. This is another instance of something that is better for the pro than the students. The students may not have anyone else they feel comfortable playing with, so their lesson gives them an opportunity to play. But I think you can become overly dependent on the pro and take lessons past the point of maximum benefit. Once you reach the stage where you should be putting into play what you've learned by constant practice, you can probably do that as well *without* the pro as with him.

TEACHING AIDS

One of the best forms of practice is still what we all did as kids— hitting the ball against a schoolyard or handball wall or some other kind of backboard. A wall is the most consistent of opponents, always returning the ball.

Ball machines are valuable teaching aids for the same reason. You can practice the same shot over and over again. They can also be set in such a way that you never know what kind of shot is coming at you. That way, you duplicate game conditions as you practice.

HOW MUCH PRACTICE

How much practice is desirable is an individual thing. Most competitive players today practice for a half hour or so the morning of a match. They'll hit, hit, hit, maybe emphasizing a particular stroke, such as serve or cross-court backhand.

When I played competitively full-time, I felt that since I was making it to the semifinals in most tournaments, I was getting in a lot of tennis and needed correspondingly less practice work than if I were being eliminated from tournaments in the early rounds. So I wasn't one to go out and just hit thousands of balls, unlike some of the others, who'd hit balls for two hours before a match and then wonder why they hurt.

To me, the important thing was that, with a minimum of practice I felt keen and fit to play and had my touch. Likewise, someone making it to the later rounds of a tournament needn't do much running and calisthenics because there's enough exercise in the competition.

AMATEUR LESSONS

You can learn valuable lessons from amateur instructors, too, though you generally get what you pay for. A friend or relative whose tennis perceptiveness you admire can provide some good tips.

Should you be the one to give lessons to your spouse? I offer the same litmus test I offered earlier: would you give him or her driving lessons?

FIVE POINTS

People would rather learn through playing than listening to a lecture. They don't want to practice grips; they want to hit some balls. So whenever I conduct a clinic, rather than get very technical and complex, I take just a few minutes and offer five points—call them axioms or tenets—that encompass the whole game. Some are so self-evident that they shouldn't have to be mentioned. But surprisingly few people abide by them. Yet no matter what your age or experience level, if you remember even one of these simple principles, your game is going to be better tomorrow than it is today.

POINT NUMBER 1: WATCH THE BALL

You've heard that advice since you were in diapers. It applies to every game in which a ball is involved. Sure, you'll sometimes see the good players stroking the ball without seeming to be watching it, but they can get away with it—sometimes. Most of us, under most game situations, can't. So watch that ball at all times.

I don't think anybody's eyes are good enough to see the racket hit the ball, but you should try to watch the ball as long as possible—right up to the racket. The better you become, the less you really have to do this. But even the stars—John McEnroe is one—sometimes miss because they shift their gaze a little too soon.

In football, we've seen the defensive back running to cover the wide receiver who's going out for the bomb. The defensive player is covering his man, but he has no idea where the ball is, and the receiver catches the ball right over his shoulder. All the defender had to do was watch that ball. You should, too.

POINT NUMBER 2: REMEMBER
TENNIS IS A GAME OF MOTION

Another simple fact: tennis is a game of motion, and you should never be standing around flatfooted while the ball is in play. Never be caught on your heels. You should always be up on the balls of your feet, your knees slightly bent, your body in motion, ready to move. Watch Borg receive serve; he's in motion as if he's preparing to bolt out of the corral. He wants to be ready to make that first move quickly. Social players worry that being in motion while awaiting a serve can lead to "zigging" when you should be "zagging," but you're not moving that much that it's a real threat.

The importance of remembering that tennis is a game of motion applies to every phase of the game. There might be a tendency for the receiver's partner to be relatively stationary, figuring there will be at least two strokes before he'll get a chance at the ball. But if you watch good players, you'll see that the instant the ball is hit the net man is moving. He wants to be ready, and he knows what every tennis player finds out the hard way: you're never ready too soon.

POINT NUMBER 3: GET YOUR RACKET BACK EARLY

What I consider the most important *technical* aspect of the game is probably the single most difficult thing for people learning the game —get your racket back early. Watch the good players in action, and you'll see they never seem to be hurrying to hit the ball. It always looks as if they have plenty of time. The reason is simply that when they see the ball coming, the first thing they do is get the racket back. *Then* they start for the ball.

You should do the same. As soon as you see the ball coming and decide whether you're going to take it on your forehand or backhand side, take your racket back before you move your feet or do anything else. It's more important to get your racket back early on the backhand side than the forehand because the racket has to travel a longer distance in preparation. You can cheat a little on the forehand, your arm's already around there, but not on the backhand. Get your racket back early and then move to the ball, and you'll be ready to hit it when you get there.

Otherwise, if, like too many players, you get the racket back at the last moment, you'll have to hurry the shot. Worse than what this will probably do to your stroke is what havoc it's going to play with your arm. Sore arms are common among people who are late getting their rackets back. Don't be one of them.

POINT NUMBER 4: HIT THE BALL OUT IN FRONT OF YOUR FRONT FOOT

Always try to contact the ball out in front of you. Never let the ball get behind you. If you're right-handed, hit a forehand out in front of where your left foot is planted; hit a backhand in front of your right foot.

Ideally, *every* shot in the game—not only ground strokes but serves and especially volleys—should be hit out in front of you. Sometimes you don't have enough time to do it, but if you possibly can, hit the ball out front. Doing so gives you options you don't have once the ball gets behind you. When a ball gets behind you, especially on the backhand, it's difficult to get power or to hit cross-court. You're limited, and your opponent knows you're limited, so he covers the shot he knows you're going to have to hit. You can drill the hardest shot in the world down the line, but if I know it's coming there, you're not going to make a point on it.

POINT NUMBER 5: KEEP YOUR WRIST FIRM

As a beginning player, keep in mind that tennis is an *arm* game, not a wrist game, so you should keep your wrist relatively firm when you make contact with the ball. Don't let it wobble. As you become more advanced, you may use your wrist a little, but please, not until you've mastered stroking with a firm wrist. Start out by learning to hit the ball the orthodox way; then, as you get better, you can start developing your own individuality and playing characteristics and doing things with the ball that make you a different player from someone else. But you can't start out hitting the ball like Borg.

When you watch the champions, keep in mind that their style is not necessarily what yours ought to be. The conventional way works for the majority of players. That means your wrist should be firm when you contact the ball.

There isn't any missed shot that can't be traced to one of these five points. Think about them, and the next time you miss an easy shot, see if you haven't goofed on one or more of these basics. Bet you have.

HOW SWEET IT IS

As you practice, keep in mind that it's essential for the ball to meet the racket in the middle of the strings. Everything else is secondary. Having your racket ready, whether you're going to hit a ground stroke or a volley, saves you time and increases the chances that you'll hit the ball with the "sweet spot" of the racket and thus make the solid shot you want.

TIGHTEN YOUR GRIP

When you hit the ball, you want to be sure the racket is hitting the ball, not the ball hitting the racket. So you should have a firm grip on the racket. But you can't maintain a viselike grip because that will tire your hand. So the thing to do when you're waiting for the action to begin—say, your partner is about to serve—is to cradle your racket in your nonhitting hand while keeping a loose grip on the racket with your hitting hand. Then, as you get ready to swing, tighten your grip on the racket.

If you want to develop a firm grip, squeezing a rubber ball or a tennis ball is probably as good an exercise as any. Actually, tennis playing in itself will develop strength in your wrist, as well as your hand and arm. When I was a younger player my right arm and shoulder were considerably bigger than my left, and I had a lot more strength in my right hand than my left, so I know that playing develops strength. Unless you're having a problem with holding the racket firmly enough, you don't have to do much more than play the game.

As far as how to grip a racket, I feel there's no single *right* way. Many ways are correct, providing you find them comfortable. I hold the racket differently from most everyone else. I have the same grip for a forehand as I do for a backhand. That's not to say that's right, but neither is it wrong. A lot of people disagree, but unless the way you grip is adversely affecting your stroking—and an instructor will point this out—stick with what's comfortable.

TWO HANDS FOR BEGINNERS?

Mal Anderson says that he never liked playing against a two-handed swinger. He preferred, he says, to play against Ken Rosewall's excellent backhand than Pancho Segura's "tremendous" two-handed forehand shot. It was easier to anticipate where Rosewall was going to hit the shot than to anticipate Segura's. "A good two-handed player can hold the shot longer and still have the required control of the racket head to play that great shot. They have so much more power and they can use a little more wrist to disguise it."

Many of the top players today use two hands, at least on the backhand, so it's not surprising that a lot of social players think using a two-handed grip will help upgrade the quality of their play.

My feeling is that, unless a person learned to play with two hands and is comfortable with that style, the advantages are not enough to make switching worthwhile. True, you can get more power into your strokes with two hands on the racket, but only if you get there in time to hit. Stroking with two hands demands greater mobility.

You have to be able to move a lot quicker to get into position to hit the ball with two hands than you would if you were stroking one-handed. As you get older, moving that quickly becomes increasingly more difficult. Logically, if any switch were to be made, it should be from two hands to one in later years because using just one hand allows you to reach a little farther and does away with the urgency of being in position that two hands requires.

POINT-LESS HITTING

Some people feel they're practicing more, and possibly getting more exercise, when they're just hitting the ball with someone rather than playing a game. That's fine, but you should aim to get to a level of play good enough that you enjoy competition. I think most people would prefer to play a set rather than just rally the whole time they're on the court.

PLAYING SOMEONE BETTER

An old axiom of tennis is that you should always try to play against someone better. The trouble is, according to a second axiom, that he or she doesn't want to play you. The first axiom is true—it's a good way to develop your playing to a higher level—but the second isn't always so. It doesn't always follow that the better player won't play a lesser player.

If your child, for example, wants to improve his game, and you're a better player, you should play the youngster. It's better for him or her to lose to you than to keep beating all the twelve-year-olds around. By constantly playing people you can beat, you'll never know if you're really improving or not, or, if you are, how much better you're becoming. So try to upgrade your competition.

If you're playing for enjoyment and not worrying about becoming a world champion, there's nothing wrong with playing with and against the same people week after week, even year after year. Plenty of prime-timers have regular tennis groups that have played together for as long as they can remember. From a strictly tennis viewpoint, you should make sure that the standard of play is about equal for all the players. It spoils the game to have three experts and one rank novice. It's equally important, if you're playing for reasons of sociability, that you enjoy playing with them. You know one another's moves, certainly, but it's a nice challenge to try to fool one another once in awhile.

You can mix things up occasionally by bringing in an outsider to your game (and by playing in other groups as well), but if you enjoy one another's company and playing style, there's no reason not to play with the same bunch as often as possible.

SEND THESE MIDDLE-AGERS TO CAMP

Tennis camps have grown in popularity along with the tennis boom. Theoretically, they offer a good opportunity for a combination of a pleasant pastime and a learning experience. In general, they're well worth your while.

In picking a camp, I don't think it's necessarily your first priority to find one run by a "name" player. (I'd feel this way, even if I were involved in a tennis camp, which, up to now, I haven't been.) It's more important to find out whether the player whose name the camp bears is on the premises and how often. If he makes a guest appearance about as often as you consistently hit winning passing shots down the line, that's a bit of a rip-off; it means the camp's just capitalizing on his name. Most of the good camps I've heard about and would recommend are those where the player is always on the scene. Tony Trabert, for example, lives up to his commitment to be at his California camp all the time. More and more name players with camps are realizing that they have to be on location or the camps and they are going to get a bad name.

A camp is only as good as the staff, starting with the top person and reaching down to the counselors and instructors. You really have to choose on the basis of the camp's reputation and experience. As in picking a summer camp for your child, you'd do well to talk to people who have recently attended.

Tennis camps, which are especially good for youngsters, are fine for adults. But caution: some of them, the type of operation John Gardner runs, for example, saturate campers with tennis for the week or two they're there, and they're worked pretty hard. It can become a chore. Still, if you're dedicated to tennis, camp is for you.

For some adult campers, though, the *total* tennis atmosphere (instruction, practice, tournaments, films, lectures) is more of the game than they want. If you're unwilling to be this totally involved, you're probably wasting your time and money. If you're more interested in going on a vacation, with a little tennis thrown in, you'd do better to go to a resort where there's plenty of tennis playing and instruction available but a lot of other options as well.

I like to play tennis for the fun of it outside of tournaments, but if I went to a resort for two weeks, I wouldn't want to play tennis every day.

TENNIS PARTIES

When social tennis was at its peak, tennis parties flourished, and they're still popular. I've participated in several, one of which was given by the wife of a tennis-playing couple to her husband for his birthday at a tennis club. Guests were invited to bring tennis gear, and there was an opportunity for everyone to play sets, or at least games, in various combinations. It can't be very serious tennis— there's a lot of eating and drinking and abbreviated matches, and sometimes you can't do justice to any one activity. But if you approach the occasion as a party at which tennis is just one pleasant element, you can have a fine time.

ONE MORE TIME

Everybody says, jokingly, that the secret of winning tennis is getting the ball over the net and into the court one more time than your opponent. That's about as profound and meaningful as saying that everyone dies from heart failure. But when everything else is stripped away, the essence of what you're trying to do on the tennis court *is* to get it over one more time.

Whether that "one more time" comes relatively early or late in a rally will vary from match to match and from opponent to opponent. Against someone who's basically a big hitter, or a wild, erratic player who makes great shots and then misses a lot, your strategy would be to try to keep the ball in play a little longer. Rather than go for outright winners, and in the process possibly make as many unforced errors as he does, you should try just to keep the rally going and wait for him to hit a losing shot. Against a more steady opponent, you might need a different game plan. Rather than try to outsteady him and risk being beaten badly, you might want to play more aggressively.

Big hits are dramatic and low-percentage shots are exciting. But keeping the ball in play is an essential part of the game, and while the player who just keeps pushing the ball back may not look as good hitting the ball as someone trying to belt away, that player probably is winning the points that the other isn't.

Older players are no different from players in other age groups when it comes to wanting to look great while hitting the ball. Nobody can fault good appearance. But you don't want to give away points, so keep the ball in play within the dimensions of the court.

HEIGHT OFTEN EQUALS DEPTH

Sven Davidson firmly believes that hitting a shot deep is an all-important component of winning tennis. I think there are other equally important principles, but I do agree that depth is one of them.

People tend to think that the beautiful shots are the ones that barely clear the net. Many of them are, but you'll find in a given match between two good players that the ball goes over the net a lot higher than it appears to. The great-looking shot might clear the net by five or six feet! It's very difficult to get a ball to hit at the baseline deep into your opponent's court unless you get some height on the ball, although a flatter type of shot can go relatively deep without being too high above the net. The trajectory of a ball hit with topspin is high over the net but shorter than the flat shot. The spin brings it down.

Jimmy Connors probably hits the ball as close to the top of the net as any top modern player, but he also hits more balls *into* the net than most. Because he hits a pretty flat ball, there's not much margin for error, so when he has a problem it's generally one of control. But when he's playing well, he makes great shots.

SERVICE WITH A SMILE

There's a certain mystique surrounding serving, which really is undeserved. Unlike any other stroke, you control exactly when you're going to hit it, which means you can wait as long as you need to—within reason and, possibly, a club time limit—until you've got

172 of PRIME TIME TENNIS

everything together and you're fully ready. Serving is like pitching, and if you're able to throw a ball, you ought to be able to serve.

THE TOSS IS ALL-IMPORTANT

The basic problems players have with the serve are usually related to the toss. Without a consistent, regular toss, you're never going to have a consistent serve. Even the best serving motion in the world is meaningless unless it's accompanied by the proper toss. Jimmy Connors used to have an unvarying serve but recently began tossing the ball a little forward and to his left (he's a lefty), instead of straight up and back. This allowed him to lean into the ball and made it easier for him to mix up his serves and also to follow his serve to the net occasionally. He did this very well at Wimbledon and Flushing Meadow in 1982.

To be correct, a toss has to be thrown *high enough* and *forward enough*. These are the two basic components.

You should toss the ball high enough so that you can barely reach it with your racket when you're up on your toes. You should hit it at the top of its arc, when it's virtually standing still. Throwing it higher is a waste of energy; throwing it lower changes the trajectory and makes the serve less effective. Sometimes you'll notice late in a match that even a better player fails to throw the ball high enough because he's tired.

You should throw the ball sufficiently forward so that you can watch it all the way, and so that you're almost falling into the court as you hit it. To test your toss for this quality, let the ball fall to the ground without hitting it; it should land a foot or foot and a half inside the court. If it lands in back of the baseline, it means you would have been hitting your serve with your arm alone. That's wrong; you can't get your body into your serve if the ball is back. And only if you make your toss roughly the same each time can you hope to develop a consistent serve.

SAME POSITION

On one serve to a particular opponent, you want to go to his backhand; on the other, to his forehand. Should you change the way you stand? Preferably not. The better the player you are, the more you want everything, including your stance, toss, and motion, to be the same all the time, the way a baseball pitcher tries to conceal what pitch is coming by disguising his delivery and keeping it consistent. If you planned to slice a serve and therefore threw the ball out to the side, your opponent would know exactly what to expect. So, if possible, you should throw the ball and stand the same way you do for a flat serve, applying the difference at the final moment with your racket. The more you conceal, the better. Guillermo Vilas showed an improved serve at the 1982 U.S. Open (where he made it to the semifinals). Among other virtues, his serve was disguised a lot better than it had been. His manager, Ion Tiriac, commented, "Everybody squeezed on the left side of the court. I used to close my eyes in practice and knew where every serve was going. But now I don't know where the serve goes."

You might change your position for a given opponent (as McEnroe did when he served to Connors at Wimbledon, trying to get it to his backhand). But against the same player, stand the same way each time you serve, or it will be too easy for him to anticipate what's coming.

No Big Need for Speed

Speed helps the effectiveness of a serve, but it's not vital. Over the years the great servers were not necessarily the ones who hit the hardest. Rather, they were players who had three different serves— flat, topspin, and sidespin—and could deliver them all with the same toss and serving motion, so an opponent didn't know what was coming.

Every player looks a little different serving, but if you were to examine the motion of the racket from just before it contacts the ball to an equal distance after, you'd be hard pressed to tell the servers apart.

Placing versus Pace

The placement of a serve is more important than its pace. When you reach a high level of tennis, you have several basic goals when you serve: (1) you're trying to serve the ball deep into the service box, as close to the service line as possible; (2) you're trying to serve consistently to the backhand, which ordinarily is the weaker side; and (3) you're trying to mix up your serves, taking advantage of the fact that you know what you intend to do, while your opponent doesn't, especially at crucial points in the match.

No matter how hard it's hit, a deep serve is more difficult to return than a shallow one. The moment you hit your serve short, say two feet from the service line, you're in trouble, because your opponent is going to have a much easier time handling it. When a good player seems to be having a problem with serving—especially if he or she is following the serve to the net—it's probably because it was landing too short in the court. That was basically my problem when I had a bad serving day, and it's the problem most competitive players have. Often I was serving short because I wasn't tossing the ball high enough.

As far as serving to the backhand is concerned, occasionally you should vary your aim to keep your opponent honest. Hit one to his forehand every once in a while to prevent him from inching over to cover the backhand serve. Steve Denton was successful several times serving into Ivan Lendl's forehand, the Czech's stronger side, in the 1982 ATP (Association of Tennis Professionals) final, though he didn't defeat him.

If, as a good player, you've learned to develop three kinds of serves, you want to mix them up to keep your opponent off-balance. You might switch from a flat serve to sidespin a few times, and then, when your opponent thinks he's guessed your pattern, cross him up by repeating the flat serve or hitting a topspin serve. You should capitalize fully on the serving advantage, which is a big one, especially on a faster surface. If you just put the ball in play, you've surrendered that advantage, so use all the equipment you have.

GRUNTING

It's become fashionable among some of today's younger players to grunt when exerting a lot of energy on a shot, notably the serve. We didn't have that in our day—and today we tend to confine our sound-making to groans about postgame soreness and stiffness. I don't think grunting really does any good, except that, at an extremely high decibel range, it can be disconcerting to your opponent. But if you think it signals the fact you're really getting exercise out there, grunt in good health.

SERVE-AND-VOLLEY

Serve-and-volley go together like love and marriage—or they used to. We're not seeing as much of either combination these days as we once did (although serve-and-volley, at least, is starting to make a comeback, especially as surfaces for tournaments are speeded up. McEnroe plays the way we did, in this respect). The club-level player, especially the prime-timer, is not going to serve-and-volley very much, unless he happens to find it works against a particular opponent.

It stands to reason that, for the volley to be effective, you have to have a good serve. If you don't, you shouldn't follow it to the net.

You may have to slow your serve down a little bit so that you have time to get to the net. It's ironic, but older players, realizing they can't get to the net as quickly as they did formerly, try to serve harder, when they should really be doing the opposite. They probably should slow their serves down slightly to give themselves more time to get well in to the net. Theoretically, a slower serve gives the receiver more of an opportunity to make a good return, but if that relatively slow serve is hit deep in the box, the receiver is still kept back. So hitting that serve deeper is more important than unleashing one at 150 mph. A ball hit short on either the first or second serve is going to find the receiver moving in, and he'll have a relatively easier time passing you or hitting the ball at your feet as you move toward the net.

Whenever you find yourself at the net, whether it's because you've followed your serve in, your partner is serving, or for some other reason, make sure you keep your racket out in front of you and up —out and up—so you're ready to hit a volley wherever it comes. When you volley, rather than take a big swing, give the ball a little punch.

HALF-VOLLEY? GET DOWWWN!

If the receiver succeeds in getting a good return back at your feet, you're going to have to resort to the half-volley; that is, hitting the ball as it bounces or immediately after. When they half-volley, many players let the ball get back too far; they don't meet the ball out in front as they should and don't bend their knees, which results in just sort of shoveling at the ball. Instead of making a real stroke out of it and following through, they just slap at the ball.

In hitting the half-volley, you have to get your body down and make a long motion with the racket to keep the ball on it a moment extra. In effect, you're trying to catch the ball with the racket. With a smooth swing at the ball and an attempt to hold it on the racket a little longer, you're more likely to hit the ball in the center of the racket. A choppy motion may result in a mishit if not a miss.

Timing is probably a little more difficult on the half-volley than on any other stroke because you don't have a chance to see the ball bounce and decide where it's going (particularly on a poor surface, where the bounce is not dependable), and you don't have much time for the stroke. But you can avoid some of the pitfalls by meeting the ball a little farther out in front (though sometimes it's the fact that a ball has gotten past you that makes you decide to use the half-volley). As you practice to get the proper timing, remember to bend your knees and get down to the ball, and take a nice smooth swing and follow-through. The half-volley is something of a defensive shot, but you shouldn't hit it completely defensively. On the other hand, keep in mind that it requires more of a delicate touch than a regular ground stroke.

Oops

More times than you'd like to think possible, you're going to rush the net and find that your serve or your approach shot wasn't good enough to put pressure on your opponent, and now you're the one in trouble. The worse your approach shot, the more vulnerable you are. Most times you're going to lose the point, but occasionally if you guess right and move in the right direction at the right time, you might extricate yourself.

On the slim chance (about one in five) that this can happen, don't give up if you're trapped in no-man's-land. Calculate in which direction your opponent's shot is likely to come, and then either take off that way immediately, or fake the opposite way first and then take off. You might get the ball hit right at you, or your movement might shake up your opponent sufficiently to cause an error. It's better than flat-footed surrender.

NET-RUSHING DOESN'T NECESSARILY FOLLOW

I think it's foolish to try to serve an ace and be thinking of following that serve to the net. That's trying to do two things with one shot, and you'll probably miss on both counts. Granted, if the serve lands anywhere near your target area with anything near the intended velocity, it's going to be more difficult for your opponent to return the ball, and so your being at the net is likely to pay dividends. But basically your intent is to win the point with a serve your opponent can't touch. If so, you don't stop playing after you serve, but the one thing on your mind should have been getting that ace.

Trying for an ace is another tactic to keep your opponent honest. Besides, you'll occasionally get one. But more often than not, you'll realize that attempts at aces frequently are faults, in which case you're left with the small problem of having to come in with the second serve. Most of the time, your game plan should be to try to get that first serve in, deep in the box, and follow it to the net, rather than try for an ace. If you get set at the net, you're in better position to win the point, most of the time.

That's the kind of percentage tennis that Jack Kramer was so good at. His serve wasn't one that blew you off the court, but it was tough and he was consistent enough with his first serve that his opponent had a difficult time returning it. Consequently, Kramer was able to hit a good first volley and consistently win his serve.

NOT TOO FAR BACK ON THE SERVE

Perhaps because the Grand Masters aren't serving quite as hard as we used to, most of us receive serve standing right about the baseline. It was never our style in years gone by to stand six or eight feet behind the baseline (except maybe on a rare occasion, to change the tempo). Because our opponent usually was coming in behind his serve, we wanted to cut the ball off a little sooner and try to get it back to his feet. So we stood in closer to block it back before he got to the net. The habit probably carries over from those days.

Since your prime time opponents aren't likely to be following their serves to the net, you can stand as far back as you find comfortable, at a distance that allows you to hit the ball out in front.

BACKSWING

On the forehand, your backswing should go back to about perpendicular to the net and point toward the back fence. On the backhand, the objective is the same, but that takes a turn of some 270 degrees, as compared with the roughly 90 degrees required on the forehand. This is why so much stress is placed on getting the racket back early for the backhand.

FOLLOW-THROUGH

Very few of the top players have a "classic" follow-through, and in fact, most of them wrap their wrist around their hit. But no matter. Everything to do with hitting a tennis ball really happens within a 45-degree angle before you hit the ball and 45 degrees after you make contact. If everything else were stripped away from the picture of a player's swing, you wouldn't know who was hitting it. Of course, the ball doesn't know who is either. Every good player is basically the same in that 90-degree area surrounding the point of contact. It's the wind-up and follow-through that give individual players their characteristic swing.

While backswings vary quite a bit (think of Borg's, for instance), follow-through is more consistent and orthodox with most players.

One suggestion relating to follow-through is that you bring the racket through after hitting the ball so that you could theoretically catch it in your other hand in front of your body. Another guideline is that your follow-through should point to where you're trying to hit the ball.

Since the follow-through occurs after the ball is hit and gone, it really has no effect on the flight of the ball—but only with a good, extended follow-through *in mind* will you make a proper stroke. The intended follow-through is part of the groove that, combined with the backswing, gives you a nice, consistent stroke without having to think about it. It should help give you a "groovy" feeling that feels comfortable every time you swing.

OVERHEADS

Like every other stroke, an overhead should be hit in front of you. Waiting to pounce on a lob to smash it, you should have your arm up a little bit, your body turned sideways and your racket back in preparation.

Hit an overhead very much as you do a serve. I don't advocate pointing at the ball, as some suggest, because it might upset your balance.

An overhead is a fairly easy shot unless the lob is a really good one that fools you a little and gets over your head. If it's spinning, you're going to have to concentrate a lot more. You don't want the ball falling over your head, anymore than an outfielder wants the baseball going over his.

If a lob is hit with heavy topspin the player sometimes mishits it, even though it doesn't get over his head. At club level, a lob with heavy spin can be very effective because it drops very quickly and is a difficult shot to hit.

Even when a lob is not spinning, many club-level players miss it or hit it out because they either take their eye off the ball or are so eager to put it away that they rush the shot.

TO GET A SHARP ANGLE

There are basically two ways to hit a ball at a sharp angle cross-court. You can meet the ball a little sooner, or you can turn your body in the direction of your target without hitting the ball any sooner. Of course, you would not want to do anything to give the shot away—for instance, if you were attempting to pass the net man. That's why hitting the ball out front is important. That way, you can use the same motion and at the last moment, using some wrist action and meeting the ball a bit earlier, steer the ball cross-court. If you let the ball get too far back, you'll close off your shot options and give your shot away.

SPINS

Don't worry about hitting the ball with spin until you can hit it just flat consistently and well. Once you're ready for spin, here's some advice.

TOPSPIN

Some players have the mistaken notion that to hit a ball with topspin you hit the top of the ball. If you did that, all that would happen would be the ball would bounce on your side of the net, or you'd miss it. Applying topspin means you're hitting the ball with the racket coming from low to high on the back side of the ball. Bjorn Borg, with his exaggerated low-to-high motion, is the outstanding practitioner. You don't have to be quite that extreme in your stroke to get the desired effect of having the ball spin forward in a top-over-bottom motion so that it jumps up and away after it bounces.

My heavily topped forehand was the result of hitting from low to high and coming over. It didn't look like the windmill swing that Borg has. My stroke was essentially the same as everyone else's. But instead of coming through the ball, I came up and over it a little more. (On the very finish of a flat shot you can come over the ball to give it a little topspin. Many beginners turn the wrist too soon.)

I never had anything approaching classic strokes and I use one grip for everything. Instead of turning the handle, when changing from a backhand to a forehand, I change the angle of the head of the racket with my wrist so that the ball and racket still meet at the right angle. I got into that by habit. As a result, I get more wrist on my forehand. On the plus side, I was never caught with the wrong grip.

On the volley, most players don't change their grip because they don't have time to. They would probably use a backhand grip for both volleys.

TOPSPIN LOB

I've been credited with introducing the topspin lob. Hitting anything with exaggerated topspin was considered very unorthodox in my younger days, but I had the kind of forehand that lent itself to this stroke.

In a magazine article, Noel Brown, a contemporary of mine, commenting about my heavily topspun forehand and heavily sliced backhand, both of which were considered unorthodox, said, "After twenty-five years, he's gained control of basically unsound strokes." That was a good description of my game.

Because topspin came to me so naturally, I decided to experiment with applying it to the lob. That struck me as a potentially good surprise shot in doubles. So I worked with it and developed it to the point where I could hit it very well, providing that I was set and the ball bounced relatively high.

The objective, when hitting a topspin lob, is to apply enough spin so that it just makes it over the head and reach of the player at the net and then, when it lands, jumps away from him and takes off. It's a nice extra offensive weapon to develop.

Unfortunately, in recent years, I've been the victim of some poetic justice. It's amazing how many topspin lobs I find working against me now.

UNDERSPIN OR SLICE

You apply underspin to a ball when you want it to come back after it bounces. A ball hit with underspin goes through the air in a straighter line and tends either to stop or head back toward its origin after it lands. You apply underspin by hitting the ball with a high-to-low stroke at its back.

Spin is used to advantage all the time, and we're seeing more spin than we used to.

The use of more or less spin is appropriate at different times, but that's a little bit advanced for the club-level player. Learn how to hit the ball properly first; spin can come later on.

DROP-SHOT

Use underspin to hit a drop-shot, which is a shot that lands barely beyond the net. The person with a natural underspin stroke has an advantage in that he or she can use pretty much the same motion as on a deeper stroke, and then take a little off the swing. In this way, the shot is not expected, and a good drop-shot depends on deception to be effective. It's much more difficult to accomplish for someone who generally hits with topspin all the time because when that player sets up to hit with underspin, it's a dead giveaway.

Be selective about when you choose to use a drop-shot, which requires a very delicate touch. Wait for a short ball that gives you some time to set up to hit it. Then if your opponent is well back or off to the opposite side, drop it over. Don't overuse the stroke, or your opponent will be expecting it all the time. Of course, at our age plenty of players can *expect* a drop-shot with certainty and still not be able to *reach* it.

AGAINST SPIN

To effectively return a ball that has spin on it, you have to concentrate more because it's doing tricks.

One objective in returning the ball is to take some of the spin off. If a ball comes to you with a lot of topspin, you can remove some by hitting it relatively flat or with underspin, rather than trying to put the same spin back.

Some of the younger players try to meet topspin with topspin, but they don't really gain much. The excessive topspin they use is good for control, but it does not produce a heavy, hard-hit ball. Although I was one of the first to use a lot of topspin on my forehand, I think you can overdo it. It was a natural stroke for me, but as mentioned, when I used it a topspin stroke was considered unorthodox.

You seldom see forehands hit with underspin, except maybe on an approach shot. McEnroe, for one, pushes his approach shot with a little bit of underspin. It's difficult to hit with a lot of topspin on the approach shot because that type of swing pulls you away from the ball. But if you swing *under* the ball, you're coming in to it, and you'll be moving toward the net as you hit it, so it's much easier to approach with underspin. That's why you don't see the players who use excessive topspin come to the net that much. For instance, Borg and Vilas are uncomfortable coming to the net, and when they do they usually hit a flatter ball on their approach shot.

If the ball coming to you is heavily sliced (meaning it has a lot of underspin), you could counteract it with some topspin. An unwritten law says that you don't hit a slice against a slice.

GETTING THE RUNAROUND

A fine time to convert a defensive posture into an offensive one is on the return of service.

If your forehand is considerably better than your backhand and you have the time, it often pays to run around your backhand and return the serve with your stronger shot. This is best done on your opponent's second serve, which ordinarily will be slower than his first. Whenever you do it, it should surprise your opponent a little and provide you with more offensive power.

If you're right-handed and you do this when you receive a serve in the deuce court, you'll be closer to the center of the court, a desirable neighborhood. But if you run around your backhand in the ad court, you've moved yourself farther off the court than you would have been had you returned the serve with your backhand. Then, if your shot isn't a really good one, you're in trouble. So there's a time and place for the runaround.

A word of caution: don't continually run around your backhand during rallies just because your backhand is weak. The only way to develop your backhand is to use it.

NEITHER FEINT NOR FAINT

If you want a quick review of your past misdeeds, just hit a short lob in reach of a zealous opponent who has a powerful overhead. As you're waiting for the smash, your sins will pass in review. Aside from prayer at that moment, your only chance of salvaging the rally is to pick a likely destination for the ball to land and head for it. In a situation like this, there's no time to try to fool your opponent; besides, he's probably looking at the ball, not you, so feinting (or fainting) would be a waste of time and leave you devoid of hope. Of course, even if you correctly guess where the ball is headed, and you get there, you're still probably not going to save the point because you're going to be in an extremely defensive position.

DON'T "CHOKE UP"

I don't think an older player should start "choking up" on his or her racket for better control. Grasping the racket at a point too far from the end will make it feel entirely different, besides shortening your reach. I think, generally speaking, you should get used to holding the racket at the same point on the handle, and if it's better control you want, just don't swing as hard.

"WRONG-HANDED" PLAYERS

It takes a bit of a mental adjustment when you realize that your opponent is holding the racket in his "wrong" hand, the left.

How much playing against a lefty bothers you depends primarily on your style of play. Southpaws used to be pretty tough for me because my backhand was the weaker of my ground strokes and the left-hander's serve always came into my backhand with lots of spin on it. Players like Don Budge and Tony Trabert were not bothered by lefties because their backhands were so strong that a serve there was essentially a serve to their strength.

Oddly enough, lefties usually don't like to play another lefty because they don't encounter lefties as often (although there seem to be more southpaws than ever now, including some of the very best pros, notably Vilas, McEnroe, and Connors).

If you apply the same basic strategy against a left-handed opponent that you do against a righty, you have to remember the obvious—that a lefty's backhand is opposite that of a righty's. Sometimes you remember too late. If I wanted to hit to a lefty's backhand, I had to hit to what was my usual right-handed opponent's forehand. This was difficult to keep in mind because a left-handed opponent was more of a rarity. So sometimes I'd forget and play right into his strength.

By the way, although I didn't like to receive from a lefty, I did like to serve against one. I had a natural wide-swinging serve that went to a lefty's backhand, so there I had an advantage. But on balance, I found it a little tougher to play a lefty.

PLANNING AHEAD

I'm asked sometimes how many shots I plan ahead in a game. It's usually not possible, or even wise, to plan very far ahead because there are too many variables that can alter even the best thought-out strategy. You should have a basic plan, however, and you might plot out your moves a couple of shots ahead of time, according to that plan.

For example, you might decide to serve constantly to your opponent's backhand and come in to the net. Or you might plan to come in on the second shot, or to aim the first volley to the open court. You might have a plan to set your opponent up and fool him on a particular shot—perhaps constantly serving to his backhand, and then suddenly surprising him with one down the middle. Against a particular opponent, your game plan might be basically to come to the net constantly.

The game plan you start with is obviously built around your basic playing style. But if it isn't working, you've got to change your plan.

A Change in Plans

I played my own game against every opponent, but if I found it wasn't working, I started doing something different very soon. There were days when nothing would work, but at least I wasn't figuratively banging my head against the wall, continuing with what obviously was a losing plan.

I remember the match at Forest Hills in which Frank Sedgman beat me so badly that it took him only forty-five minutes to complete the crime. But I tried everything I could think of. I stayed back, I came in, tried slowing the ball down, tried speeding it up. You try something different in the hope that it will upset your opponent a little and change the way the tide is going. It may not help at all, but you won't know if you don't try.

This is the complaint some observers had about Jimmy Connors for a long time. His attitude seemed to be, "I've got to win the way I play; I'm not going to try anything else." I often saw him go down the drain without ever altering his plan. The year Manuel Orantes beat him at Forest Hills for the U.S. Championships, you could tell the match was over after the first set. Connors was just hammering away at the ball while Orantes was popping it back, hitting drop-shots, and Connors was like a bull butting a stone wall. He should have tried a drop-shot or something to mix Orantes up and try to get him out of his groove, but Connors just kept hammering away. Orantes killed him, 6–2, 6–2, 6–3.

I don't think Jimmy really has the equipment to play a lot of different ways. Essentially, he hits the ball hard, and that's it. But, to give him due credit, in 1982 he made an adjustment, albeit a small one, that I think was very significant: he threw the ball slightly more forward when he served, and he was successful, winning both Wimbledon and the U.S. Open.

Even Borg has made adjustments. He realized that he had to start coming in on grass, and he began to serve better and come to the net. I'm sure he wasn't comfortable doing it.

Sven Davidson recently suggested that the intellectual level of the game has declined since we were at our peak. "Sure," I told him, "none of the current players could be as smart as we were." But Sven was serious. He was thinking of generations of tennis players, he said, not just ours, but also those who came before. Sven said when he watched Vilas play Wilander in the 1982 French Open, he was "very sadly disappointed." He said that Wilander, whose achievement was "great to watch," knows "only one type of play." Wilander, he noted, was not yet eighteen, and perhaps at that young age one should not be expected to know more than that. But, Sven continued, Vilas was about twenty-nine and had been around the game for a long time, had the physical equipment, and yet "he plays the same game over and over, and it's a losing game. He just kept on playing. He doesn't do what Vic Seixas did twenty-five years ago—change a losing game."

Thanks for the compliment, Sven, but it should be reemphasized that changing doesn't guarantee winning. Also, it should be pointed out again that by the time the 1982 U.S. Open rolled around, Vilas had changed his game, at least to the extent that he was varying and disguising his serve a lot more.

When Ivan Lendl met Steve Denton in the finals of the 1982 ATP Championships, he changed his strategy. One thing he did was to take the pace off his serve, and he managed to get 80 percent of his first serves in. "I tried to serve wide so I could get an open court and so he would have to do a little running," Lendl said. Ivan also took some pace off his blistering ground strokes and rallied from the baseline against Denton, a 6-foot-2, 190-pound serve-and-volleyer. "His body is so huge, it's hard to move," Lendl said. "So that's what I was playing for." It worked, and Lendl won the championship.

Sometimes you'll see a fellow suddenly change what's been working for him for some inexplicable reason. For instance, he's been going to the net consistently on his serve, and it's been successful. Then suddenly he gets to 30–40 and stays back. Why a player would change a winning form is something I can't figure out, but that's what makes horse races—and tennis matches.

WHAT'S IN A GAME?

Now that you've absorbed all the tips and gotten your tennis act together, how do you find competition at your own level? For that matter, how do you determine just what your own level is?

THE ROUND ROBIN GETS THE SEED

Play in major tournaments is usually based on single elimination, with players seeded (or ranked) according to their current performance records (aided by computer) and how they fared in the given tournament in recent years. The number one player is the top seed, and so on down the line. Beyond a given number of seeded players, others get into the tournament by virtue of their ranking, or by winning qualifying rounds. Matches are drawn so that the top-seeded players meet players from the bottom of the heap in the early rounds. This way, if all goes as anticipated in the elimination tournament (one lost match and you're out), the better players will compete against each other in the later rounds. Usually, the draw is structured in such a manner that hopefully the number one and number two seed meet in the finals.

Often, however, the luck of the draw plays a role in who makes it to the late rounds. One player may have had a series of easy opponents, while another had very tough ones. To the extent that in an elimination tournament no two winning players will have competed against the same opponents, it's not a perfect test of ability. But, obviously, it's just not practical to have a round robin, where everyone plays everyone, when you have 128 entrants in the tournament. (You might, however, make it elimination until the quarter-finals, and round robin after that.)

Round robins are feasible when there are few players involved, such as the eight-man Grand Masters. Until recently, in fact, our grand finals tournament used a round robin format. As a player, I liked it because we got to play four days instead of three, and you weren't out after one loss. Under certain circumstances, a round robin is a good system, but you have to be careful of the format, it does have some drawbacks. Occasionally, you're confronted with a match that doesn't mean anything to one of the players, and he dogs it a little bit. (This happened at Madison Square Garden during the Grand Masters tournament.)

At the club level, for people playing purely for fun, a round robin is a lot more sociable way of running an event. You get to play with everybody, and you can even keep mixing up the doubles partnerships. After a few games, you change partners and opponents. It's also very good for convention groups and resort play. It's a good way to get the guests mingling so that they became acquainted. In golf, it's called a *scramble*.

You don't have to be exceptionally good to participate in and enjoy round robin tournaments that take place at conventions and outings. If you're part of a firm or industry that has an annual event at which tennis is a part, even if it's not at the same place every year, you'll get to know one another's ability very quickly; therefore, rankings can be established as the basis for good matches.

In clubs where there is a permanent membership, you'll often find a challenge ladder on which the best player is placed number one, and the others rated from there on down. Then if someone thinks he can beat—or would just like to play—the person above him on the ladder, he issues a challenge. If he wins, he rises to the next rung.

All these systems have their benefits in different situations.

RATINGS

A key to arranging competitions that are enjoyable for all the participants is to make sure that opponents are evenly matched, and it's been my experience that the best way to rate players is to watch them hit a few balls, rather than depending on them to rate themselves. The pro at your tennis club or resort might do the rating or the matching up if he's had a chance to observe players in action on the court. He might decide that Fred and Bob can give Jack and Jerry a good game, or that Frank and Murray would play a fairly even match, and try to arrange competitions that way. But if there is no pro and games are arranged with no idea of how anyone plays, there's too much chance of a mismatch, and then it's no fun for anyone.

When players are asked to rate themselves, most often it comes down to chance because there's so much leeway—whether it's on an A, B, C scale or advanced, intermediate, beginner ranking. It's very subjective. A player with an inflated opinion of himself may brag that he's an advanced player when he really isn't, while another fellow may be too modest to place himself in the advanced level, even though he qualifies. Leaving personality quirks aside, the cream of the playing crop at one club may be only on an intermediate level at another. The definitions of A, B, C and advanced, intermediate, beginner may vary from place to place or individual to individual. It's almost impossible to get a truly accurate rating system in this way.

A serious attempt has been made to overcome this problem by the National Tennis Association (NTA) in cooperation with the United States Tennis Association (USTA) and the United States Professional Tennis Association (USPTA). They developed what they hope will be a universal rating system, by which every player will be able to rate himself or herself objectively. It's designed to eliminate the use of ambiguous traditional terms (A, B, C and advanced, intermediate, beginner.)

Known as the National Tennis Rating Program (NTRP), the classification system identifies and describes levels of tennis ability and assigns a numerical rating. Using the system, players may rate themselves, have a teaching pro rate them, or rate themselves and then have a pro verify their ratings. The sponsoring organizations believe that the NTRP allows players "to achieve better competition, on-court compatibility, personal challenge and more enjoyment in the sport." A nice potential side effect of the system is that a middle-aged player, for example, will be able to find good, even competition among players of different age groups, as well as his own.

The NTRP chart of pro verification guidelines, with general characteristics of various playing levels, is on pages 192–95. Ratings range from 1.0 for the player with "No concept of waist-level stroke. Most often swings from elbow at eye-level. Most likely avoids backhands or misses completely. No knowledge of service motion or procedure. Little knowledge of scorekeeping and basic positioning" up to 7.0 for the player "Generally committed to tournament competition as a life-style and frequently depends on tournament winnings as a portion of his income."

Most players, of course, are somewhere in the middle. To give you a sampling of the characteristics of some of the other ratings, a 2.5 player is "Well prepared for moderate shots. Follows through on most shots. Fairly consistent on set-ups," but on his backhand "Still has grip and preparation problems, lack of confidence, no follow-through. In serving, he's "Starting a full motion, can be consistent on the second serve, no directional intent." He has "weak court coverage, cannot return lobs, can return serve on forehand consistently, cannot adjust to variance in serves, usually remains in the initial doubles position."

Two levels up is the 3.5 player, who, on his forehand, has "Good consistency on set-ups. Still lacks depth on difficult shots. Has directional intent on moderate balls." On his backhand, he has "Preparation problems. Starting to hit with directional intent on easy shots. Starting to follow through instead of punch." He's "Starting to serve with some power and control. Tries to direct serves. Usually flat serves. May be trying to learn to use spin." He "Moves up and back well, covering court fairly well, with doubles partner can effectively cover the net."

Qualities are also rated under the headings of "Volley" and "Special Shots."

There are some aspects of the national rating program that are of particular interest. For instance, it's recommended that you qualify on *all* points of a preceding category before placing yourself at a given level. Gradations are now in .5 increments, but once the NTRP is established the ratings can be made finer. Players within a .5 difference in ratings are considered to be generally compatible in ability: they are capable of having close matches, but the player with the higher rating usually wins. If a player has a stroke deficiency but can play competitively with a player who does not have such a deficiency, the two players may be rated at the same level. For example, if you can't hit a topspin serve but you have enough other abilities, you can play a close match with someone who can hit that kind of serve.

The NTRP doesn't rate men and women on the same scale, so when you rate yourself, you should use players of the same sex as reference points. But if you want to compete against someone of the opposite sex, there ought to be a .5 difference in the woman's favor if the two of you are to be competitive. For instance, a man with a 3.5 rating should have a fairly equal match with a woman who has a 4.0 rating. (When a man reaches the 6.0 level, a woman needs to be close to a 7.0 level to be competitive.)

Don't confuse the terms *ranking* and *rating*. The NTRP rates players' abilities based on performance in an open adult category, while ranking is based on achievement in sanctioned tournaments, many of which are based on age divisions. Players should rate themselves based on their current ability, regardless of their past rankings or achievements.

To determine a team's eligibility for a doubles event, according to the sponsoring organizations, use individual player ratings rather than a combined rating. In a doubles tournament where 4.5 is established as the maximum, no player on a team should be rated higher than 4.5 to qualify. This, says the USTA, is more equitable than basing the event on a maximum *team* rating of 9.0 composed of, say, a 3.0 player and a 6.0 player. "Allowing so many different levels into an event may be fun at a tennis party, but it makes for incompatible play in competitive situations," comments the USTA. To the extent that a doubles game is as good as its weakest player, I tend to agree.

The initial rating is provisional and may change as competition shows it to be incorrect or as the player improves. While rating by a pro is more objective, rating yourself can be very accurate. The NTRP has drawn up the following list of guidelines and rating categories.

NATIONAL TENNIS RATING PROGRAM

PRO VERIFICATION GUIDELINES

(General Characteristics of Various Playing Levels)

Rating	Forehand	Backhand	Serve	Volley	Special Shots	Other
1.0	No concept of waist-level stroke. Most often swings from elbow at eye-level.	Most likely avoids backhands or misses completely.	No knowledge of service motion or procedure.	Makes little contact with the ball at net or doesn't go to net at all.		Little knowledge of scorekeeping and basic positioning.
1.5	Late preparation; No follow through; Erratic contact; No direction.	Avoids backhands when possible. No change of grip.	Inconsistent toss and motion: Infrequent contact on center of strings; No follow through; No backscratch or full swing; Frequent double faults.	Only FH volley; Infrequent success.		Little knowledge of procedures; Difficulty with scorekeeping.
2.0	No directional intent. Infrequently in position. Can keep a rally of up to 3 hits when set up.	Grip problems; No follow through; Erratic contact; No direction; Faces net.	Mostly ½ swing; Frequently a back-forth motion; Can frequently get the ball into play; Double faults still common.	Frequently swings; Reluctant to play net; Avoids BH; No footwork; Successful on set-up FH's; No depth.		Can keep play moving in singles and doubles.
2.5	Form developing. Well prepared for moderate shots. Follows through on most shots. Fairly consistent on set-ups.	Still has grip and preparation problems. Lack of confidence; No follow through; Can compensate frequently for a ball coming to the BH side.	Starting a full motion; Can be consistent on the second serve; No directional intent; Frequently no backscratch.	Can angle FH volley when set up. Does not bend for low volleys (usually drops racket head). Still uncomfortable at the net, especially on the BH side. Grip problems.	Can lob intentionally.	Weak court coverage; Cannot return lobs; Can return serve on FH consistently; Cannot adjust to variance in serves; Usually remains in the initial doubles position.
3.0	Fairly consistent with some directional intent; Lacks depth control.	Little directional intent. Frequently prepared; Usually lacks follow through; Can be consistent on set-ups.	Developing rhythm; Little consistency when trying for power.	Consistent FH volleys; Frequently uses FH racket face on BH volleys; Can be offensive on set-ups. Inconsistent BH volley when using BH racket face; Has trouble with low and wide balls.	Can occasionally handle balls hit at the feet (but not with a good half-volley form). Can make contact on overheads; Can lob consistently.	Can frequently cover lobs in doubles; Recognizes offensive doubles play; but weak in its execution; Can return serve on the BH, but with little directional intent. Developing match play sense.

Level	Forehand	Backhand	Serve	Volley	Overhead / Approach shots	Overall / Tactics
3.5	Good consistency on set-ups. Still lacks depth on difficult shots; Has directional intent on moderate balls; May have good preparation, but still weak on deep shots.	Preparation problems; Starting to hit with directional intent on easy shots; Starting to follow through instead of punch.	Starting to serve with some power and control. Tries to direct serves; Usually flat serves; May be trying to learn to use spin.	More aggressive net play. Some ability to cover side shots. Using proper footwork; Can direct FH volleys; Consistent contact, but little offense on BH volleys.	Can use full overhead swing on shots within reach. Recognizes approach shots and half-volleys; Can place the return of serve.	Moves up and back well. Covering court fairly well. With doubles partner, can effectively cover the net.
4.0	Dependable most of the time with consistent depth and control; Can control running FH; Starting to develop topspin; Frequently may try to hit too good a shot off the FH.	Player can direct the ball with consistency on each shot; Returns difficult shots defensively; Little control on running BHs; Still lacks depth.	Places both first and second serves; Frequent power on first serve with some control; Starting to use spin; Tends to overhit first serve.	Depth and control on FH volley; Can direct BH volley, but usually lacks depth; Developing wide and low volleys on both sides of the body.	Can direct easy overheads; Can poach in doubles; Can hit both offensive and defensive lobs; Follows aggressive shots to the net; Hits to opponents' weaknesses.	Has more confidence, but rallies are still commonly lost due to impatience. Not yet playing good percentage tennis; Has developed teamwork in doubles.
4.5	Very dependable; Uses speed and spin effectively. Tends to overhit on difficult shots; Offensive on easy shots.	Can hit with depth. Usually not offensive; Can control direction and depth, but not under pressure.	Aggressive serving, with limited double faults; Uses power and spin; Still developing spin and direction on second serve; Frequently hits with good depth.	Can handle a mixed sequence of volleys; Good footwork; Has depth and directional control on BH; Developing touch; Most common error is still overhitting.	Approach shots with good depth and control; Can consistently hit overheads as far back as the service line; Starting to hit drop volleys; Can change pace on groundstrokes.	More intentional variety in game; Covers up weaknesses well; Plans tactics more than one shot ahead.
5.0	Strong shot with control, depth and spin; Uses FH to set up offensive situations; Has developed good touch; Consistent on passing shots.	Can use BH as an aggressive shot with good consistency; Has good direction and depth on most shots. Difficult shots are returned without intent of direction or depth, but can frequently hit winners off of set-ups.	Serve is placed effectively with the intent of hitting to a weakness or of developing an offensive situation; Can mix topspin, slice, and flat serves; Good depth and spin on most second serves, and few double faults.	Can hit most volleys with depth, pace and direction; Can hit either flat or underspin volleys. Plays difficult volleys with depth; Given opportunity, volley is hit automatically for a winner.	Has added drop shot and lob volley to repertoire; Approach shots and passing shots are hit with a high degree of effectiveness.	

The 5.0 player frequently has an outstanding shot around which he can mold his game or protect weaknesses. Has sound strategy in singles and doubles and can vary game plan according to opponent. This player has become "match wise," and "beats himself" less than the 4.5 player. Covers court well, plays percentage tennis, and has good anticipation. Hits mid-court volley with consistency, but may lack depth. Serve return is consistent, and can gain offense against a weak second serve. Overhead can be hit from most any position on the court.

5.5   This player can hit dependable shots in stress situations; Has developed good anticipation, and can pick up cues from such things as opponent's toss, body position, backswing, preparation, etc. Can analyze and exploit opponents' weaknesses.

6.0 to 7.0   These players will generally not need NTRP ratings, as their rankings or past rankings speak for themselves. The 6.0 player frequently has a teaching knowledge of the game and often travels from city to city for competition. The 6.5 player frequently makes travel-for-competition a part of his life-style, and sometimes earns a portion of his income from prize-winnings. The 7.0 player is generally committed to tournament competition as a life-style and frequently depends on tournament winnings as a portion of his income.

© USTA, NTA, USPTA, 1979 (REVISED 1981).

SELF-RATING GUIDELINES

TO PLACE YOURSELF

A. Begin with 1.0. Read all categories carefully and then decide which one best describes your present ability level.

B. Be certain that you qualify on all points of all preceding categories as well as those in the classification you choose.

C. When rating yourself assume you are playing against a player of the same sex and the same ability.

D. Your self-rating may be verified by a teaching professional, coach, league coordinator or other qualified expert.

E. The person in charge of your tennis program has the right to re-classify you if your self-placement is thought to be inappropriate.

NTRP RATING CATEGORIES

1.0 This player is just starting to play tennis.

1.5 This player has limited playing experience and is still working primarily on getting the ball over the net; has some knowledge of scoring but is not familiar with basic positions and procedures for singles and doubles play.

2.0 This player may have had some lessons but needs on-court experience; has obvious stroke weaknesses but is beginning to feel comfortable with singles and doubles play.

2.5 This player has more dependable strokes and is learning to judge where the ball is going; has weak court coverage or is often caught out of position, but is starting to keep the ball in play with others of the same ability.

3.0 This player can place shots with moderate success; can sustain a rally of slow pace but is not comfortable with all strokes; lacks control when trying for power.

3.5 This player has achieved stroke dependability and direction on shots within reach, including forehand and backhand volleys, but still lacks depth and variety; seldom double faults and occasionally forces errors on the serve.

4.0 This player has dependable strokes on both forehand and backhand sides; has the ability to use a variety of shots including lobs, over-heads, approach shots and volleys; can place the first serve and force some errors; is seldom out of position in a doubles game.

4.5 This player has begun to master the use of power and spins; has sound footwork; can control depth of shots and is able to move opponent up and back; can hit first serves with power and accuracy and place the second serve; is able to rush net with some success on serve in singles as well as doubles.

5.0 This player has good shot anticipation; frequently has an outstanding shot or exceptional consistency around which a game may be structured; can regularly hit winners or force errors off of short balls; can successfully execute lobs, drop shots, half-volleys and overhead smashes; has good depth and spin on most second serves.

5.5 This player can execute all strokes offensively and defensively; can hit dependable shots under pressure; is able to analyze opponents' styles and can employ patterns of play to assure the greatest possibility of winning points; can hit winners or force errors with both first and second serves. Return of serve can be an offensive weapon.

6.0 This player has mastered all of the above skills; has developed power and/or consistency as a major weapon; can vary strategies and styles of play in a competitive situation. This player typically has had intensive training for national competition at junior or collegiate levels.

6.5 This player has mastered all of the above skills and is an experienced tournament competitor who regularly travels for competition and whose income may be partially derived from prize winnings.

7.0 This is a world class player.

Since the NTRP is not based on age divisions, you can check the rating level you've chosen by asking yourself, "Can I play competitively against *any age* player of my sex who is rated at the same level that I have rated myself?" If your answer is "yes," your self-rating is probably accurate. But remember, the rating categories are generalizations about skill levels, and you may find that you actually play above or below the category that best describes your skill level, depending on your competitive ability.

Above all, remember that there's no substitute for on-court performance as a measure of playing ability.

CHANGES

The only change I'd like to see in the game is in the foot-fault rule. When I was playing full-time, the rule stipulated that the server had to keep one foot planted on the ground and that the other could not swing over an imaginary plane at the baseline before the ball was hit. As I mentioned, if I stood back three inches from the baseline my natural service motion normally would not carry me over that plane. This solved the problem for me.

However, because the combination was too difficult for the linesman to call—he had to watch your feet and listen for the sound of the ball—the parts of the regulation that required maintaining contact with the ground and swinging over were eliminated. The rule now simply says, in effect, that you must not touch the line or any part of the court with either foot until you hit the ball. What that does, though, is allow you to take a flying leap into the court, as long as you hit the ball before you land. That's ridiculous.

It reminds me of something else the International Tennis Federation (all countries) Rules Committee experimented with some years ago in an attempt to counter a player's net rush. The feeling was that a good grass-court player had too much of an advantage when he served on grass. The fellows with the big serves on bad grass were flying up to the net, volleying the return of serve, and never having their serve broken. So the rules-makers tried to take away the advantage by stipulating that the ball had to bounce on his side before the server could go to the net. They also moved the server back three feet. But it didn't accomplish what was intended. It was like proposals to raise the basket in basketball. That wouldn't help the little fellow, because the big man is still going to be closer to it. The proposed serving rules didn't help the player who had the weaker serve. The good server still had the advantage.

The answer in that case was to make the court better by slowing it down, so that the receiver had a better chance to make the return. That was what was done, and now many matches are played on slower courts, and you don't have that net rushing problem anymore. What you do have, however, is the server taking a flying leap on his serve with the result that on cement or grass he's into the net almost before the ball.

It's sometimes questionable whether he's actually hit the ball before he lands. So a player often gets away with something that gives him a big advantage. Yet, if his foot should touch the line on his serve— which really doesn't have any bearing on the return of serve—the foot fault is inevitably called. It doesn't make any sense. To prevent all this jumping into the court with two feet, why not reinstate the foot-fault rule requiring the server to maintain contact with the ground behind the baseline until the ball is hit?

I'm not proposing that we hamper the server by reinstating the rule about not swinging the foot over the imaginary plane. But we should go back to insisting that the server keep a foot on the ground until the ball is hit. Otherwise, with the trend returning to faster surfaces, including cement, the serve-and-volleyer is going to start to dominate again.

Except for that one change, I think the game is great as it is. Some people have commented that the public can't understand the scoring —the love, 15, 30, 40, deuce, ad, and so on. But I learned to play and keep score when I was five—and I was no "brain." Certainly, an adult ought to be able to do as well.

Some tournaments use Van Alen's no-ad scoring system, counting points in sequence from one on. But to this fuddy-duddy, it doesn't seem like the right game.

TRIPLES

Now that I'm on record as wanting tennis to remain virtually unchanged, I feel it's only fair to let you know about a small revolution in the making. You're all familiar with singles and doubles; now some people are putting forth *triples,* specifically designed for older Americans and as a learning tool for youngsters where court space is limited. That's right—three players on a side.

It may be blasphemous to say so, but it could be fun, although I don't imagine it's really going to catch on sufficiently to change the game. I anticipate players running into each other and swatting one of their partners with the racket, but it does have the advantage of less running for each player and the potential for a greater variety of offensive and defensive formations. I haven't yet sampled the game, despite threats by a friend at the USTA to get me to play it.

Proponents of triples, particularly Geoffrey Godbey and Frank Guadagnolo of Pennsylvania State University, lay the groundwork by pointing out the game's metamorphosis from a dainty, elitist sport to a highly competitive one played by one-third of the U.S. population, ages twelve and up. They cite such changes as the introduction of open tennis, indoor tennis, yellow balls, larger rackets, foot-fault rule changes, team tennis, and the like. The game, they say, continues to evolve, and the next step is triples.

Contending that triples is a good way to learn the game because the players don't have to cover as much ground and can concentrate on strokes, they say beginners may keep the ball in play a little longer than with singles or doubles. For the better players, they continue, triples is an interesting, fast-paced game involving more complex strategies and rapid exchanges. It gives a chance to play to those who can't cover the ground for long periods of time in singles or doubles (the elderly, overweight, physically impaired, pregnant, or slow-moving). The game obviously accommodates more players, thus alleviating overcrowding on the courts, and reduces the individual's share of court costs.

Essentially, the game uses the rules of doubles, but there are some special regulations. At the start of each point, all players, except the one receiving serve, must be behind the baseline or its extension. The rules relating to foot fault apply to all players but the receiver. The teams alternate serves, and by the end of six games, each of the players will have served a game. Only one player is allowed to receive in the forehand court in an entire game; only one in the backhand court. A tiebreaker is 13 points, with the victory going to the first team to score seven points.

Getting a high proportion of first serves and returns into play, hitting deep ground strokes, and good lobbing are important, as they are in singles and doubles. But teamwork is even more important in triples than in doubles. It is less likely that a single player can dominate the game or compensate for less-skilled partners.

The serving team has several options after serving: keep everyone near the baseline; send the server to the net; send one or both non-servers to the net. There are rationales for doing any of these. But it doesn't make sense for all three players to go to the net since they're likely to get in each other's way and can be lobbed over.

Soft serves, even underhand serves, are acceptable because, with three opponents, it's much more difficult for the receiver to hit an outright winner.

Triples makes more tactical demands and offers a greater opportunity for socialization. Learning doubles, and even singles, may be easier after starting with triples, in which players can practice hitting ground strokes with less running. Thus it's claimed, they master the strokes faster while actually playing sets of triples. As Godbey and Guadagnolo say in their booklet "Triples" (available from the USTA), "Triples is a game of tennis which is played a little more in the mind and a little less in the body. It is going to be the next revolution in tennis."

I thought I'd pass it along.

PART-TIME TENNIS

THE WEEKEND WARRIOR

As I mentioned earlier, the 1957 Challenge Round in Australia was my farewell to full-time tennis. At thirty-four, I felt it was necessary to begin the transition from athlete to businessman. I might explain why that transition was more critical then than it is now. Prior to 1968 there was no such thing as open tennis. All of the major tournaments in the world were "amateur," as was the Davis Cup competition. Once a player turned professional, he could no longer compete in these important events, and his play was limited to barnstorming tours and a few purely professional tournaments. In tennis, at least, the word *amateur* had the connotation of being not as good as a *professional*, but that really was not the distinction. What those terms distinguished was whether or not a person was eligible to play in a particular event. All the players were pretty much equal, and I've never really quite believed in the theory that when you turned pro you suddenly became a better player.

Pro tennis as we know it today was in its infancy when I retired from full-time tennis, and only a handful of the best players could make enough money out of tennis to pursue it as a career. The game was just not popular enough among the masses and with the media to attract the kind of sponsorship it presently enjoys. The head-to-head tours, whereby the leading pro was usually challenged by the most recent top amateur, provided most of the tennis excitement in the pro game, and despite all the fine efforts of Jack Kramer, first as a player, then as a promoter, the results rarely received big-time coverage by the media.

To make any money out of tennis then, you had to turn professional when you were the dominant amateur and defeat the reigning pro on your first tour. If you lost that first time around, your value decreased sharply. With the likes of Kramer, Gonzales, Sedgman, and Trabert around, I saw little chance of making it big enough in the pro game to warrant my turning pro, plus I was already thirty-four years old. How many more years could I realistically figure on playing at my best? I may have been a little off in my judgment, for as I look back, I believe I could have played another six or seven years, barring any unexpected injuries. Today's players are proving that you can play well into your late thirties at top level, and, of course, my old friend and rival, Ken Rosewall, was still going strong at forty-three. With the added incentive of money, the mental keenness and desire tend to remain longer, and I always believed that was tougher to maintain than good physical condition.

There was one other alternative. Quite a few of the better amateurs became teaching pros after they felt that they had given the circuit their best shot. That way they stayed in tennis, and many of them are among the finest teachers and coaches today. Fellows like George Toley, Bob Harmon, Eddie Moylan, Tut Bartzen, Pancho Segura, Alex Olmedo, Welby Van Horn, Sammy Giammalva, and Dennis Ralston, to name a few, were able to make the switch from player to teacher smoothly and successfully. In my opinion, this is not an easy change to make, and I can think of many players, myself included, who had no desire to go this route.

Having little or no yen to teach, I opted to go into business and remain an amateur tennis player. In this way, I felt I could earn my living outside of tennis and continue to enjoy playing on a part-time basis. I figured I could play a few tournaments during the year, thus keeping my hand in the game, and reap the enjoyment of competing without suffering the accompanying pressure I'd learned to live with for so long. By making tennis secondary in my life, I felt I could still enjoy winning occasionally while somehow rationalizing the losses that were sure to come. I was to find this process more difficult than I had imagined, and to this day I don't think I have gotten used to the idea of losing.

Around 1955, during the last two or three years I played full-time, I also explored several fields that I contemplated pursuing upon retirement. I had pretty much narrowed down the possibilities to television, insurance, and the investment business. I had had a certain exposure to television as a player, having been interviewed and done some commentary from time to time, and the idea of being either a sportscaster or an announcer appealed to me. I can remember growing up as a youngster in Philadelphia being told that I should learn to speak like a radio announcer, devoid of any telltale accent. I've never forgotten that and honestly believe I come very close to not having any noticeable accent. Tennis was not ready, however, for any full-time commentators, and the general sportscasting field was loaded with real pros and was not yet welcoming former athletes into the fold on a wholesale basis. Because of the uncertainties of this industry, and my age, I decided it was not the career to follow.

It didn't take me long to abandon the idea of the insurance business either. I'd heard from so many friends that it was a natural field for former athletes to enter. Here they could capitalize on their name to the fullest. Without casting any aspersions on the many good friends of mine in the insurance business, I reflected on how I felt when a well-meaning insurance agent called on me. Albeit ever so necessary, I always found myself trying to figure out how to avoid his well-planned approach. Why is it no matter how much insurance one has, it's just never quite enough?

In any event, I came to the conclusion I would be too uncomfortable selling insurance. It takes a certain type of personality to be a successful insurance salesman, and I wasn't sure that I fitted the mold. What, then, was I best suited for? I had talked at length with a number of friends both in and out of the investment business, and after a careful analysis of my attributes and the challenges and opportunities in the industry, I decided that was for me. Here was a pursuit, not unlike insurance, in which starting in at thirty-four was not a disadvantage, there was no need for capital outlay to get going, and you were more or less your own boss, with your income dependent upon your own initiative and willingness to work. This appealed to me and seemed at the time to be a type of activity that would be easier to adapt to after the gypsy life of a touring tennis player. I also felt that, unlike buying insurance, everyone is interested in the idea of making money through investments, and I could become genuinely enthusiastic about trying to sell an investment idea I myself believed in.

So I became one of the first of the tennis players of my era to enter the securities business. Others were to follow, and a few, such as Ham Richardson, Dick Savitt, Chuck McKinley, and Gil Shea, are still active in one way or another in the business. After a series of interviews, in 1957 I joined the Philadelphia office of Goldman, Sachs & Co. and started my training to become a registered representative, or, as it's more commonly called, a broker. Goldman was and is one of the top companies in the industry, and I was proud to be a part of such a fine firm.

I didn't play much tennis during the next few months, concentrating instead on learning the business so that I would be more than just another jock in the world of finance, trying to get by on a bit of a name and reputation. Fortunately, I had majored in business at the University of North Carolina, so I had a start in the right direction. Having been on the international tennis circuit for eight years, though, hadn't made it any easier to hit the books again. I'd almost forgotten how to knuckle down and study.

The transition took about a year. In addition to learning as much as I could about the nature of the business, there were practices I had to discontinue and routines I had to establish. Though never a late morning sleeper, I had to get into the habit of rising at a set time each day. I had to reacquaint myself with suits and ties on a daily basis instead of the sports clothes I'd become accustomed to. I put my foot down, however, when it came to wearing a hat. With the exception of the time spent in the service, I'd never worn a hat, and to this day I still don't own one. Attending business lunches and entertaining clients were also new experiences for me, having been for so long on the receiving rather than the giving end of such customs. And then there was customer tennis. I had never been one who particularly enjoyed social tennis to start with, so playing this kind of game was really work for me. Having been so thoroughly competitive for so long, I found it difficult to play without trying hard to win. Unlike golf, tennis is almost impossible to handicap adequately.

Some changes in attitude also followed. When I stopped playing full-time tennis in 1957 and went into the business world, I was determined that I wasn't going to let myself go to pot, as a lot of people do who are very athletic and active for a period and then stop. Unless I exercise a lot, I don't feel well, so I tried to play fairly often after work and on weekends, even though it wasn't on a competitive basis.

I was starting to play for exercise rather than to exercise to play. In so doing, I became more like the person who plays tennis just for fun. To keep a little bit of competitive edge, I did play a few tournaments during the year, especially at resorts, which I really enjoyed. But the competitive edge soon lost some of its sharpness. That wasn't all bad. When tennis became my avocation rather than my vocation, psychologically I was able to put it second, and so I coped a little better with losing.

Gradually, I began to enjoy my new life. I found my work most interesting and challenging, and the changeover seemed to be taking place relatively smoothly. I still hankered to compete now and then, and found I could use my normal vacation time in the winter months to play a couple of tournaments in warmer climates. As a result, I continued to play in Puerto Rico and Jamaica on the so-called Caribbean Circuit.

In earlier years, when we were playing the Florida–Caribbean circuit in the springtime, a tournament would end on Sunday, and you'd have to be somewhere else the next day for the start of another competition. If you made it to the final of the first tournament, this presented some difficulty. To ease the problem, the tournament sponsors would arrange for you to play a nonexistent person in the first round, held on Monday, of the second tournament. They did this by putting some phony, funny-sounding names like Bud Budweiser or Sonny Schlitz in the draw (rather than just granting an out-and-out bye, which they apparently considered too much of a special privilege). Since the player didn't exist, he couldn't show up, and you'd win by default and thus have Monday free.

Once I arrived in Miami from Jacksonville, where I'd made it to the finals on Sunday. I looked at the draw and saw that I was supposed to play "Homer Shoop" in the first round. "That's a good one," I thought, "they've come up with a really good name they haven't used before." As I was thinking this, a fellow tapped me on the shoulder and said, "Hello, I'm Homer Shoop." Homer, who was a banker from Indianapolis, turned out to be a supernice guy. But his tennis game went with his name; he hit nothing but weird-looking spin shots all the time.

As a businessman, I also discovered some weekend tournaments, mostly on the East Coast, which were fun and didn't take time away from my work. Two other events in which I continued to compete were Merion (Pennsylvania State Grass Court Championships) and Forest Hills (Nationals). While this may sound like a lot of tennis for a working man to play, it really wasn't much compared with playing full-time. It was, however, enough to keep me from losing the match-play toughness so necessary to winning.

There were some other players of my era who pursued this type of tennis activity. In addition to some of those I've mentioned who were fellow brokers, others, such as Ron Holmberg, Mike Green, Clark Graebner, Tom Brown, Donald Dell, Straight Clark, and Gene Scott, would pop up on the scene every so often in weekend tournaments as well as some of the major events. All of these players had been at one time or another seasoned circuit performers, and many of them still played quite well on occasion. Because we would frequently play havoc with the draws by upsetting some of the current favorites, this group became known as the "Weekend Warriors." I like to think of myself as one of the leaders of this band not only because I was one of the oldest, but because I produced some real surprises for quite a few years.

For example, at the Nationals in 1958, I was drawn in the first round against Kurt Nielsen, seeded seventh that year, and I managed to beat him in five sets. I also made it to the quarterfinals before losing to Ashley Cooper, the eventual winner. In the same tournament in 1959, I upset Ramanathan Krishnan, seeded fifth, in the third round, 6–3, 6–4, 6–2, and in the 1962 Nationals, I defeated sixth-seeded Jan Lundquist in the third round, 6–4, 6–3, 6–3. One of my most satisfying wins as a Weekend Warrior occurred in the 1966 U.S. Championships when I managed to beat Stan Smith, 6–3, 6–4, 2–6, 2–6, 6–4, in the first round. Stan was on his way up and not yet the force he would become, but I was forty-three and playing in my twenty-fifth National Championship, and it was gratifying to win a five-setter at that stage. I played in four more Nationals at Forest Hills and had the distinction of playing in the last match held in the stadium there before the shift to Flushing Meadow, a Hall of Fame doubles. I thought it was particularly fitting since I had played my first National match on that same court thirty years earlier.

The year 1966 proved to be a very unusual and interesting year in tennis for me. In addition to the win over Smith, I managed to win a weekend tournament in Detroit, beating Ron Holmberg in the finals, and played a match at Merion that put my opponent and me into the record books. It was that third-round encounter against Bill Bowrey, an Australian Davis Cupper at that time. We started at 4 P.M. and finished at 7:55 P.M., and I was the winner by 32–34, 6–4, 10–8, in the sixth longest singles match of all time. (The sixty-six-game first set is the second longest ever in singles, and was actually the longest for a couple of years). There were only three service breaks, but I guess what will always stand out the most about the match is the fact that Bill was twenty-eight and I was a month shy of forty-three. Obviously, there was still some fight left in this old boy. The culmination of the year came when the national rankings were announced and I was placed ninth. This was my thirteenth time in the top ten, the first time being twenty-five years before, in 1942, when, interestingly enough, I was also ninth. No other American, man or woman, comes close to that quarter-century span, I'm proud to say.

"MUG HUNTING"

Incidentally, when I first stopped playing full-time, I avoided playing in tournaments in and around my hometown, Philadelphia, despite the pressure for me to play in them. But I resisted because once you've played at the top level, you don't have much fun playing competitively at a lower level—like driving a Model T Ford after you've had a Cadillac, you get no kick out of winning a local competition if you've won a national or world competition. Eventually, somebody you shouldn't lose to will beat you, and then it's a big deal, while it's no big deal if you win. Why bother to go through all that? It's an individual matter, of course. It's not a matter of refusing to support local tournaments. But once you play one, you have no excuse not playing the others.

A lot of players who have played top tennis continually enter local tournaments they know they'll win and take home trophies. It's called *mug hunting*. Not that I'm being snobbish about it, but I never wanted that. I simply decided that I would play competitively only against somebody who *should* beat me. Those of us in the Grand Masters had played against each other twenty to thirty years earlier, so winning and losing was still just as important to us as ever. I didn't *want* to lose to Frank Sedgman or Sven Davidson, but at least when I did, I was losing to someone I had lost to before, someone I had beaten before, and someone of my own vintage.

Open tennis came along in 1968, the greatest thing that ever happened to the game. Even though I was, by then, a full-time businessman and a part-time tennis player, I felt so strongly in favor of this move that I immediately declared myself professional. If I say so myself, it didn't create much of a stir in the sporting world. I didn't even call a press conference. But by this simple declaration, I, and many others of my era, put our stamp of approval on the opening of the sport to all tennis players. Wimbledon led the way, as Wimbledon always had, welcoming the pros back into the 1968 draw. Forest Hills followed, as did the other major tournaments and the Davis Cup. As prize money and sponsorship began to grow, the media became interested, and tennis was suddenly booming, as a participant as well as a spectator sport.

Along with the sudden growth in the number of people playing tennis, a rapid expansion in all types of businesses directly related to the game also took place. The tennis apparel industry, for one, is now estimated to be a billion-dollar industry, not including shoes. Equipment companies sprang up by the hundreds, offering a variety of rackets as well as new tennis paraphernalia. Indoor tennis facilities appeared almost overnight in those areas of the country where there are lengthy winters and have even oversaturated some cities. There are more and more tennis camps around the country, and hundreds more teaching pros to provide good instruction. Even the medical profession is busier, with more sprains, tears, pulls, and breaks to take care of, not to mention the bane of all tennis players, the tennis elbow. Needless to say, as an aging warrior, I've had to become much more aware of such things.

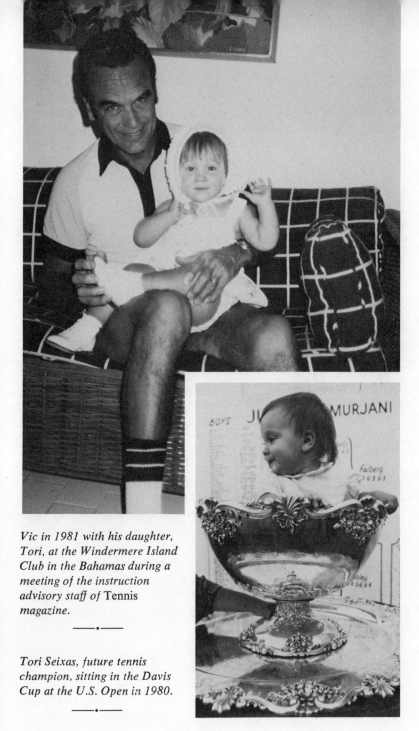

Vic in 1981 with his daughter, Tori, at the Windermere Island Club in the Bahamas during a meeting of the instruction advisory staff of Tennis *magazine.*

———•———

Tori Seixas, future tennis champion, sitting in the Davis Cup at the U.S. Open in 1980.

———•———

*Tennis definitely is a sport for a lifetime
—whether you've been playing it regularly
since you couldn't see over the net (for
reasons of youth), you're learning the
sport for the first time (and can't see over
the net for reasons of age), or you've
resumed playing after a hiatus of some
years.* Photo by Betty Cleveland, courtesy
of the U.S. Tennis Association

———•———

Playing and enjoying tennis all your life
help you keep fit and feel younger and
better. If you're physically healthy, you
can start playing tennis at almost any age.
Photo by Betty Cleveland, courtesy of the
U.S. Tennis Association

If you're never too old to take up tennis, it follows that you're never too old to take lessons either. These prime time players are enrolled in senior tennis classes in Princeton, New Jersey. Photo by Betty Cleveland, courtesy of the U.S. Tennis Association

GIVE THE DEVIL
HIS DUE

When I was a pilot in World War II, one airplane I always wanted to fly, but never did, was the B–26 Marauder, a medium-class twin-engined bomber used almost exclusively in the European theater. It had an excellent combat record, and the pilots who flew it swore by its performance. It had one drawback, however: more pilots were killed in training in this plane than in any other in the Army Air Corps. In the vernacular of flyers, it was considered a "hot plane." In layman's terms, the wings were rather short relative to the body of the plane. This meant less lift, less gliding capacity, and a higher takeoff and landing speed. It also made it a lot more dangerous during the training period and until the pilots became accustomed to its characteristics. This accounts for the high fatality rate.

It may be just as well that I never got to fly this airplane, or I may not have been around to tell this tale. But I did get to read the pilot's "Tech (Technical) Orders," which describe the B–26, its characteristics, instrumentation, and equipment, as well as complete operating instructions. I have never forgotten the opening sentence of the thick manual on the B–26: "Aerodynamically, this airplane will not fly!" After making that statement, they proceeded to tell you how to fly it.

There is an analogy of sorts between that apparent contradiction and what I am about to attempt. Comparing sports greats of different eras is virtually impossible and usually results in futile controversy. Now that I've said that, I'll attempt to make some comparisons and

207

ultimately present my top ten male tennis players. Since I cannot honestly evaluate any player I never saw perform in his prime, I will not go back beyond the days of Don Budge in the late 1930s. From Don to the present, however, I have personally played against and/or witnessed the play of every champion I will mention. In view of what I have just said, my apologies to my good friends Fred Perry, Ellsworth Vines, Jack Crawford, and the fabulous Frenchmen, René Lacoste, Jean Borotra, and Henri Cochet, all of whom are among the greatest ever to have played the game. Among those no longer with us, Bill Tilden, Bill Johnston, Tony Wilding, Norman Brookes, and Gerald Paterson also would deserve recognition. Many aficionados of tennis, in fact, consider Bill Tilden the greatest of all time. By limiting my ranking to those I've seen and played, however, I feel qualified to argue with anyone concerning their place in the history of the game.

Before proceeding any further, I should spell out some of the criteria I have used to arrive at my conclusion. Obviously, to achieve greatness a player must win a sizable number of major titles on different surfaces against top opposition. He must also remain at the top long enough to prove he was not just a flash in the pan. Many players have shown genius on occasion but were unable to sustain it long enough to be called true champions. We've often heard someone say of a player, "On a given day he could beat anyone." The day after is a different matter. Our sport has had more than its share of performers who play like world-beaters one day and beginners the next.

I guess the ultimate compliment to a player is attaching an era to his name, such as the Tilden Era, the Budge Era, the Laver Era, and so forth. I would certainly like to have included myself in that elite group, but I don't recall ever hearing anyone speak of the Seixas Era! In any event, I cannot conceive of anyone's being associated with an era without having proved *consistent* greatness, which is perhaps the key to any ranking.

We also have to keep in mind the fact that open tennis came along in 1968. Many players who reached the top and turned pro prior to that year were not playing the major tournaments and Davis Cup for some of the years they were in their prime. Pancho Gonzales is a notable example. He turned professional in 1949 at age nineteen after a meteoric rise to the top of the amateur ranks. From 1949 to 1968 he could not compete against the leading players in the world until they turned pro, so he garnered very few major titles. Yet he dominated the pro ranks for most of that period, and many consider him the greatest ever. Pancho's turning pro was one of the reasons I think the United States wasn't more successful in Davis Cup competition in the 1950s. One or two players can make a big difference. Players in other countries turned pro, too, but not until somebody equally good could take over. When Gonzales turned pro, there really wasn't another Gonzales around.

There is no disputing that it would be easier to come up with a ranking over this span of about a half a century had tennis been open the whole time. Many more head-to-head confrontations would have taken place between the greats than actually occurred, and many of those who won major titles might not have won them, had the field included *all* the world's best players at the time.

I mentioned surfaces and the ability to win on various types of courts. Perhaps this should be stressed more. To be a great champion, in my opinion, one has to be able to win on a variety of surfaces. To be able to achieve results on clay, or hard courts as they are called in Europe, but not on faster surfaces keeps a player from being considered really great. Conversely, a serve-and-volley type player who lacks consistency from the back court on slower surfaces doesn't really qualify as a true champion. In recent years, we've seen any number of really fine slow-court players who weren't around when the quarterfinals were being played at Wimbledon, and a like number of big servers who couldn't win two rounds at Roland Garros, France.

Keeping all this in mind, let's take a chronological look at the great champions of the past and present, starting with Don Budge. Winner of the first Grand Slam of Tennis (French, Wimbledon, United States, and Australian), Don is truly a player after whom an era was named. Totally dominant on all surfaces as an amateur in 1937 and 1938, he was also the mainstay on the Davis Cup team that wrested the trophy from the British, who had held it for four years. In 1938, his Grand Slam year, he again led the team to victory over Australia, winning both singles matches. Possessor of what many consider the greatest backhand of all time, Don was also an excellent doubles player, teaming during this period with Gene Mako. In what is often called one of the greatest tennis matches of all time, Budge defeated Baron Gottfried von Cramm of Germany in the Interzone final of the 1937 Davis Cup at 8–6 in the fifth set. This was the final match of the tie that stood at two-all, and Don was behind 4–1 in the fifth set. At this point, he is reputed to have said to his captain, Walter Pate, at the changeover, "Don't worry, Cap, I'll pull it out." This he did, and the United States went on to defeat Great Britain 4–1 in the Challenge Round. Don often speaks about that match and never fails to mention what a fine player and great sportsman von Cramm was. Most of the people who saw the flaming redhead play in his prime agree that he was virtually unbeatable, and many claim he would have easily handled the serve-and-volley players who followed a few years later. While this is one of those debatable points, it is hard for me to see how anyone who ever played could have served and come to the net against the Budge backhand with any amount of success. Taking the return early with that famous brushing motion, Budge's accuracy and consistency were almost unbelievable. While not a serve-and-volleyer himself, Don could, and did, attack most of the time and was not uncomfortable at the net. His fine doubles and mixed doubles record attests to the well-rounded nature of his game.

After his Grand Slam year, Budge turned pro and dominated the barnstorming tour for the next couple of years until a little fellow with a funny walk and a heady game came along. His name was Robert L. Riggs. It's rather unfortunate that Bobby Riggs will always be better known to sports fans as the male chauvinist who lost to Billie Jean King in the famous battle of the sexes. Students of tennis, however, will be quick to tell you what a fine player he was. In 1939, he played his one and only Wimbledon and accomplished the hat trick, winning the singles, doubles, and mixed doubles. In the same year, he played in the last Challenge Round before World War II. Big-time tennis took a back seat to the war during the next six years, and Bobby was unlucky that this was during his peak years. He was still the top pro in 1947, however, until meeting and succumbing to a younger and stronger Jack Kramer.

Before we leave this particular period, two players deserve some comment. In 1940, W. Donald McNeill was the U.S. champion, beating Riggs in a five-set final. Don was also the French titlist in 1939. His career was also shortened by the war and he played very little after it, opting instead for a future in advertising. Those of us who remember Don and his slashing, attacking style of play are quick to point out, however, that for a short period of time he was a really great player. I daresay very few of the present-day players will recall his name or know who he was, but some of us remember well how tough he was.

The other player I'd like to mention is Frank Kovacs. As I mentioned earlier, Frank, known as the "clown prince" of tennis, was probably the best player who never won a major title. It was his unfortunate lot to have had Riggs as his major adversary during his peak, and he just couldn't beat Bobby. They met in numerous finals over a couple of years and I don't recall Frank's ever winning. He had a particularly strong backhand and a colorful style, which included occasional antics on and off the court. He is supposed to have said to Don Budge one time, "How's the second-best backhand in the game?"

Frank Kovacs was indeed one of the real characters of the game, but the big handsome guy of Hungarian descent was joyfully colorful and entertaining and never obnoxious or offensive on the court. He is yet another name that most current tennis enthusiasts would not recognize, but to the real students of the game, he was one of the best.

When John Bromwich was asked to name the toughest player he had ever faced, he paused for a moment and then replied, "Kramer." Asked why, Brom replied, "Because when you play Jack, you run to your right to return his shot, then you run to your left for his next shot, then you run to your right and barely reach his next shot, then you run to your left and don't quite reach his next shot, and that's the way every point goes." The period after World War II until about 1953 belonged to Jack Kramer. Much as Budge had done earlier, Big Jake virtually dominated the sport, first as an amateur, then as a pro. After winning Forest Hills for the second time in 1947, Jack turned pro and proceeded to defeat Bobby Riggs in their barnstorming tour. He then continued his undefeated way by beating back the successive challenges of Pancho Segura, Pancho Gonzales, and Frank Sedgman before deciding to give up the playing part of the game and move into promoting. He was the mainstay of the U.S. Davis Cup team in 1946 and 1947, and with partner Ted Schroeder won most of the doubles matches they played. Jack is credited with having perfected the "big game" that most of the leading players thereafter emulated. He had no particular weakness unless it was a tendency toward injuries, for he played much of his career with bothersome blisters or back problems. In my opinion, Kramer personified percentage tennis at its best. While his forehand was his big weapon, his serve was probably better than most people realized, and his relentless attacking style was well suited for the difficult indoor conditions under which the pros played back then. All in all, Big Jake was a dominant force in the game and certainly one of its greatest players.

After Kramer came Gonzales. Out of nowhere, Big Pancho came east and won the U.S. Nationals in 1948 when he was only nineteen. He repeated that victory in 1949 in a classic five-set final win over Ted Schroeder. He promptly turned pro, depriving the United States of a mainstay on its Davis Cup team that might have kept the big mug on American shores for years to come. Instead, it went down under, where many of us tried in vain to bring it back, succeeding only twice in the next decade. Pancho turned back the challenge of a succession of the world's best during that period, including Sedgman, Hoad, Rosewall, and Trabert. No question about it, Big Pancho picked up where Kramer left off and was the master during most of the 1950s. Turning pro so early undoubtedly precluded his winning Wimbledon and many of the other major world titles, but his dominance over the players who had won these titles is evidence that he was the best player of his time.

The 1950s produced quite a few great players, mostly Australian and American. Frank Sedgman, who led the charge in 1950 that took the Davis Cup to Australia, gave both Kramer and Gonzales all they could handle in their pro tours and won most of the major titles in the world in singles, doubles and mixed doubles before turning pro at the end of 1952. It's difficult for me to be completely objective since this was my playing era, but to me, when at his best, Frank was one of the world's greatest players. He was also a great doubles player, as his record clearly demonstrated. With partner Ken McGregor, he won the Grand Slam in 1951 and almost duplicated the feat the following year. Many believe Frank was the best his country produced, and it produced many a great champion over the years.

Two others come immediately to mind, namely, the "whiz kids" Ken Rosewall and Lew Hoad. After Sedgman turned pro, the job of holding the Davis Cup fell on the shoulders of these youngsters. That they were able to successfully defend in 1953 when not yet nineteen years of age is a tribute to their greatness. With the notable exception

of Wimbledon, Rosewall managed to win just about every title worth
winning, as did Hoad, with the exception of the U.S. Championship.
Together they won all the major doubles titles at least once. Lew's
career was cut a bit short due to chronic back problems, but while
he was in his prime, he was devastating. Lew had a great serve and
was exceptionally strong, and when he got everything going, no one
hit the ball any harder. The racket was like a matchstick in his hand
and his wristy, flicky shots were ahead of their time. Indeed, many
think he led the way into the "table tennis" type of shots you see
nowadays. Rosewall, on the other hand, was just the opposite in
style. Slightly built and a converted southpaw, Ken had a somewhat
labored serve, not a major weapon, although his control with it was
excellent. Ken's major attributes were his speed afoot and one of the
finest backhands in the game. I doubt if Rosewall, unlike Hoad, has
ever had an injury or physical problem. His effortless stroke pro-
duction and perfect footwork have helped to give him such a long
and illustrious career. Currently in his late forties, he's still winning
matches and tournaments against players fifteen years his junior.
While the Wimbledon title eluded him, it's a great tribute to this fine
player that he reached the finals no less than four times, the last in
1974 against Jimmy Connors when Ken was just a few months shy
of his fortieth birthday. As pros, both Ken and Lew were beaten by
Gonzales, but Pancho is on record as saying that Hoad was the only
player he feared.

The list of fine Australian players during the fifties and early
sixties goes on and on. After the whiz kids came Ashley Cooper,
Mal Anderson, Neale Fraser, Roy Emerson, Fred Stolle, and eventually Rod Laver and John Newcombe. The United States was a distant
second in those days, but we had a few who broke through the
Aussie grip on occasion. My doubles partner, Tony Trabert, had two
French, two U.S., and one Wimbledon singles titles before leaving
the amateurs in 1955. I can also personally attest to Tony's ability
in the left court in doubles. He, as did those before him who turned
pro, found Gonzales just too tough. Dick Savitt and Ham Richardson
were Americans who challenged the Australian domination of this
period. Savitt's big win was Wimbledon in 1951, but he was also
close to major titles on other occasions. Alex Olmedo, the trans-
planted Peruvian, had a couple of good years, winning Wimbledon
in 1959, and almost single-handedly returning the Davis Cup to the

United States in 1958. Jaroslav Drobny was king for a while on the slow courts in Europe, and a popular winner of Wimbledon in 1954. Overall, though, the period belonged to Pancho Gonzales, whose big serve and catlike court coverage make him high on the list of all-time greats.

If the 1950s belonged to Gonzales, the 1960s belonged to Rod Laver. The only two-time Grand Slam winner (1962 and 1969), Rocket Rod fashioned his game after Lew Hoad's and improved on it. If Hoad had any weakness, it was his inability to hit over his backhand with consistency. Rod made this shot look easy, as he did with almost every other shot in the game. He won twenty major titles over the decade of the sixties, including four Wimbledon singles, two of which were after open tennis began in 1968. From 1962 to 1968, had tennis been open, he might well have won a half dozen more. Winning the Grand Slam in 1969 against all comers stands out as perhaps the greatest achievement in tennis. There were other fine players during this period, including Roy Emerson, who lost in three of the four Grand Slam finals to Laver in 1962; John Newcombe, who amassed twenty-five major titles during his ten-year career at or near the top; and Tony Roche, Chuck McKinley, Dennis Ralston, Arthur Ashe, Stan Smith, and Manuel Santana, to mention a few. Emerson holds the distinction of having won the most major titles in singles and doubles, a resounding twenty-eight between 1959 and 1971. Despite all this, one name stands out head and shoulders above the others during the 1960s: Rod Laver.

The 1970s saw the tennis boom come into full bloom and more and more fine young players making the headlines. Most of the top performers during that period are still active, and it may take awhile for some to emerge as true champions. Here again, however, one man stands alone at the top of the heap, Bjorn Borg. Probably the finest athlete ever to play the game, Borg has been virtually unbeatable on the slow surfaces and has managed to garner five straight Wimbledon singles crowns on grass. There are those who believe he is the greatest tennis player ever. My own opinion is that he is the best ever on slow courts, but on grass or fast hard courts, there have been quite a few who would have beaten him. I say this in spite of his magnificent Wimbledon record, for if you stop and think, there haven't been any great serve-and-volley–type players around. In fact, until John McEnroe came upon the scene, Borg was the best serve-and-volley player on grass! When I think back to Gonzales, Kramer, Sedgman, Hoad, Laver, and a host of others who attacked constantly, I feel that Borg, as great as he is, would not have beaten the really top net-rushers on the faster surfaces.

I feel equally confident that, with Borg's great stamina, athletic ability, and disposition, there has never been anyone better on the slow surface. Taking his record into consideration, one has to acknowledge his greatness, and if anyone ever deserved an era named after him, it's Bjorn Borg. The other champions of the 1970s worth mentioning include Jimmy Connors, Guillermo Vilas, Stan Smith, and Arthur Ashe. Right at the end of this period, John McEnroe emerged. He is currently the best player in the world and no doubt will eventually take his place on the list of all-time greats. Perhaps he will be the player of the 1980s and have an era named after him. Having already won U.S. and Wimbledon titles, he's well on his way. At a time when there are so many fine players, it's more and more difficult to dominate the game, and winning the coveted Grand Slam seems more and more remote. While I honestly feel the level of play nowadays at the top is no better or worse than twenty-five or thirty years ago, the standard is much higher down the line. There are many more good players now than when I was playing, which makes it tougher to win the big tournaments.

I'd be hard-pressed to characterize one generation of tennis players as superior to another. There may be some differences in style, but not very much in quality. When we were at our peak, I think we had more good players than when Budge was playing; today there are more good players than when we were playing. Because we're getting a quantity of good players and the depth of talent is much greater, there are better players at lower competitive levels. Consequently, it's become increasingly difficult for the players at the top to win consistently; they're playing much tougher competition day-in and day-out.

Obviously, the big purses offered to professional tennis players have enticed a lot of good athletes to the game, which is why we find the depth of talent that we do. But I don't think the fact that they're playing for 100,000 dollars makes them play any better. I don't think there's a connection between performance and dollars, except for the possibility of easing up in certain situations in the knowledge that even losers earn big bucks.

People will comment, "Look at all the money these guys are getting; no wonder they're killing themselves out there." It may not be intended, but the implication in this sort of comment is that today's players try harder than we ever did. But that's faulty reasoning. Today's players sometimes get thirty thousand dollars or more when they lose! I'm not saying they don't try, but there have been times —I've seen it—when a player tanks after losing the first set. The big money cushions the loss. When we played, if you lost you got nothing. You just waited for the next tournament. So if any players killed themselves trying, *we* did.

Well, the moment of truth has arrived. After all that I've said about these great players, past and present, the time has come for me to rank my top ten for the past half-century:

1. Don Budge	6. Lew Hoad
2. Jack Kramer	7. Ken Rosewall
3. Pancho Gonzales	8. Bjorn Borg
4. Rod Laver	9. John McEnroe
5. Frank Sedgman	10. Roy Emerson

I have a confession to make. While I had no trouble selecting the top of my list, I found it more and more difficult at the bottom. Budge, Kramer, Gonzales, Laver, and Sedgman are five who absolutely belong there; their records are all the evidence you need. But then you have someone like Rosewall, who played so long and so well, yet on a given day was not that great a player. Hoad played for a much shorter period but had a fantastic record. You have to weigh how much longevity should count.

Conceivably, Bobby Riggs should be on the list. He'd certainly head my list of all-time great eccentric or flamboyant players. It was not easy leaving him off. Emerson was a question mark; I had to decide between him and Newcombe, and I was probably swayed a little bit by the fact that I never had much respect for Newk's game, despite his great record. He didn't impress me as much as Anderson, for example, who had a great record, but not as great as Emerson's. Yet he might have been the superior player. My partner, Tony Trabert, is another who belongs there among the greats.

The players I finally settled on represent portions of six decades, back to the 1930s, and, I think, reflect the fact that every time period produces great competitors.

If there are those out there who agree with my selections, I would appreciate hearing from them.

Meanwhile, fellow prime-timers, go out and establish your own playing record, approaching the game of tennis with the resolve of the seventy-five-year-old about to marry a girl in her twenties. Warned that the disparity in age could prove to be fatal, he shrugged and said, "If she dies, she dies."

SENIOR
TOURNAMENTS
■|■

USTA Senior National Championships Tournament Schedule

Each year the USTA publishes the Senior National Championships Tournament Schedule, which lists the USTA national tournaments for men and women, ages 35 to 80, including events for mother-daughter and father-son doubles. The requirements for entering these national championships include one USTA championship and winning at least one other tournament. For the latest schedule and further information, write USTA Education and Research Center, 729 Alexander Road, Princeton, New Jersey 08540.

Sectional Tournaments for Seniors

The USTA is divided into seventeen geographical sections. Each section features age-level tournaments for seniors. Write for a schedule in your region at the address given below.

For Maine, Massachusetts, New Hampshire, Rhode Island, Vermont, and part of Connecticut—
New England Tennis Association
P.O. Box 223
Needham, MA 02192

For New York, part of New Jersey, and part of Connecticut—
Eastern Tennis Association
202 Mamaroneck Avenue
White Plains, NY 10601

218

For Pennsylvania, Delaware, part
of West Virginia, and part of
New Jersey—
Middle States Tennis Association
939 Radnor Road
Wayne, PA 19087

For the District of Columbia,
Maryland, part of Virginia, and
part of West Virginia—
Mid-Atlantic Tennis Association
P.O. Drawer F
Springfield, VA 22151

For Alabama, Arkansas, Georgia,
Louisiana, Mississippi, North
Carolina, South Carolina,
Tennessee, part of Kentucky,
and part of Texas—
Southern Tennis Association
3121 Maple Drive, N.E., #29
Atlanta, GA 30305

For Florida—
Florida Tennis Association
520 N.E. 118th Street
Biscayne Park, FL 33161

For Puerto Rico and the U.S.
Virgin Islands—
Puerto Rico Tennis Association
P.O. Box 40456
Minillas Sta.
Santurce, PR 00940

For Indiana, Michigan, Ohio,
West Virginia, part of Illinois,
and part of Wisconsin—
Western Tennis Association
1024 Torrence Drive
Springfield, OH 45503

For Minnesota, North Dakota,
South Dakota, and part of
Wisconsin—
Northwestern Tennis Association
2200 First Bank Place East
Minneapolis, MN 55402

For Iowa, Kansas, Missouri,
Nebraska, Oklahoma, and part
of Illinois—
Missouri Valley Tennis
Association
4045 Merle Hay Road
Des Moines, IA 50310

For part of Texas—
Texas Tennis Association
P.O. Box 192
Austin, TX 78767

For Arizona, New Mexico, and
part of Texas—
Southwestern Tennis Association
3739 South Siesta
Tempe, AZ 85282

For Utah, Wyoming, part of
Colorado, part of Idaho, part of
Montana, and part of Nevada—
Intermountain Tennis
Association
2903 Laredo Place
Billings, MT 59102

For Alaska, Oregon, part of
Washington, and the province
of British Columbia—
Pacific Northwest Tennis
Association
P.O. Box 02322
Portland, OR 97202

For northern California—
Northern California Tennis
Association
645 Fifth Street
San Francisco, CA 94107

For southern California—
Southern California Tennis
Association
609 N. Cahuenga Boulevard
Los Angeles, CA 90004

For Hawaii—
Hawaii Tennis Association
P.O. Box 411
Honolulu, HI 96809

SENIOR TENNIS PUBLICATIONS

In addition to the titles listed below, the USTA has a number of publications available. For a free annotated publications list with prices, write USTA Education and Research Center, 729 Alexander Road, Princeton, New Jersey 08540.

Directory of Tennis Programs for Seniors, compiled by the USTA Education and Research Center, revised edition 1983. A resource guide for organizations interested in offering tennis activities for seniors.

Tennis for the Mature Adult, by Dr. Jim Montgomery, 1980. Explores the needs and goals of the mature tennis player and dispels the myth that the older player cannot learn new techniques after middle age. Contains chapters on fitness programs, practice, motivation, physical precautions, and play.

Winning Tennis After Forty, by Jason Morton and Russell Seymour with Clyde Burleson, 1980. National singles and doubles champions on the national over-45 circuit, Morton and Seymour combine their fifty years of playing and teaching experience to demonstrate how you can turn the skills and experience you already possess into winning tennis strategies and tactics—by relying on brains rather than brawn. Contains sections on accuracy, mental toughness, and strategy.

221

EEVeTeC: The McGregor Solution for Managing the Pains of Fitness, by Dr. Rob Roy McGregor and Stephen E. Devereux, 1982. EEVeTeC stands for equipment, environment, velocity, technique, and conditioning. Presents a self-help system for every athlete to avoid or eliminate common aches and pains associated with fitness. Topics include anatomy of activity, getting into shape, picking your sport, general conditioning, increasing your tolerance for stress, tennis, running, and other sports.

Speed, Strength and Stamina: Conditioning for Tennis, by Connie Haynes, Eve Kraft, and John Conroy, 1975. An eight-week conditioning plan for all ages and abilities, describing exercises for both on and off the court.

The Tennis Player's Diet, by Connie Haynes and Steven Kraft, 1978. A discussion of the basics of good nutrition, with vital information for players who want to enhance their match performance by increasing and sustaining energy and balancing fluid loss.

SENIOR TENNIS CAMPS

Each year the USTA Education and Research Center prepares the *Worldwide Tennis Camp Directory*, which is published in *World Tennis* magazine. The camps listed below are taken from the *1983 Directory* and include camps with adult only or adult and junior programs and where tennis is the primary focus and activity, as opposed to general camps and resorts where tennis is a major activity but not the primary focus. Each listing includes the address of the camp business office for obtaining additional information, number of courts, student/instructor ratio, and when the camps are open.

ARIZONA
John Gardiner's Tennis Ranch
on Camelback
5700 E. McDonald Drive
Scottsdale, AZ 85253
24 courts, 3:1 ratio, weekly
sessions October to May.

Wickenburg Inn Tennis & Guest
Ranch
P.O. Box P
Wickenburg, AZ 85358
11 courts, 5:1 ratio, September
to May.

ARKANSAS
John Newcombe Tennis Center
Fairfield Bay Resort
P.O. Box 152
Fairfield Bay, AR 72088
10 courts, 5:1 ratio, 2- and 5-day
sessions April to October.

CALIFORNIA
Bear Valley Tennis Club
Box 794
Twain Harte, CA 95383
6 courts, 5:1 ratio, 5-day
sessions June to August.

Big Bear Tennis Ranch
Box 767
Big Bear City, CA 92314
15 courts, 4:1 ratio, weekend
sessions in September.

Ed Collins USD Tennis School
University of San Diego
Alcala Park
San Diego, CA 91110
8 courts, 6:1 ratio, June 12–17
and July 24–29.

John Gardiner's Tennis Camp
P.O. Box 228
Carmel Valley, CA 93924
15 courts, 3:1 ratio, April to
November.

Mammoth Tennis Camp
Box 918
Mammoth Lakes, CA 93546
3 courts, 6:1 ratio, 5-day sessions
May to September.

Rancho Bernardo Inn Tennis
College
17550 Bernardo Oaks Drive
San Diego, CA 92128
12 courts, 5:1 ratio, 2-, 4-, and
5-day sessions all year.

The Vic Braden Tennis College
22000 Plano Trabuco Canyon
Road
Trabuco Canyon, CA 92678
17 courts, 6:1 ratio, sessions all
year.

COLORADO
Copper Mountain Tennis Camps
Copper Mountain Racquet Club
P.O. Box 3195
Copper Mountain, CO 80443
6 courts, 4:1 ratio, 2- and 5-day
sessions July and August.

John Gardiner Tennis Clinics
P.O. Box 38
Keystone, CO 80435
14 courts (2 indoor), 4:1 ratio,
weekend and weekly sessions all
year.

FLORIDA
All American Sports Tennis
Academy at Amelia Island
366 Madison Avenue
New York, NY 10017
19 courts, 4:1 ratio, 3-, 4-, 5-,
and 7-day sessions all year.

Andy Garcia Tennis Clinic
590 Ocean Drive
Key Biscayne, FL 33149
10 courts, 4:1 ratio, January to
April.

Fred Stolle's (H.I.T.) High
Impact Tennis
P.O. Box 630578
Miami, FL 33161
16 courts, 4:1 ratio, 5-day
sessions all year.

Gary Kesl's Inverrary Tennis
Academy
3366 Spanish Moss Terrace
Lauderhill, FL 33119
38 courts, 4–5:1 ratio, 4-day
sessions November to May.

Harry Hopman's International
Tennis
Bardmoor Country Club
8000 Bardmoor Boulevard
Largo, FL 33543
42 courts, 4:1 ratio, sessions all
year.

Laver's International Tennis
Resort
2350 Jaeger Drive
Delray Beach, FL 33444
37 courts, 6:1 ratio, 1-, 3-, and
5-day sessions all year, evening
clinics available May to
December.

Nick Bollettieri Tennis Camp
5500 34th Street West
Bradenton, FL 33507
32 courts, 6–8:1 ratio, July 31–
August 6.

Ponte Vedra Club/Mincek
School of Tennis
P.O. Box 1264
Ponte Vedra Beach, FL 32082
15 courts, 4–6:1 ratio, June to
August and 2 weeks in March,
April, September, and October.

GEORGIA
All American Sports Tennis
Academy at Callaway Gardens
366 Madison Avenue
New York, NY 10017
21 courts, 4:1 ratio, 3-, 4-, 5-,
and 7-day sessions all year.

HAWAII
Tennis in Hawaii at Kiahuna
Beach & Tennis Resort
c/o U.S. Sports Development,
Inc.
980 Magnolia Avenue
Larkspur, CA 94939
10 courts, 5:1 ratio, March
10–17.

IDAHO
Elkhorn Tennis School
P.O. Box 394
Sun Valley, ID 83353
18 courts, 4:1 ratio, June to
September.

John Gardiner's Tennis Clinics
The Ranch at Sun Valley
c/o William A. Harding
2121 So. El Camino Real
San Mateo, CA 94403
10 courts, 4:1 ratio, weekend
and weekly sessions August to
October.

ILLINOIS
Ramey Tennis Schools at Knox
College
Route #6
Owensboro, KY 42301
10 courts (3 indoor), 4:1 ratio,
June 5–July 23.

INDIANA
Ramey Tennis Schools at
DePauw University
Route #6
Owensboro, KY 42301
16 courts (5 indoor), 4:1 ratio,
June 24–26 and July 22–24.

IOWA
Herb Lipsman Tennis Camps
Cedar Rapids Racquet Club
252 Blairs Ferry Road NE
Cedar Rapids, IA 52402
11 courts (5 indoor), 5:1 ratio,
May to July, with Seniors
Program May 23–27, June 27–
July 1, and August 15–19.

KANSAS
Bryce Young's Bethany Tennis
Camps
Bethany College
Lindsborg, KS 67456
12 courts (5 indoor), 6:1 ratio.

KENTUCKY
Ramey Tennis Schools
Route #6
Owensboro, KY 42301
6 courts (3 indoor), 4:1 ratio,
April 10–October 16.

MASSACHUSETTS
All American Sports Tennis
Camp at Amherst College
366 Madison Avenue
New York, NY 10017
46 courts (10 indoor), 4:1 ratio,
June 9–August 24.

All American Sports Tennis
Camp at Mount Holyoke College
366 Madison Avenue
New York, NY 10017
10 courts, 4:1 ratio, May 25–
September 7.

Total Tennis (Williston-
Northampton School,
Easthampton, MA)
Box 1106
Wall Street Station
New York, NY 10268
20 courts (7 indoor), 4:1 ratio,
summer sessions.

World Tennis Clinics on
Martha's Vineyard
4821 Arlington Avenue
New York, NY 10471
5 courts, 3:1 ratio, 6-, 7-, and
8-day sessions in July.

MICHIGAN
The Homestead Tennis Clinics
The Homestead
Glen Arbor, MI 49636
9 courts, 4:1 ratio, June to
September.

Irish Hills Tennis Camp
Box 36371
Grosse Pointe, MI 48236
13 courts (3 indoor), 4:1 ratio,
June to August.

MINNESOTA
Jack Roach Tennis Camp at
St. Olaf College
4948 Newton Avenue So.
Minneapolis, MN 55409
17 courts (5 indoor), 4:1 ratio,
weekend and 4-day sessions June
to August.

SETS Tennis Schools (Steve
Ehlers Tennis Schools, Inc.) at
Carleton College
Minneapolis Tennis Center
600 Kenwood Parkway
Minneapolis, MN 55403
26 courts (4 indoor), 4:1 ratio,
weekend, miniweek, and weekly
sessions July to August.

Tennis and Life Camps
Gustavus Adolphus College
St. Peter, MN 56082
21 courts (4 indoor), 4:1 ratio,
June 9–July 31.

MISSISSIPPI
"Tennis World" Diamondhead
5300 Diamondhead Circle
Bay St. Louis, MS 39520
8 courts, 5:1 ratio, sessions all
year.

MISSOURI
Bearcat Tennis
Southwest Baptist University
Bolivar, MO 65613
5 courts, 4:1 ratio, June.

Northwest Missouri State
University Camp of Champions
Lamkin Gym 107
Maryville, MO 64468
13 courts (3 indoor), 5:1 ratio,
June 26–30 and July 3–7.

NEBRASKA
Cornhusker Tennis Camp
University of Nebraska
Bob Devaney Sports Complex
Lincoln, NB 68583
29 courts (5 indoor), 4:1 ratio,
June 11–12.

NEVADA
Lakeside Tennis Club
P.O. Box 5576
Incline Village, NV 89450
13 courts, 6:1 ratio, weekend
and weekly sessions May to
October.

NEW HAMPSHIRE
Tamarck Tennis Camp
Franconia, NH 03580
12 courts, 4:1 ratio, 3-day
weekends May to June.

NEW JERSEY
Alex Mayer's Camp Tennis at
Centenary College
1 Brockden Drive
Mendham, NJ 07945
16 courts, 4:1 ratio, August
8–14, August 8–11, and August
12–14.

Frank Brennan Tennis Academy
The Peddie School
Hightstown, NJ 08520
19 courts (5 indoor), 4:1 ratio,
June 22–25.

Frank Brennan Tennis Camp
Ramapo College of New Jersey
Box 126
Ramsey, NJ 07446
12 courts, 3½ :1 ratio, June
12–18.

Rutgers University Tennis Clinic
& Camp
1010 River Road
Piscataway, NJ 08854
12 courts, 6:1 ratio, weekly day
program June to August

NEW MEXICO
Inn of the Mountain Gods
Tennis Camp
P.O. Box 259
Mescalero, NM 88340
8 courts (2 indoor), 4:1 ratio,
6-day sessions January to
October.

Tennis Ranch of Taos
c/o Kurt's Tennis Shop
Drawer BBB
Taos, NM 87571
8 courts (2 indoor), 4–5:1 ratio,
2-, 3-, and 5-day summer
sessions.

NEW YORK
All American Sports Tennis
Academy at Southampton
366 Madison Avenue
New York, NY 10017
21 courts (5 indoor), 4:1 ratio,
3-, 4-, 5-, and 7-day sessions
May 8–September 25.

Pat Panzarella's St. Bonaventure
Tennis Camp
Box 14
St. Bonaventure, NY 14778
8 courts, 6:1 ratio, July.

World Tennis Clinics at
Easthampton
4821 Arlington Avenue
New York, NY 10471
2 courts, 3:1 ratio, 4-day sessions
May to September.

World Tennis Clinics at Montauk
4821 Arlington Avenue
New York, NY 10471
2 courts, 3:1 ratio, 3- and 4-day
sessions May to September.

World Tennis Clinics at
Southampton
4821 Arlington Avenue
New York, NY 10471
2 courts, 3:1 ratio, 3- to 7-day
sessions May to September.

World Tennis Clinics at
Westchester
4821 Arlington Avenue
New York, NY 10471
11 courts, 4:1 ratio, day camp.

NORTH CAROLINA
Davidson College Tennis Camps
Davidson, NC 28036
17 courts, 4:1 ratio, June 5–10.

John Newcombe Tennis Center
Rte. #70, Box 80
Sapphire, NC 28774
8 courts, 4:1 ratio, April to
October.

Mary Lou Jones Tennis Camp
St. Mary's College
Raleigh, NC 27611
14 courts (2 indoor), 4:1 ratio,
May 23–June 3.

Welby Van Horn Tennis at
Pinehurst Hotel & Country Club
Box 259 Gracie Station
New York, NY 10028
30 courts, 3–4:1 ratio, April to
November.

Western Carolina Tennis Camp
P.O. Box 542
Black Mountain, NC 28711
5 courts, 4:1 ratio, 2- and 4-day
sessions May to June and August
to October.

OHIO
Dave Power Tennis School at
Mad River Mountain Resort
11275 Chester Road
Cincinnati, OH 54246
2 courts, 5:1 ratio, weekend
sessions May to August.

Oberlin Tennis Camp
Oberlin College
Oberlin, OH 44074
19 courts (7 indoor), 5:1 ratio,
2- and 3-day sessions June to
July.

Ramey Tennis Schools at
Wittenberg University
Route #6
Owensboro, KY 42301
12 courts, 4:1 ratio, June 17–
July 30.

OREGON
Janet Adkisson's Tennis
Adventures at Salishan Lodge
3320 122nd Place NE
Bellevue, WA 28005
7 courts (3 indoor), 4:1 ratio
(seniors camp, 6:1 ratio),
January to April.

Oregon Tennis School at Mt.
Bachelor Village Resort
290 West 37th Avenue
Eugene, OR 97405
6 courts, 5:1 ratio, May to
September.

PENNSYLVANIA
Fighting Scots Tennis Camp
Edinboro State College
116 Miller Research Center
Edinboro, PA 16444
12 courts, 10:1 ratio, July 11–15
and July 18–22.

Fritz Schunck Tennis Camps
7-Springs Resort
Champion, PA 15622
14 courts (2 indoor), 4:1 ratio,
May to September.

Greyhound Tennis Camp
Moravian College
Bethlehem, PA 18018
17 courts (3 indoor), 5:1 ratio,
June 23–26.

Fred Perry–Jack March Tennis
Academy at Bedford Springs
Hotel
Bedford, PA 15522
11 courts (3 grass), 5:1 ratio,
August 1–28 (four one-week
sessions with a supplementary
"Weekend Adult" program).

Van der Meer Tennis University
P.O. Box 5902
Hilton Head, SC 29938
14 courts (4 indoor), 6:1 ratio,
February to November, Seniors
Clinic February 7–12.

TEXAS
The Hockaday Junior Tennis
Camp
11600 Welch Road
Dallas, TX 75229
12 courts (2 indoor), 4:1 ratio,
May 16–19.

John Newcombe's Tennis Ranch
P.O. Box 469
New Braunfels, TX 78130
24 courts (4 indoor), 4–5:1
ratio, sessions all year.

Lakeway World of Tennis
One World of Tennis Square
Austin, TX 78734
26 courts (2 indoor), 4–5:1
ratio, sessions all year.

Walden Tennis Camp
Walden Racquet Club
11800 Walden Road
Montgomery, TX 77356
16 courts (4 indoor), 6–8:1
ratio, June 10–12, July 8–10,
and August 12–14.

VERMONT
All American Sports Tennis
Academy at Topnotch
366 Madison Avenue
New York, NY 10017
15 courts (4 indoor), 4:1 ratio,
3-, 4-, 5-, and 7-day sessions all
year.

Cortina Inn Tennis Resort
Killington, VT 05751
8 courts, 4:1 ratio, May to
October.

Ian Fletcher Tennis School at
Bolton Valley Resort
Bolton, VT 05477
8 courts, 4:1 ratio, 2- and 5-day
sessions June 12–September 11.

John Gardiner Tennis Clinics at
the Sugarbush Inn
5700 E. McDonald Drive
Scottsdale, AZ 85253
11 courts, 3:1 ratio, Memorial
Day to September.

Killington School for Tennis
Killington Road
Killington, VT 05751
8 courts, 4:1 ratio, 5-day sessions
May 27–September 11.

Windridge Tennis Camp
Box 3185 J
Jeffersonville, VT 05464
22 courts (2 indoor), 4:1 ratio,
4-day sessions May and
September.

World Tennis Clinics at Mount
Snow
4821 Arlington Avenue
New York, NY 10471
5 courts, 3:1 ratio, 3- and 4-day
sessions September.

VIRGINIA
All American Sports Tennis
Academy at Boars Head Inn
366 Madison Avenue
New York, NY 10017
19 courts (3 indoor), 4:1 ratio,
3-, 4-, 5-, and 7-day sessions all
year.

Blue Ridge Tennis Camp
Dyke, VA 22935
12 courts (4 indoor), 5:1 ratio,
July 14–17.

Eric O'Neill's University of
Richmond Tennis Camps
2423 McRae Road
Richmond, VA 23235
17 courts (4 indoor), 5:1 ratio,
one weekend session each month
from May to August.

4 Star Tennis Academy at the
University of Virginia,
Charlottesville
Dept. WTQ
P.O. Box 790
McLean, VA 22101
16 courts (3 indoor), 4:1 ratio,
weekend and weekly sessions
May to June.

Van der Meer Tennis University
at Sweet Briar College
P.O. Box 5902
Hilton Head Island, SC 29938
15 courts (1 indoor), 6:1 ratio,
June 6–11, June 13–18, June
20–25, and July 25–30.

WASHINGTON
Janet Adkisson's Tennis
Adventures at Roche Harbor
Resort
3320 112th Place NE
Bellevue, WA 98005
2 courts, 4:1 ratio, May to June
and September.

WISCONSIN
Medalist Bachman-Laing Tennis
Camps at Lawrence University
10206 N. Port Washington Road
Mequon, WI 53092
15 courts (6 indoor), 6:1 ratio,
June to July.

Nick Bollettieri Tennis Camp at
Wayland Academy
5500 34th Street West
Bradenton, FL 33507
15 courts (4 indoor), 6–8:1
ratio, July 31–August 6 and
August 7–13.

Warhawk Tennis Camps
University of Wisconsin–
Whitewater
Roseman Building
Whitewater, WI 53190
21 courts (6 indoor), 6:1 ratio,
June 24–26.

INDEX